WIDE OPEN

HarperEntertainment
An Imprint of HarperCollins*Publishers*

WIDE OPEN

A LIFE
IN
SUPERCROSS

Jeremy McGrath

WITH
Chris Palmer

HarperCollins books may be purchased for
educational, business, or sales promotional use.
For information please write: Special Markets
Department, HarperCollins Publishers Inc.,
10 East 53rd Street, New York, NY 10022.

FIRST EDITION

Designed by Adrian Elizabeth Leichter

Printed on acid-free paper

Library of Congress Cataloging-in-Publication Data
McGrath, Jeremy, 1971-
    Wide open : a life in supercross / by Jeremy McGrath with Chris Palmer.– 1st ed.
        p. cm.
    ISBN 0-06-053727-2 (hardcover : alk. paper)
    1. McGrath, Jeremy, 1971- 2. Motorcyclists–United States–Biography. 3. Motocross
I. Palmer, Chris (Chris M.) II. Title.
GV1060.2.M36A3 2004
796.72'092–dc22   2003056773

04 05 06 07 08 ❖/RRD 10 9 8

FOR ANN AND JACK MCGRATH

HAVING PARENTS LIKE YOU HAS MADE ALL THE
DIFFERENCE IN THE WORLD. I AM THE PERSON
I AM TODAY BECAUSE OF YOUR UNCONDITIONAL
SUPPORT, ENCOURAGEMENT, AND LOVE.

This is what motocrossers do when no one is looking. This is what we do in the dry air, the dusty wind, and the unforgiving sun. We ride. A Supercross race is merely a snapshot of my life. A clip. A highlight. What I do when the world is watching. It's my reason for being, yes. But between those races is where life happens. And a huge part of my life is preparation.

That's why my longtime mechanic and friend, Skip Norfolk, and I were at the KTM practice track in Corona, California, on that warm, sunny, dusty day the twenty-first of September 2002. I had just signed with KTM after five years on a Yamaha. Riding a brand-new bike is like getting to know a complete stranger. If you don't know anything about that person you have to ask. I ask by riding. Again and again and again.

How does it handle in the corners? How broad is the power delivery? Do I feel comfortable thirty feet in the air? Is this bike faster than Ricky's? And about a thousand other things I have to know before I pull up to the starting gate under the lights of Edison International Field in Anaheim for round one of the AMA Supercross Series in January.

I had already put over fourteen hours on the new bike over the past two weeks and was beginning to feel pretty comfortable on it. Skip and I had wrapped up another five-hour session and were close to having the bike completely dialed. He gives the rear suspension a couple of clicks, documents the day's findings in his logbook, and loads up the truck.

"I'd better take it out for one more quick spin," I gladly tell Skip. Staying late at the track was nothing new for us. For the better part of the last thirteen years we've spent countless hours going over an infinite number of suspension and carburation settings. Besides, you never know exactly how long it'll take to work the kinks out of a motorcycle, so Skip gave the thumbs up so we'd have a jump on tomorrow's testing. "Just two more laps, Skip."

Skip flicks his stopwatch and I blast down the first straightaway. I guide the bike in and out of a tight hairpin, as easily as I would point and click a mouse, then shoot for a sixty-foot triple jump. With a blip of the throttle in second gear, I'm sent thirty-five feet into the lower atmosphere. I like the view from up here. I've seen it many times in my thirteen-year career. So good I take my right foot off the footpeg and swing it over the bike behind me like I'm going to dismount my KTM in midair. The nac-nac. Been doing it that way before there was anything called the X Games.

Upon returning to earth, I grab a handful of brake, but not too much, snake in and out of another turn, then head for a tricky rhythm section—the meat and potatoes of a Supercross course—made up of a small triple, another triple, and a big double. Negotiating a 200-pound motorcycle with a hair-trigger temper through a technical section like this requires upper body strength, a gymnast's balance, and the precision of a scalpel-wielding surgeon. Now do that at full speed. One mistake and you'll actually need a surgeon.

I smoothly pogo the first triple, gas it, hit the second triple, then more gas before the double. But there's a bit of a problem. As I come off

INTRODUCTION

the second triple jump, my bike bogs down. The high-pitched scream of the 250 two-stroke motor is reduced to a suffocated low rumble as it starves for gas. This is never a good sound.

I've built up too much momentum to avoid the double, so I hit it as planned—bogged out engine and all. The idea is to land smoothly down the backside of the landing jump. But it isn't going to happen. The bike dies. With my KTM gasping and choking, it takes an unwanted nosedive, ejecting me over the handlebars. I'm sailing through the air without my bike, praying for a soft landing I know isn't coming. Luckily, I've got my feet out in front of me. I land on the face of the landing jump almost as if I've jumped out of a window. Unfortunately, that window was three stories high. It isn't really a bad crash. At least it doesn't look that way. Even though I land on my feet, I hit with such force that my body folds completely over like I'm trying to touch my toes—with the back of my neck.

The human body can only bend so far forward before unnatural things begin to happen. In my case, the top of my right femur pops out of my hipbone, tearing away the ligaments and muscles that were holding it in place, and shoots out of the back of my right ass cheek. Regardless of what kind of pain you've dealt with in your life, a dislocated hip will make you cry.

I've crashed plenty in my career, suffered a broken wrist here, a broken leg there. I've been knocked unconscious, had double vision for six weeks, and nearly had my rib cage crushed. (And I've had it pretty good.) But I was thirty years old and now I knew the meaning of agony. My leg was paralyzed with pain. It shot up my back and through all my extremities. I lay there on the track in a fetal position—because I couldn't straighten out my legs—while Skip came rushing over. If I had to lie there in that pain for ten more minutes it would have been way too long.

It would last for another four hours. "I've never seen anyone in so much pain," Skip said. Me neither.

He immediately called 911, then started to check me for injuries and tried to keep me still. Skip cut off my Thor motocross pants so he could inspect my leg. He wanted to make sure my femur wasn't cracked in half and that my feet still had color. After he saw that I could wiggle my toes, he cut the side of my underwear to reveal the dislocated hip. He tried his best to keep my mind off the incredible pain. All I could do was wince and grit my teeth until the ambulance arrived.

He brought over the tent he used to shade himself when he works on the bike and set it up right over me on the track. After twenty-five minutes, the ambulance arrived. Paramedics loaded me up and gave me morphine for the pain. It didn't help. The half-mile drive from the track to Interstate 15 was murder. It's a steep, winding, bumpy dirt road. Every dip in the road went straight to my hip. By that time my body was frozen with pain.

You don't know what to do in a situation like this. You want to just call out, but to whom? There was nothing right then and there that was going to make the hurt go away. The only thing I could do was grit my teeth and accept it. And that's a lonely feeling.

Skip instructed the driver to take me to Tri-City Medical Center, the better of the local trauma centers. (Good mechanics know everything.) He then called my doctor who was in New York, my wife, Kim, and my parents. Everyone met up at the hospital within the hour as frenzied as can be. As they rushed me into the emergency ward, worried faces and confusion reigned.

The doctors tried unsuccessfully to pop the hip back in by treating the muscles with electroshock therapy and forcing the bone back manually. Skip likes to say the strongest thing on my body, other than my head, are my legs. But because of the pain, I resisted the doctor's efforts by tightening up my legs. I tried as best I could to relax, but my muscles just weren't cooperating. There were six people holding me down.

After struggling with me for twenty minutes, they finally gave me some more morphine to knock me out, then reset the hip while I was under. I was so looped out I could barely tell what was going on. I just knew I wasn't going into the light.

The doctors came out and told everyone that I was resting comfortably (yeah, right). Just then, Skip happened to look at his stopwatch. It read 3:49:27. Three hours, forty-nine minutes, and twenty-seven seconds. I had clicked off two fifty-two second laps before I crashed. The rest of the time I was dying from intense pain.

Injuries happen. There's no way around it. It's a part of this sport you accept long before you throw a leg over the bike and regret every time you're writhing in an emergency room. But this one weighed heavy on my mind. I was thirty years old with ten AMA Supercross and outdoor motocross national championships under my belt. I was the best rider in the sport with the most wins, the guy they say is the reason the sport went from our backyards to your living room. The king of Supercross is what people call me. Kim and I live in the house of our dreams, and my bank account says I never have to work again.

But man . . . that crash. In the following weeks of rehab I still couldn't get it off my mind, because I knew what it signified, what no other mishap in my career ever had. The beginning of the end.

But this is the life I chose, what I do under the lights of Edison International Field in Anaheim or on the sandy, whooped-out straightaways of Southwick. What I do with my friends, for my fans, about my problems, and when everything is on the line.

And, oh yeah, what I do when no one is looking.

WIDE
OPEN

I was not allowed to go in the street. Nowhere near it. The sidewalk, yeah, but the street was way off-limits. Strict orders from my dad, Jack. I knew the consequences: I'd pretty much get my butt kicked. So for once in my life I decided to listen. Okay, my life consisted of about three years at this point, but when you've got a Big Wheel and you're as gnarly as I am, staying on the sidewalk is a tall order. But I had my fans to think about. The older kids from the neighborhood would gather on my block to see my daredevil act. San Francisco is all about super steep hills. And what more does a young show-off need than steep hills and a Big Wheel?

I was too small to ride a bike, but that didn't stop me from hanging it out. I had pretty much mastered the art of charging down the sidewalk and jumping in and out of the apron lips at the end of driveways. Those old Big Wheels had holes on the seats so you could adjust the seatback. I think I used to use the notches furthest back because it was just my style. I would fly down the sidewalk and get some pretty good height out of the aprons. We're talking a couple of inches here. When I got to the bottom of the sidewalk, I had to pitch it hard to the right or risk rolling into the street. The trike's plastic tires never really grabbed that well, but I hung it so far out I could make the turn every time. The sidewalk would be black with skid marks from those plastic knobbies.

The kids gathered along the sidewalk and flipped out when I raced down the hill. They were so entertained they would take turns pushing me back up the hill over and over again. I would wear those tires down to a nub. I must have gone through ten Big Wheels on that hill.

It didn't take me long in life to figure out that I was a show-off. And that was only the beginning. Next year I would be four.

Camping with the McGraths

My dad had always been a sort of weekend warrior motorcycle enthusiast. When he wasn't training to be a mechanic at the local Chevrolet dealer, he spent his time with motorcycles. He loved being on two wheels. My mom, Ann, never discouraged him either. It was just another way they could spend time together. He taught my mom how to ride and they would often spend their weekends on or around motorcycles. Because of that, my first experience with motorcycles was a family one. My daredevil Big Wheel days were long past when my dad began taking us on trips to Hollister Camp grounds just outside of San Francisco.

I remember how beautiful the park was. There were these huge redwoods that stretched to the sky. The trails seemed like they went on for days. They had a motocross track with really good, wet dirt, too.

My dad had an old-school Maico that was even old by mid-seventies standards. As far back as I can remember he always owned one kind of bike or another. Never a brand-new bike, more of an old beater. He had some pretty worn out bikes but always had them running right. I can't picture him not tinkering with something.

Hollister is where I first threw a leg over a motorcycle. Problem was, my legs didn't exactly touch the ground. Actually, it was more like my dad lifting me up and sitting me on the gas tank, but to me I was riding. We'd be tooling around the trails, me sitting on the gas tank and holding onto the handlebars while Big Jack steered. My mom wasn't far behind. My dad got her an old Yamaha IT 175 enduro bike. It was a

World's Fair, Spokane, 1973.

mellow four-stroke so she could handle it pretty well. It didn't even have full-on knobbies. They were some sort of half street-half trail deal. The IT had this purple steel gas tank with a metal Yamaha emblem on the side. I mean it was ancient, but it made weekends at Hollister fun. My mom loved to ride up hills, and she got pretty good at it. Coming back down the hill was her problem. She was too scared to ride down so Big Jack had to trudge up the hill and ride her bike down for her. My mom sort of slid down the hill on her butt. Even back then there was something about motorcycles that fascinated me. When you were riding you were free. Even at four years old I could feel it.

HOW TO GET STARTED IN RACING

You made your decision: You want to be the next Jeremy McGrath. Big dream, but you've got to start somewhere. Follow these quick steps and you should be on your way to your first race. (It's a foregone conclusion that you already know how to ride.) As far as your first win goes, you're on your own.

Choose Your Weapon

The mini pilots of Team Green may go through ten bikes a year. You only need one. A brand-new 80-cc bike retails for around $3,500. But you shouldn't have too much trouble finding a late-model, well-maintained bike for half that in the local classified ads.

Team Salvation Army

Since you haven't earned a Thor sponsorship yet, get yourself a long-sleeved jersey, goggles, a helmet approved for motorcycle racing, and a pair of boots. Borrow them if you have to. It isn't necessary to look like the pros in your favorite motocross magazines. Safety is the key. Matching gear is optional.

Find the Tracks

Knowing where to race is half the battle. Ask someone at your local riding spot if there are nearby tracks to race. More than likely somebody will know where or someone who does. Quiz the guys who work at the local motorcycle shop and check the bulletin boards there, as well. You'll need a license from one of the major sanctioning bodies (AMA, NMA), which you can acquire at the track for a fee of about $30.

Know Your Limit

There are several different levels you can race on: local, regional, and national. Your local racetrack is the best atmosphere to hone your skills and get over your nerves. Regional racing is a bit more involved, as you will be required to travel your state to various tracks and line up against riders who are semi-serious about motocross.

Jeremy McGrath

The national level (the national championships at Ponca City, Loretta Lynn's, World Mini GP) is for serious racers who oftentimes have sponsorship deals to fund their racing efforts.

Recruit Your Parents

Minicycle racing is a family sport. It's very difficult to start a racing career without the support of your parents. You need someone to supplement your paper-route money and take you to the races. If something goes wrong at the track, your parents will be there to help you handle it. If your parents can't make it to the races, your racing buddy's parents will be glad to offer moral support.

Moment of Truth

On the day of your first race, arrive at the track early. Make sure you know what time practice starts. It's a good idea to prep your bike the night before so you can concentrate on the race. Go to the rider's meeting before the race. They'll announce it over the PA system. (Just follow everyone else if you don't know where you're going.) Ask a lot of questions throughout the day.

Sometimes it's the only way to learn. Don't try to be a hero. Just finish the race. And above all, have fun. Isn't that why you ride in the first place?

Fast and the Furious, Sort of

Speed is what united my parents in the first place. They met at a party but totally didn't dig each other. After two years passed, speed brought them together. My dad was big into San Francisco's illegal drag-racing scene.

One night my mom and her girlfriend were driving down the street when she saw my dad in his '56 Corvette. They pulled over and chatted. He asked her out for a hamburger but said he had to go racing first. So he picked her up at midnight, and they went to Mel's Diner in San Francisco and talked about cars and motorcycles and life all night long.

My dad quickly got my mom to ride along for the underground races. She loved it immediately. They went to every car racing spot in San Francisco. The cops crashed the scene often. Sometimes my parents ran, sometimes they got caught. One time they were racing on El Camino Real, one of the hottest strips in San Fran in the sixties. They were at the front of the line when the cops crashed the party. They got out of there quick, laying rubber all the way down the strip. Big Jack ducked into a nearby housing development and pulled into somebody's open garage. There they sat for twenty minutes with the engine shut off until the coast was clear. Something clicked between them that night. They both loved the speed and excitement. The element of danger that went along with street racing didn't scare my mom away. She could see it was a part of my dad and she liked what she saw.

Evel Who?

If there was any question about where I got my penchant for stunts, you didn't have to look any further than my dad. He was forever trying to pull these little feats of risk on two wheels. I guess you could say he turned out to be a great role model. One of his most memorable stunts came not long after my Big Wheel exhibitions. Out in front of our house he set up a three-foot-high sawhorse in the street. He took a flimsy plank of wood—about eight feet long and two feet wide—and placed it on the sawhorse. This board was more like a trampoline than a launching ramp. Any kind of weight at all would make it flex.

He laid one end on top of the sawhorse without attaching it. It was definitely a sketchy situation, but my dad didn't care. He loved to show off, and a shaky ramp wasn't going to stop him. All sorts of kids and parents gathered on the sidewalk to watch him. He fired up my mom's old

Jeremy McGrath

IT and rode up the block. Big Jack is not what you'd call a svelte guy by any means. He goes about 260 with a pretty huge belly. Keep in mind the old IT only had about four inches of suspension travel.

Jack with T-bucket.

He rode down to the end of the block and got the bike up to a good thirty miles an hour, his long hippie hair blowing everywhere. He hit the ramp and, by an act of God, everything stayed in one piece. The plank flexed like a Twizzler and shot my dad fifteen feet through the air. He's actually gonna make it! But one thing my dad forgot about those old IT's is that the tool kit and airbox are located underneath the seat. To get to them you have to pop up the seat from one side like you're opening a cooler.

When he sailed off the ramp, the seat popped open in midair. On the landing the bike sounded like it was going to explode into a thousand pieces. At least I think that was the bike. My dad came down squarely on the popped-up seat and totally racked himself. The bike got squirrelly, but he managed to save it. He almost killed himself, but it was pretty funny. Afterward he was completely embarrassed but at least he made the jump. And his kid was impressed. My dad's stunts definitely had an effect on me. They were so cool. I wanted to be just like that. Except for the part about the seat.

Sun City

My dad finished his mechanic training, my mom quit her job at the bank, and they decided to leave the big city for the country life of 1970's Southern California. My great grandparents had lived in So-Cal since 1930, so they thought that would be a good place to raise a family. When my sister Tracy was born in 1975, my parents knew it was official. We moved in with my great grandparents in Sun City for a month until we found a home on Hawthorne Street just a few minutes away. We were only an hour north of San Diego, so we weren't completely out of touch.

When they bought the house in Sun City, my parents also got some land down the street on which my dad opened up Jack & Ann McGrath's Auto Shop, where they've worked ever since.

Hawthorne Street is actually a dirt road. Since we were out in the desert, everything was pretty much dirt. In this part of California, the lanscape is cluttered with huge boulders. Some the size of watermelons, others as big as elephants. We also had about

Our house and land where I first started riding.

three acres of land surrounded by rusty wire fencing to go along with the house. One thing was certain, Sun City was the perfect backdrop to nurture my budding daredevil personality.

Sun City also gave me the only memories I have of my great grand-parents, Stanley and Belle McGrath. I used to ride around with them in their beat-up green Nova. It had this super huge bench seat in the back that I used to sit on with no seatbelt. Belle was a crazy driver. Not too careful. She used to just fly all over the place and I'd slide from side to side every time she whipped it around a corner.

Superman

I didn't even need a bike to satisfy my daredevil appetite. One Halloween my mom got me a little Superman costume. So naturally I thought I could fly. I couldn't remember which foot to take off from so I decided to find a nice high place. The roof of our house would do just fine. Look-ing back, I'm glad we only lived in a one-story house. I climbed through the window out to the roof, got a good running start, and dove off. Fully extended, I was flying! For like a half a second. Then I came crashing down to the unforgiving earth. It's a good thing none of those water-melon-sized boulders were there to cushion my fall. When my face hit the ground the impact caused me to bite a hole in my tongue, and I was spitting up blood everywhere. The big difference between Superman and me was that I had my mom to patch me up. And from then on the roof was off-limits.

My First Bike

At the time I was able to occupy myself just riding my bicycle around and partaking in the occasional act of mischief. Since our move south, the family didn't spend as much time with motorcycles. My dad had one at his shop, but he didn't have a chance to ride it that much since he had a business to run.

We didn't get a lot of rain in that part of the California. When the wind would pick up it made for some pretty nasty duststorms. But when it did rain, the area was susceptible to minor flooding. About 1977, we had one of those rainy spells. When the water washes away, whatever was laying around often got buried in sand. One day on his way home from work, my dad saw this pair of minibike handlebars sticking out of the ground on this guy's property. Upon closer inspection, he saw that it was a complete bike, and he asked the guy if he could buy it. It was an old beater that hadn't run in years, but my dad gave him something like fifty bucks to take it off his hands.

He took it down to the shop and began to rebuild it in his spare time. On my sixth birthday he gave me my very first bike. It had a Briggs & Straton lawn mover engine with a pull-cord starter. He buffed up the frame and painted it orange. At the time the blocks on Chevys were orange, so he used what he had left over from the shop. The seat was a piece of foam wrapped by car-seat upholstery stapled to a piece of plywood. The brake pedal was just a long lever connected to a piece of metal that would rub directly on the tire when you pressed it. It wasn't a factory works bike, but it was mine.

He taught me to ride it right there in the parking lot of the shop.

At the Sun City house, age 4.

The lot is about two-thirds the size of a tennis court, and my dad instructed me not to go out in the street. I'd heard that one before. Not to mention a thick fog had rolled through, making it impossible to see more than twenty feet in front of your face.

For about ten minutes I'm riding my new mini-bike around in circles. I got the hang of it pretty easily. My dad was so excited that his son was finally riding a motorcycle. But circles get old, so I shot across the lot, straight out of the front gate. I was putting down the middle of the road with cars zooming by as my dad ran out of the lot screaming for me to stop.

I did.

Eventually.

Hmm, Tasty

The street rule was still in effect so I did most of my riding out in the pasture behind our house where we used to raise livestock. Back then we pretty much lived off the land. We had cows for beef and milk and chickens for eggs. We'd get the cows when they were just calves and feed them 'til they were ready for slaughter. Then we stored all the meat in this huge freezer. At first I thought the cows were pets. The first two we got I named Pebbles and Bam Bam. They would be out grazing while I rode around them on my minibike. I remember the day

Silver Lake Mammoth.

Jeremy McGrath

the slaughter guy came. But I didn't realize what had happened since I didn't actually see it. The next day I went riding and Pebbles and Bam-Bam were gone. After I was done riding around, I came in for dinner. I didn't realize it, but we had Pebbles that night.

I Didn't Get This Scar Playing Tiddlywinks

The minibike was cool, but after a while I just stopped riding it. I was way more into riding my BMX bike. Especially since most of the kids in the neighborhood had bikes too. We rode BMX all day, ten or twelve hours sometimes. When I got home from school the first thing I would do was grab my bike and race off to meet my friends.

My first BMX race, San Bernardino, age 11.

We had this uphill driveway with chain-link fences on both sides that fenced in the property in front of the house. The gate to the driveway wasn't at the bottom of the street but up near the house. Since it was on a hill and didn't latch properly, it wouldn't stay open. Usually, we had to prop it open with a rock or something. One day I got home from school and wanted to prop the gate open so I could just zoom out of the house on my bike to the street without having to stop, but I couldn't find a rock anywhere. I wandered almost all the way down to the street until I saw one on the other side of the fence. There was no way I was going all the way back up the driveway and around the fence to get it. So I tried to hop the fence, because that's what eight-year-olds do. I climbed the fence and jumped off the top when a wire that was sticking out gashed me from my nipple to my belly button. I started bleeding like crazy.

Since I was home alone I just ran up to my bed and tried to go to sleep despite being a walking bloodbath. When my mom got home a few hours later there was blood everywhere—on the floor, the pillow, my sheets. My mom came into my room and thought I was dead. I didn't get stitches but I probably should have. Somehow my mom was able to stop the bleeding. I still have that scar to this day. I made up a story about how I crashed trying to pull off some crazy jump. For some reason I wanted to make it sound like I got hurt trying to do something cool.

PREPARING FOR THE RIDE

Chances are you don't have a big-time factory mechanic like Kawasaki's Jeremy Albrecht to prep your bike. That means before you ride, it's up to you to give your trusty steed a good once-over. Whether you've planned a Sunday afternoon trail ride or are pulling up to the gate of a 250 Supercross, failure to properly perform a preride inspection could lead to mechanical problems or even injury. Here are a few things that should be on your checklist:

1. Check the air pressure. The last thing you want to discover when you're two hours from anywhere is that you've got a slow leak in one of your tires. Keep in mind that different temperatures affect air pressure (your tires may seem flat in colder weather). Know

Jeremy McGrath

what type of terrain you'll encounter and set pressure accordingly.

2. Bleed the air from your fork. Chances are you keep a close watch on your suspension settings. To alleviate any unnecessary stiffness, use a screwdriver to release excess pressure from the bleed screws on the forks.

3. Be sure to check whether all of the spokes on your rims are properly tightened. Loose spokes could potentially break when you're landing off a jump. That's never a good thing. While you're at it, check for small objects in your tires (glass, nails) that could cause punctures.

4. Check all of your major cables. See that the throttle and clutch cables aren't loose and adjust accordingly. This is a good time to make sure all the levers, shifter, and brake pedal are functioning properly.

5. One of the most integral moving parts is the chain. Check it before each ride for wear. Chains will stretch after excessive use. Most people don't replace the chain until it breaks. Try to stay ahead of the curve. Tighten the chain so there is a three-finger gap between it and the rear of the chain slider. Apply chain lube.

6. It would be wise to quickly check all major nuts and bolts (motor mounts, axles, triple clamp, etc.). This only takes a few minutes but can save you a world of trouble.

7. Now make sure you've got a tank full of gas and turn the petcock to the on position. Have a nice ride.

By 1979 the "stay out of the street" rule had all but disappeared. Partly because there are hardly any sidewalks in Sun City and partly because my dad was at the shop all day when I would ride my bike. My bike was pretty much my main transpo.

I had a rad Mongoose that I was totally proud of. I was always trying to trick it out as much as I could. My dad bought me a blue ACS Z-Rim, which were some of the coolest wheels at the time. They were made out of some sort of fiberglass composite that would flex under stress. When the rims got bent you had to put them in the freezer to straighten them back out. My dad bought just the front rim; I had to earn the money myself to buy the back rim. It was his way of teaching discipline and trying to instill an appreciation for money. Those rims were so cool it didn't take me long to earn the money for the back one.

I had my Mongoose set up just right. On my Z-Rims I rotated Comp III and Snake Belly tires. I ran

A'me grips and anodized ACS hubs. I really took pride in my bike because it was all I had.

Going into town was a trip—a six-mile bike ride if you wanted to go to McDonald's or the bike shop, Sun City Schwinn. We'd pretty much get into whatever mischief we could find when we weren't jumping curbs or seeing how long we could do wheelies. Sometimes we would harass old people or get chased off by various shop owners. Other times we would get like twenty kids together and ride all day to Lake Perris. It was a three-hour ride away. We'd get to the lake and swim for about half an hour before we had to make the ride back.

How Not to Ride a Motorcycle

There was a kid in my neighborhood named Jeff Castle who had a brand-new 1980 Yamaha YZ 80. I was so envious of that bike because it was a real motorcycle, unlike my Briggs & Straton. Even though I was spending most of my time on my bicycle, my dad managed to scrape up enough cash and buy me a used 1979 Suzuki RM 80. That was my first real motocross bike, and my dad took it upon himself to teach me how to use the clutch and gears. We're back in the parking lot of his shop. He fired it up and rode it around to warm it up.

Everything was going fine until he decided to really crack the throttle and the bike did a massive wheelie. Picture a 260-pound man standing an 80 straight up. He's off balance and stuck on the gas. He was totally scared out of his mind. I don't think he realized that little Suzook had so much kick. At this point he's heading straight for a chain-link fence that surrounds the lot. And he can't turn since the front wheel is in the air. He managed to set the front wheel down and ran smack into the fence. The bottom of the fence wasn't really secured to the ground, so he rode halfway under the fence before getting pinned on the motorcycle. He was hanging off the back with the chain-link fence holding the bike upright. I had to push the bike over so he could get free.

Somehow I knew that wasn't the way it was done.

Jeremy McGrath

I got pretty good on the RM quick. I learned to handle the bike up and down hills, through the sand, and full throttle in top gear. Everyday I looked for new challenges, some small way to push the RM a little more. Not far from Hawthorne

On my Suzuki RM 80, age 10.

Street there was a riding area we called Finger Point Hill. At the top of this thirty-foot-high hill was a large rock shaped like a finger that pointed to the sky. That hill seemed like a mountain to us. Eventually, I got the nerve to conquer it on my Suzuki. I just grabbed a handful of throttle and held on.

Looking at that hill today it seems so small. You could probably ride a BMX bike up it, but it felt like such an accomplishment back then. I came home all excited and told my dad I'd climbed the hill way before Jeff Castle and his new YZ 80. Needless to say my dad was equally pumped.

Tracy, Please Wake Up!

Sometimes obstacles don't always come in the form of hills and rocks. Sometimes they are shaped like people. I came home from riding one afternoon all stoked after clearing a big obstacle or something. By now I could hang the RM out pretty good. I pulled in our driveway and twisted the throttle for one last blast. My sister Tracy was standing at the top of the driveway, at the gate, when she saw me coming. She immediately started to freak. She was only six, so I'm sure getting hit by a motorcycle was not in her plans. I was in second gear wringing it out. I must have been going about twenty mph, and instead of being smart, I decided not to slow down. She tried to get out of the way at the last second, just as I attempted to maneuver around her. I ended up steering right into her, which sent her flipping up in the air. I crashed so hard it was like a huge mushroom cloud of dust floated up over Sun City. My elbows were totally thrashed and my Tough Skins took a serious ripping. My dad came running out of the house when he heard the screaming.

I was in big trouble. Big Jack was fuming.

He didn't even have to ask questions. He slapped me on my helmet so hard I flipped over on my head. He was so pissed that his face turned beet red and seemed like it stayed that way for days. Luckily, my sister wasn't hurt.

Hemmet BMX

By 1981, I was spending every second that I wasn't sleeping or in school on my BMX bike. If I wasn't trying to clear ridiculous obstacles, I was

Jeremy McGrath

in my room working on my ride. That Mongoose was pretty much an extension of my body. One of the kids I rode with was an older boy named Corey Collum. He was about seventeen and all the kids looked up to him because he raced BMX. He must have thought I was pretty good because he suggested that I should race, too. Corey helped me convince my dad to let me give it a try.

My dad agreed, so we loaded up our bikes in the family's wood panel Plymouth wagon and headed for Hemmet BMX Track. It was a small local track, but it was bigger than anything I had been on to that

point. The track had a lot of smooth rollers, double jumps, and a giant tabletop. I entered the ten-year-old beginner class. For some reason I wasn't nervous at all. I was actually pretty excited. I knew what I could do on a bike, so I was confident. There were only a few other kids in my class that day and I smoked them. I also threw in a touch of style over the tabletop for good measure. At least I thought it was style.

From the first day I was hooked. It was the competition. I loved showing people that I was the fastest or could jump the highest. Plus I'm a showoff. When there is something that I'm good at I love to show people what I can do. The showman in me just takes over. This wasn't lost on my dad. He gave me the nickname Showtime, and it fit so well everyone started calling me that.

Shortly after I started racing, I got a brand-new Hutch. The Mongoose was cool, but that thing must have weighed thirty-five pounds. Hutch was top of the line back then. It was light, sleek, and so fast. It had titanium bear-trap pedals that would shread your shins if you slipped a pedal. My dad was really enthusiastic and wanted me to have the best equipment. He would always yell encouragement from the berms when I passed by. A lot of fathers get out there and act like maniacs, but my dad pretty much kept it to constructive critiscm. But don't get me wrong, he loved winning just as much as I did.

I had ridden my bike so much before I began racing that it didn't take me long to transfer my skills to the racetrack. Jumping, cornering, and sprinting just seemed so natural to me. The competition made it that much more fun. Within a couple months I ran roughshod through the beginner and novice classes and moved up to expert. To turn expert you have to accumulate a certain number of points and wins. It usually takes about a year if you race regularly. Like I said, I was pretty fast. I began to venture farther away from the old Hemmet track to race as many races as I could to rack up as many points as possible toward the state championship. A championship was awarded to the overall points leader for each age group and class. I was gunning for the title in eleven-year-old expert class.

In California, there were so many tracks and so many kids racing then, you had to go out four or five times a week to stay in the points hunt for the state championship. Throughout the rest of the country racing BMX was usually a weekend pursuit. You could race Saturday and Sunday with maybe a special weekday race thrown in. But out here they ran races daily.

Each week we loaded up the Plymouth and traveled to tracks like

Jeremy McGrath

Holding my triple race trophy,
Bandit, San Bernadino, age 12.

Coal Canyon BMX in Corona or Orange County YMCA BMX track in Anaheim. One day at Orange County I met another eleven-year-old expert from Mission Viejo named Brian Lopes. Like me, he was one of the fastest eleven-year-olds around, so we hit it off right away. During the summer we'd spend the weekend at each other's house riding BMX and motorcycles for as long as we could stay awake. But mostly we raced. Sometimes up to thirteen times a week.

Our BMX week would start on Saturday and my dad would end up putting over 100 miles on the old Plymouth wagon driving us around to the races. We began at Coal Canyon in Corona, where the races started at nine A.M. From there we went across town to Snipes BMX for the noon race. Then it was off to the Corona YMCA track for the three o'clock start. Finally, we'd head back home for the seven o'clock evening race at Lake Elsinore BMX.

On Sunday we did the whole routine again. During the week we probably raced four out of the five weeknights. We did this for almost three years. During the school year I adjusted my race load depending on how much homework I had. Most of the time I just did homework in the car on the way to the race.

When you raced as often as I did, you start to bring home a lot of trophies. I was so excited when I first started getting them. It was such a cool feeling to get your trophy at the trophy presentation. But after a while trophies didn't mean anything to me. In fact, we ran out of places to keep them. Most tracks had it set up so you could sell back your old trophies for a few dollars. I got so many it was hard to even sell them. There are still a couple hundred sitting in storage at my parents house.

Duned

By thirteen, I was getting good enough to qualify for the big out-of-state nationals. I got my first sponsorship from VDC, a small California bike company, but I was ignored by the big teams like GT or Diamond Back. Still, it was cool to have someone interested in my racing. They helped me get to some of the nationals, because my parents didn't really have the money for me to go racing out of state. And even when they did, it seemed something would always happen to prevent me from going.

Once, before the National Bicycle League (NBL) Grands in Tennessee, the year-end championships, my dad took us to ride three-wheelers at these beautiful rolling sand dunes called Whitewater in Palm Springs. My dad had a home-built three-wheeled contraption with a Yamaha 360 engine. He was up to his old tricks when he tried to tackle the biggest dune out there. When he hit the gas on that old thing, it rattled your teeth loose and cleaned out your ears. He blasted up the hill and tried to hang on with everything he had. He was almost to the top when he flipped out and the bike went flying.

That was the good news. The bad news was that somewhere during that stunt he lost his wallet. Now, we were just about to fly to Tennessee for the Grands. He had nearly $1,500 in the wallet to send my mom and me and now it was gone. He had been saving for months to pay for our trip. He stayed late at the shop nearly every day to make the extra cash. We looked everywhere, on every dune, for that wallet, but couldn't find it. There would be no trip to the Grands. I was bummed out but I could tell my dad was really crushed.

Burned Out

At the end of the 1984 season, I was really starting to get burned out. Completely toasted. I had just put in another year racing a schedule that was totally bananas. At thirteen, I won the NBL Gold Cup and the California State Championship. I finished the season with 24,893 points, and even beat out Brian, who finished the year fourth with 19,793 points.

To give you an idea of how we much raced that year, the points leader in Connecticut had just 3,596 points. See what I mean? I loved racing BMX, but I definitely needed a bigger challenge.

Clockwise from top left: Bobby Pease, me, Pat Killam, and Cory Collom at the BMX National.

You want to go faster, right? Who doesn't? You can hop your bike up all you want, but if you don't know how to ride it you won't go anywhere. Follow these easy riding tips and you may just shave a second or two off your lap times.

Don't Loop Out

One of the most common causes of crashing is looping out (flipping over backward). If you hit a jump with too much throttle and are too far back on the seat, you'll loop. If you find yourself in this predicament, hit the rear brake and pull in the clutch. That will instantly level the bike out.

Keep It Down

The key to any race is getting a good start. Wheelie too high on the start, and you'll lose ground because you'll have to shut off the throttle. If your front wheel gets up too high on the start, simply pull in the clutch a bit and the rpm's will drop just enough to lower the front wheel.

Whoops, I Did It Again!

Everyone has a theory about how to go fast through the whoops. Here is a simple one: Pick a tall gear, maintain your speed, and go in a straight line. Changing your speed or line in the middle of the whoops is a surefire way to go down.

Turn For the Better

You're more likely to make that great pass going into the turn than coming out. But you've got to come in smokin'.

Jeremy McGrath

Late as you possibly can, pull in the clutch and the brakes at the same time. Brake only can kill the motor, but pulling in the clutch releases the suspension from the torque effect of the motor.

You'll Flip Over It

Another common get-off is the mid-air endo, which is usually followed by an unwanted face plant. If your nose starts to dive, crack your throttle wide open. The momentum of the spinning rear wheel should level the bike out and save your face.

On my fourteenth birthday, November 19, 1985, my parents decided that I was ready for my first brand-new motorcycle. One of their friends worked at Malcolm Smith Motorsports in Riverside. My dad always had Yamahas, so he wanted me to have one, too. That birthday wasn't unlike any other. My parents gave me my presents and that was pretty much that. Afterward, my mom asked me to come out on the porch to help with the laundry. So I did. What I didn't know was that my parents had already sneaked outside. When I came out on the porch my dad flicked the lights on. Right there on the porch was a brand-new 1986 YZ 80. No more secondhand bikes for me. I was so overwhelmed I just started crying. Man, I couldn't believe it. My mom said getting me the bike was their way of showing me thanks for staying out of trouble and such. My face pretty much said it all. They were just happy that I was happy. Ask my mom and she'll tell you that night on the porch was one of the happiest moments of her life.

First Race at Perris

That YZ was so fast to me. That year the YZs had been totally redesigned and Yamaha dropped the traditional yellow-and-black color scheme for red and white. I had been riding that clapped out RM for six years and that made the YZ feel like a factory ride. When I showed up with that thing at the local riding area, all the other kids were pretty stunned. One of the guys who rode BMX with us all the time was Raymond Hensley. He had an 80 and raced motocross as well. I guess he was tired of me constantly smoking him on BMX, so he suggested that I race my YZ. At that point I was so over racing BMX and riding my bicycle that I thought I should give motocross a try.

Raymond and I talked my dad into letting me race. Actually, it wasn't that hard. My dad loved to watch me compete, especially when I'd show off. One day in June of 1986, Ray and I loaded up our 80s and drove thirty-five minutes to the local track, Perris Raceway. It was carved right out of hills that were covered with huge, smooth boulders that looked like they were sprinkled there by God. Perris was a fast track with a lot of jumps and elevation changes.

I entered the 80 beginner class. I didn't look like much of a Supercross star back then. I wore my old BMX gear and borrowed some clapped-out boots from a friend. Back then there were so many kids that they ran the 80 novice and beginner at the same time. They dropped the gate for the novice class then sent the beginners twenty seconds later. Raymond rode novice. When the bikes went screaming off the starting line it reminded me of my first BMX race. That's because I wasn't really nervous at all. I just loved trying to beat the guy next to me. Whether it was off the line, over a tabletop, or in a corner, I wanted to come out on top. It's like I was programmed to compete or something.

I won the first moto of the beginner class. Even finished ahead of some of the novice riders who had a twenty-second head start. For the second moto, I lined up on the gate with the novice class. I picked out a spot on the gate, but I wasn't going to go. I had to wait until the rest of the beginners pulled up. But something just came over me. I got so excited when the novice gate dropped I just took off with the novice class. Honestly, I couldn't tell the differences in the classes. I finished third with the novices in the second moto, ahead of Raymond Hensley. But since I raced with the wrong class I didn't get an overall score for the day. It didn't matter. I knew that this was what I wanted to do. BMX was done. I decided to spend every moment on my bike practicing, play riding, and racing.

After school I'd come home and roost up every inch of our three-acre lot. We had a tractor that I used to fashion some makeshift jumps on the property. But because of where we lived, there was terrain to ride as far as the eye could see. I could leave our backyard, ride away from my house, and not turn around until it got dark. That's how far we could ride! There was every type of surface: sand, hard-packed dirt, hills, jumps, and long straightaways. It was a perfect training ground for a budding young motocrosser.

Every now and again my bike would throw a chain or get a flat. I had seen my dad work on my bike so many times that I could pretty much do everything myself. Besides, when everyone is out jammin' you don't want to go bother your dad at work to turn the wrenches for you. I made a habit of cleaning the air filter or tightening the chain each time before I rode so I could get peak performance. I imagined that I was a Team Honda factory rider and my bike had to be in tip-top shape. Learning to work on my bike helped me when it came to working with my professional mechanics. Understanding their job makes both of our lives easier. These days so many young kids have no idea how to work on their bikes and that's ridiculous.

Racing motocross was a breath of fresh air. The races were just once a week, as opposed to thirteen times on BMX. I felt like I was back to being a kid without stressing over having to race every night of the week to stay atop the points. There was also a little more time for me to do my schoolwork, which made my mom happy.

A couple months after my MX debut, I started my freshman year at Perris High School. My bus stop was the farthest from school. I mean it took and hour and fifteen minutes to get there. And that's by highway.

My senior photo, 1989.

We got out of school at 2:30 and sometimes I didn't get home until 4:00. When daylight savings ended I'd only have an hour to ride at best. That was the main reason I never played team sports in high school. It would take time away from riding.

Full-Time Mini Pilot

We became regulars at Perris Raceway, Glen Helen in San Bernardino, and De Anza in Moreno Valley. It got to the point where I was finishing on the podium almost every weekend in 80 novice. I realized immediately how BMX helped my riding. I had the habit of staying low to the ground over jumps and rhythm sections. The best BMX racers ride with pure poetry. In BMX you have to be perfect on a jump or you'll crash hard or get passed. It's all about staying as low as possible over jumps. For me, that carried over. I tried to do little things like land perfectly off of jumps or hold the throttle a second longer diving into a turn. Most young motocrossers are so squirrelly they are a hazard to their own health. But I was smooth. I learned early how to set myself up for obstacles three or four jumps in advance. I studied the track like a textbook. The more jumps there were, the better I was. Right away I could identify the faster line in and out of the corners. I loved the technical aspect of racing and tried to concentrate on solid fundamental riding. Anything to make me a smoother rider, because I knew the smoother I was, the faster I could go.

Jeremy McGrath

Hi, I'm Ryan . . . And This Is Phil

One thing cool about racing was that I could meet other kids who were as into it as I was. At Perris, I met an 80 rider named Ryan Hughes. He introduced me to his friend Phil Lawrence, who had a Yamaha that always seemed to be the cleanest at the track. Ryan had a cool sense of humor and was tough as nails. We hit it off immediately because we had the same exact interests: motocross and girls. He was a couple of years younger than me and Phil but was just as fast.

When we weren't racing, we were riding together. I would get my parents to drive me up to Beaumont to spend the weekend at Phil's or to Escondido to stay at Ryan's.

One of the places you could always find us was Reche Canyon, not far from Phil's house. Reche Canyon was one of the best riding areas in all of Southern California. It had almost every type of terrain you could think of. Huge sections of it were nothing but jumps carved out by nature. No tractor or shovel had ever touched the place. It was almost like a natural Supercross track. It's almost impossible to meet someone who was into motocross at that time who didn't ride there. One of the Reche Canyon regulars was a kid named Buddy Antunez. He was like the cool guy of the crew. He always had everything: the latest clothes, a brand-new turbo Toyota Supra, and tons of bikes. He was also the fastest 80 rider around. But he never had a big head, so he and I became friends.

Another regular was a shrimp of a guy named Tommy Clowers who could ride his ass off. He and Buddy always knocked heads, but that just added to the fun. Today Tommy goes by The Tomcat and is one of the best freestyler motocrossers out there. Sure, you've seen him ripping up the Step Up comp at the X Games, but he got his start on the racing scene.

On an average day we'd have a posse of ten guys out in the canyon at once. You could ride for hours and not cover the same ground twice. Right in the middle of everything was this huge mountain that we all used to race up. When we got to the top it seemed like we could see forever. Sometimes we shut our bikes off and raced back down the hill with no engines. It would be dead silent except for ten kids screaming at each other and laughing all the way down the mountain.

Despite our nonstop thrill ride out in the canyon, there was also an element of danger to riding at Reche. First off, it was illegal. Much of the area was privately owned. But not by any of us. Private property sucks for MXers. When the cops didn't have anything better to do they would come after us. But the chase was always short. Sometimes we'd go exploring and cut across some old guy's desert property. Because no one could catch us, some maniacal property owners started shooting at

Racing, 1987.

us. I don't know if they were trying to scare us or just had terrible aim, but no one ever got hit. We'd hear bullets whizzing by us and not even be all that worried. Because when we were riding we felt invincible. We were lucky to hit Reche Canyon in its heyday. Thirteen years

later the area has become victim to park service laws and suburban sprawl as the ever-expanding SoCal construction monster continues to gobble up prime real estate that would otherwise serve as proving grounds for future Supercross stars.

Buddy was also friends with two brothers, Jeremy and Joel Albrecht, who rode for Team Green, Kawasaki's squad of ameteur hotshots. Because they lived right on the edge of Reche Canyon, their house became Grand Central for young motocrossers across the state.

The Albrechts were like spoiled rich kids without acting like snobs. I got along with Jeremy and Joel right away because we were all so into motocross. The first time I walked in their garage I was blown away. They had about fifteen bikes all lined up in a row. Their dad hired a mechanic that would come over and work on their bikes for them. "Man, I hate working on my bike," Jeremy Albrecht used to say. (That proved motocross is not without a sense of irony since Jeremy would become one of the most successful motocross mechanics of all time. He currently wrenches for James Stewart, Jr.)

I knew they were getting factory support, but this was ridiculous. It also helped that their father was loaded. They lived in a huge house their dad gave them after he split from Mrs. Albrecht. I guess it was to keep them happy. The fact that there was no parental supervision kept us kids happy. Jeremy was sixteen and Joel just fourteen, and they lived there by themselves. Their dad gave them money every month to live on. It worked for us. Picture this enormous house with no food or furniture, doors wide open, and teenage kids everywhere.

We were at the age where girls were the only thing that could pry us away from our bikes. Sometimes there would be as many girls at the house as guys. That is, if they didn't mind the soda cans and porno magazines lying everywhere. It seemed like sleeping bags and backpacks covered every other inch of the floor. It was our own private Animal House. On any given night there were twenty kids crashed out all over the house. If you didn't have anywhere to go, you knew you could always go to the Albrechts.

Jack the Mini Dad

Back then there was a race series called Yamaha MX Classic. The series had a contingency program in which you could earn YZ Bucks, which were redeemable for parts and gear at area Yamaha dealers. It was a much needed incentive program for a race family like ours, because motocross is an extremely expensive sport. In 1986, an 80cc bike cost about $1,500. (Triple that for a 2004.) If you want to be competitive you need the best aftermarket modifications, too. Then there's travel, entry fees, and insurance until you're out of money. We were a typical middle-class family as far as income goes, so we didn't have tons of green to spend on racing. There were also times when things got pretty tight.

To help finance a racing career, riders often have sponsors (bike shops, apparel, parts companies) that give the kids product in exchange for sticking the company's logo on their front fender. The fastest kids are often sponsored directly by one of the Big Four bike manufacturers—Honda, Yamaha, Kawasaki, and Suzuki—and get free bikes and parts. It's in the manufacturer's best interest to create good relationships with riders (and vice versa) during their grassroots careers. I didn't have any sponsors, so I needed every dollar.

Luckily, I was winning a lot and my dad was into my racing pretty hardcore. I think in some ways he lived his racing dream through me. So naturally he wanted to protect my interests at all costs. One weekend I raced the Yamaha MX Classic at Sunrise MX Park in Adelanto, which is just north of San Bernardino, three hours east of L.A. There was this one kid in my class named Joshua Dunn, who was about seventeen. This kid was like twice my size. I was about 5' 7", and he towered over me. He even had a beard and a mustache. Joshua was beating us on a regular basis and my dad was not happy about it. So at this particular race he just smoked us and took all the YZ Bucks. After the race, my dad goes over to Dunn's father and gets in a nasty shouting match right there in the pits. The two dads are calling each other every name in the book. "Your son's too old to race against fourteen-year-olds," screamed big Jack. Finally, my dad had enough and hocked a huge loogie in the guy's face. Race officials had to separate them. Needless to say, Joshua Dunn was no longer in my class after that.

My dad got a little carried away, but he was pretty tame compared to the way a lot of the dads behaved. The Mini Dad is one of the most notorious figures in the sport. Known for his complete bloodlust, win-at-all-cost mentality, and four-letter vocabulary, the Mini Dad can be found trackside at every major national in America.

Minicycle racing can be more cutthroat than the pros. And that's before the gate drops. Accusations fly like mud in the mini world. "Little Johnny's motor is bored out!" "You're lying about your kid's age!" "His wheels are too big!" "He's running an '88 brake set and this is '87!" You get just about everything under the sun when you have parents who want to win more than their offspring. Manufacturers go at it, too. But it's usually just talk. It would be bad news if a manufacturer had another team's bike torn down only to find it perfectly legal. As much as parents complain, they often stop short of protesting a manufacturer, because it may affect their kid's future career. There are only five manufacturers to play ball with. Why limit your options before you even get started?

A strong showing on the national scene can mean the difference between starting your pro career under a factory umbrella or hitting the highway as a privateer and covering your own expenses.

Overzealous parents have always been a part of the high-stakes world of amateur motocross. Sometimes it gets messy. Ezra Lusk, a kid from Georgia with a super fast KX 60, who'd jump anything, ended up in a nasty legal tangle with his parents over money that lasted well into his pro career.

I never had that problem with my parents. They always knew when to throttle back and never forgot rule no. 1: Racing is supposed to be fun.

By the end of the 1986 season I had ridden my YZ into the ground. Motocross bikes are super durable, but after racing week in and week out the bikes get worn. I had earned enough YZ bucks to buy a brand-new 1987 YZ 80. And since we were getting serious about racing, my dad somehow scraped up enough and bought a second YZ to rotate so the bikes wouldn't wear out so fast. But I still wasn't sponsored by anybody. Ryan had a full ride with Team Green. "When they sent me six bikes I thought I had made it," said Ryno about being sponsored. And Phil got bikes and parts from Yamaha. But I got nothing. That always annoyed my dad that people constantly overlooked me. "Man, this is hard because we just can't afford it," Big Jack said. He wasn't mad at me, but the fact was, I was beating kids who were sponsored by shops and gear companies! Yet I still wasn't getting any love from them.

A lot of fast area kids got help from Yamaha, but they looked right past us. "There's a guy at Yamaha named Mike Guerra who never gave a shit about the McGraths," my dad would say. "We'd beat all his kids and he would never even acknowledge us."

I hated that, too, but all I could do was to keep riding and keep winning.

Team Green (with Envy)

I couldn't help feeling jealous when I would see kids who rode for Team Green. At the grassroots level of motocross, the best of the best ride for Team Green. It's the closest thing a kid can get to being a factory rider. Team Green is Kawasaki's support program for the fastest amateur racers in the country. It's the equivalent of a top-flight Little League program that travels the country dominating the competition. Their riders get bikes (green KXs, of course), gear, equipment, travel expenses, and operate out of a big rig at the major events with highly-skilled Kawasaki mechanics just like the pros. The team started in the early eighties with just the 80cc class, but has since expanded to 60, 65, 100, 125, and 250 amateur classes. Imagine being little Johnny Hardluck and showing up at one of the amateur nationals and putting by Team Green's semi on your RM with its bald knobbies, worn graphics, and poorly set up suspension, wearing a ripped hand-me-down Fox jersey your cousin loaned you. It can be pretty intimidating.

It seemed like all of my friends who rode at Reche Canyon got bigtime support from somewhere, whether it was a manufacturer, a local shop, or an MX clothing company. Everybody except for me. I got nothing and it always pissed my dad off.

"When is someone going to give us some help?" my dad used to ask no one in particular.

Team Green spared no expense, throwing hundreds of thousands of dollars at its grassroots development program. For the most talented of racers, getting a ride with Team Green is like being on the fast track to the pros. That's why a spot on the team is so coveted. But getting to Team Green is not easy. Each year they receive over 5,000 young racer's resumes. Kids also have to submit report cards and weekly race reports. And you have to destroy the comp at the local level.

The list of Team Green alumni reads like a who's who of motocross. Former 250 champs Jeff Ward, Mike Keidrowski, Jeff Stanton, and Jeff Emig have all made their names on the Green machines. Even the stars of today like Ricky Carmichael, James "Bubba" Stewart, and Ezra Lusk all have lime green pedigrees and rooms full of national championship trophies.

Factory Phil

Just because I wasn't on Team Green didn't mean I didn't cherish what I had. In fact I might have cherished it too much. Ryan only had one bike at the time and we both had the same idea of how to make them look cool. You know how little kids think all those souped-up cars in *The Fast and the Furious* are so cool? Well, we thought it was the baddest thing to deck out our bikes the same way. The YZs back then were red and white, and in '87 neon colors were the hot thing. Ryno and I thought the more color you had, the better. We outfitted our bikes with pink seat covers, fork boots and grips, and orange YZ graphics. We bolted on every kind of guard there was. Guards for the brakes, frame, and pipe. Even our guards had guards. We put so much crap on our bikes we must have added thirty pounds. When I look back now I don't know what we were thinking. You'd never catch us on something that hideous today.

My first interview, 1987.

But Phil was the exact opposite. He liked his bikes clean and simple. His YZs were perfectly stock, almost like you could buy out of the showroom. He tried to emulate the pros who rode for Factory Yamaha with their perfect looking rides. Everyone started calling him Factory Phil. The nickname has stuck to this day, and Phil still keeps his bikes clean. We all wanted to be factory riders, but Phil was the only one smart enough to at least look the part.

Jeremy McGrath

Loretta's

Halfway through the '87 season, it became apparent that I was getting too big for my 80s. That spring I had earned enough YZ Bucks to buy a YZ 125. Making the transition from minis to the big bikes is no easy task. The 125s are more powerful and harder to handle. The riders are more skilled and things happen much faster on the track than in the mini class. There is more of an emphasis on skill, since the riders are much more talented across the board. But I had been preparing myself all along with my BMX-inspired love for the fundamental aspects of racing. I skipped 125 beginner and went straight to novice. I continued to race 80s until June of 1987, when I decided to sell both minis and put the money into my 125 effort. Most mini riders advance to 80 intermediate, then the highly competitive expert class, to prepare them for the rigors of 125 life. Not me. Even though I was a novice I knew I had what it took to race the big bikes.

It didn't take me very long to make the same impact in 125 novice that I had in 80 novice. In just a couple short months I had won enough local races to qualify for the AMA Youth Amateur National Championship, the Super Bowl of amateur motocross, at Loretta Lynn's Dude Ranch motocross track in Hurricane Mills, Tennessee.

More Mini Kids

Another rider I made friends with at Perris was a local kid named Derek Natvig. He was a super fast 80 expert who could race with anybody. Eventually our families became really close. Our parents were friends. Our little sisters played together. And our weekends revolved around racing. In August, I caught a ride with the Natvigs to Loretta Lynn's in their motorhome. We hitched the bikes to the back and drove the 1,673 miles to Tennessee in three days. My dad flew in and met us there a day later.

This was the big time to me. I couldn't believe I was at one of the biggest annual showcases for up-and-coming motocross talent. Anybody who was anybody was at Loretta Lynn's. Ryno and Phil were there.

So was Buddy Antunez. So was a future 250 Supercross rider from Georgia named Ezra Lusk. He was Team Green's ten-year-old wunkerkind and the favorite to win the 7-11 6occ stock and modified classes. After all, he rode an ultra-trick $7,000 KX 6o that could run with 125s on straightaways. With its aluminum parts and engine modifications, it put most pro factory efforts to shame.

Another rider who made the rounds at amateur nationals was Damon Bradshaw of North Carolina. He was simply known as The Beast from the East. A more popular and decorated amateur rider there wasn't. His mystique alone was intimidating. He had already won sixteen national minibike titles and was sponsored by Fox, the biggest MX clothing company at the time. The motocross magazines would do features on his super fast, tricked out YZ 80–the bike that made the number 68 so feared. "We Ride Bradshaw's Bike!" the headlines would scream. Bigtime pros like Rick Johnson (who was my hero), Johnny O'Mara, and Broc Glover all said Damon was going to be the next big star. By the way he rode, everyone believed it. Bradshaw was wildly aggressive and completely hung it out there, rarely letting off the throttle. While I had been toiling away at Perris with no sponsors, Damon was lighting up the national scene and getting full factory support from Yamaha.

Yamaha had sponsored Damon since May of 1985, a year and a half before I even had a real motocross 80. Yamaha gave him eight bikes for the year, two of which were tuned by factory mechanics for national events. To go with the bikes he got an $8,000 parts credit (a ton of money in '87) and had the option to sell the bikes at the end of the year and pocket the cash. His parents, Randy and Marsha, received about $25,000 a year to cover travel and other expenses while accompanying Damon to the races. Don't forget the $500 he got for a national win and $50 bucks a day to test bikes.

This was a kid we all wanted to be like. But we had no concept of the pressure he was under at such a young age. With so much expectation it was easy for people to forget that he was just a regular kid who liked the hair band Ratt and the movie *Top Gun* and got annoyed by his younger sibling just like the rest of us.

At home on my Yamaha 80, age 14.

But when you're touted as the next big thing, those things tend to get lost. Yamaha wasn't grooming him just because they liked seeing him win. A winning rider means positive publicity and high visibility for a manufacturer's product—the motorcycle. That translates into big sales at dealerships all across the country. The simple truth is that the money spent on a rider's career is nothing more than an investment back in the company in order to generate bike sales. Even though you don't realize it, that's the source of the pressure. If you're not winning, no one is going to "invest" in you.

But when you're fourteen, you don't care about that. All you want to do is ride. We just cared about the fact that Damon got more magazine coverage than some of the 250 pros. That was cool to us. And he was so cool that after a while, people just started calling him the Golden Boy.

That year at Loretta's I entered 125 novice stock and modified classes. Stock is simply a bike with no major suspension or motor modifications, not that much different from what you would find on your dealer's showroom floor. A modified bike uses aftermarket products to

WIDE OPEN

improve power, handling, and exhaust. You can run a stock bike in the modified class, which is what I did, but not vice versa.

I got a great start in the stock class and ended up winning my first ever amateur national title. In the modified class, I didn't fair so well against the souped-up bikes. I finished about sixth overall, which wasn't bad for a national, but I was bummed nonetheless. Local boy Mike Brown, who would eventually win the 2001 125 Motocross National title as a pro, won the modified class that day.

THE DIFFERENCE BETWEEN MOTOCROSS AND SUPERCROSS

The sport of competitive off-road motorcycle racing is simply referred to as motocross. But there are two distinctly different styles of racing sanctioned by the American Motorcycle Association that make up the sport: Supercross and outdoor motocross (also called Nationals). The sixteen-round Supercross series runs from January to May, mostly in football stadiums throughout the country. For each race a crew of a dozen men and several bulldozers haul in forty tons of dirt that are fashioned into triple jumps, doubles, step-ups, hairpin turns, and whoops. Each race, with the exception of the Daytona SX, is run on a Saturday night.

The outdoor motocross season begins the weekend following the last Supercross race and includes twelve rounds, which run through September. Save for a few minor suspension adjustments, riders will use the same bikes for the outdoor circuit as they do in Supercross. Motocross courses are often carved right out of a hillside and have fewer obstacles than the more technically demanding Supercross tracks. Outdoors you'll find grueling, steep uphills and super fast downhills that break into off-camber, sweeping turns with deep ruts.

Motocross race on Sunday afternoons and often have to deal with an unforgiving sun or inclement weather. Not to mention rocks the size of Nerf footballs that can be unearthed by roosting knobbies.

Motocross and Supercross also differ from a fan's perspective. In a stadium, it's hard to have a bad sight line. You can see every bit of action, from the leader to last place lapper, without leaving your seat. In the hilly terrain of a motocross course, riders often go out of sight for as much as thirty or forty seconds at a time. But at a motocross race, fans can get right up to the side of the track to cheer their favorite riders. Just be prepared to get roosted.

The last significant difference is the format. Motocross determines a winner with two thirty-minute motos plus two laps. Where you place in the second moto counts more than the first. Example: You go 1-2 and I go 2-1. I get the overall win.

Supercross is broken down into two qualifying heat races (four riders from each transfer to main), two semi-finals (five from each transfer), and a Last Chance Qualifier (two more lucky riders advance). Twenty riders go at it in a twenty-lap winner-take-all main event. The Supercross championship is determined by the rider who accumulates the most points after sixteen rounds of racing. A first place is worth 25 points, second is good for 22 points, third is 20, and so on.

Mammoth, 1987.

When I returned to Califonia from the nationals, I raced out the rest of the season in the novice class. After winning a title at Loretta Lynn's, I felt like it was time to step up. But first there was something I had to do. My last novice race came at the Barona Oaks track, which was on an old Indian reservation in San Diego. Barona Oaks was a really fast track with a lot of Supercross-style jumps, so it suited me well. But that's not why I waited for that race to move up to intermediate. At the year-end race at Barona they gave away really sweet prizes. That year winners were given rad little Honda Spree scooters. Those things were awesome, and I thought my garage could use a few. So I borrowed an 80 from a friend to race along with my 125. I ended up winning three scooters that day.

In January of 1988, I jumped to 125 intermediate. Ryan Hughes and Phil Lawrence were already racing intermediate, so naturally I felt the need to show those guys up. Or at least try. That attitude plus their refusal to lose to me led to some of the best battles of my amateur career.

If any rider even thought about proving his worth in Southern California, the Golden State series was the place to do it. The record book of the series, run all over Southern California, reads like a who's who of motocross legends. In 1988, I found out I could belong, but I still wasn't the fastest. Team Green ace Jeff Emig won the 125 class while Chad Pederson (more on him in a bit) won the 250s. Ryno finished second in both classes. I got a couple of thirds. But I could feel an upset coming. I knew I was getting faster, but I still had to ride on the ragged edge to keep up with those guys.

Since I had just turned intermediate I wasn't really fast enough to be a serious threat to them just yet.

However, I didn't get the oppurtunity to bang bars with them at Loretta Lynn's that year. I just couldn't afford to go. In fact, I missed all of the other must-race nationals that year, which included the World Mini GP in Las Vegas, NMA Nationals in Ponca City, Oklahoma, and the GNC Nationals in Lake Whitney, Texas.

Not only were my friends winning titles and bringing home trophies, they were getting seen by the factories who were labeling them as pros of the future.

Ryan was riding so well he was signed by Team Green and got six bikes to practice and race. I was happy for him, but now I was pretty much the only fast guy who didn't have any support.

Meanwhile, the Yamaha MX Classic series was now defunct and the YZ Bucks had dried up. I got occasional discounts at Sunwest Yamaha in Corona and Orange County Cycle in Garden Grove (through Ken Faught, now editor of Dirt Rider) but that was it. Somehow we scraped up enough money for a YZ 250. I raced limited duty in the 250 novice class but only because my dad felt I should have a big bike to break the monotony of constantly racing 125s.

That didn't matter much because it was getting harder and harder to compete at this level with no support. Something was going to have to give.

Jeremy McGrath

Emig Does Southern California

We still rode regularly at Reche Canyon. On occasion, Jeremy and Joel Albrecht used to invite one of their Team Green teammates out to California to ride Reche and stay at the house. Joel met Jeff Emig at the Mini Olympics in Florida in 1988. I had seen Jeff before at Loretta's and Ponca City and read about him in the motocross magazines. He was almost as fast as Damon Bradshaw and always won huge at the nationals. For a sixteen-year-old, he and his No. 47 Kawasaki got a lot of coverage. He was from Kansas City and never backed down from anybody once the gate dropped. Jeff had a reputation for getting great starts. He was fast, but to me he was just another rider who got way more support than I did. Of course, I didn't realize it then, but other than my dad, no other person would shape my career quite like Jeff Emig would.

To most of the MX world Emig was known as Fro. One day while he was living with the Albrechts, fellow racer and Emig pal, Denny Stephenson, wrote "Jeffro is a homo" on his refrigerator. Denny needed something to rhyme with homo and Jeffro is the best he could come up with. "I got flak for that for a long time," Emig says. "I just want everyone to know that I'm not gay. Even though there is nothing wrong with that."

Eventually it got shortened to Fro, and that's pretty much what everyone calls him to this day.

I began to ride with Jeff on a regular basis when he moved in with the Albrechts in December of 1988 so he could race the GMC Golden State series. Jeff would ride at Reche Canyon with our crew and proceeded to work himself into the fabric of the up-and-coming Southern California motocross culture. In 1989, the heyday of Reche Canyon, Jeff was permanently on the scene, always ready to prove he was the hottest shit on two wheels.

Any differences anyone in our pack had was always drowned out by the wail of two-stroke engines. We would get up just after the crack of dawn, go get gas, and be ripping up the canyon by 9:00 A.M. After a morning of riding we'd jump in our low rider mini trucks and caravan down to Bakers and get a taco, fries, and a soda for a dollar. You always knew when someone in our crew was coming from the rattled-out bass you could hear a mile away. Jeff had a hooked-up Mazda and J-Bone pimped a Nissan we called the Maroon Typhoon. "The fastest stock truck you ever saw," says Emig. "It was always a mystery about what was under the hood."

After eating, we took whatever money we had left to the arcade at Fiesta Village and played Super Sprint, a four-player racecar arcade game. Usually we'd linger about trying to pick up girls. Then it was back to the canyon to ride until dark. After riding rough, whooped-out tracks all day, we'd go looking for cliff or 100-foot jumps to step things up a notch.

The Reche sessions were an incredible learning experience for everyone who rode there. The fact that so many talented young riders were constantly pushing each other had to have a hand in elevating the sport, as so many Reche guys went on to factory deals.

Datsun

One bright spot that season was getting my driver's license, and soon after, I got my first car. It was a mustard yellow 1971 Datsun 1200. There was a primer spot on the hood from the time it caught on fire. When I went seventy miles per hour it started to wobble and felt like it was going to blow up. But I wasn't worried about looks or even the AM cassette radio. Even though it was a junker it was like I had a newfound freedom. I was liberated from sleepy Sun City.

Hanging out with Ryan and Phil was a lot easier, too. I was tired of having my parents drive me everywhere and I think they were sick of driving me.

Ryan lived in Escondido, which was about twenty-five minutes south, and Phil was up north a ways in Beaumont.

When I wasn't at the Albrechts I was usually at Phil's house. His parents had a separate garage behind their house that had a couple beds. Phil spruced it up a little and turned it into his room. We spent countless hours hanging out in his bedroom garage. The smell of gas and oil was overpowering, but we didn't care. If we needed fresh air we'd go out back and ride the skateboard quarterpipe.

Fright Night

When we weren't racing we were pretty normal teenagers. That means we got into our share of mischief. We never got in trouble with the

Me, Ted Parker, and Darren Hoopengardner at graduation.

law or anything, but mischief seemed to follow us everywhere. On the Fourth of July, we went around with a pack of M-80s and blew up a bunch of mailboxes. We used to hang out in a creepy orange orchard in the middle of the night and try to spook each other. Ryno had this box van he used to go to the races in. We'd invite our neighborhood crushes over and try to get to second base in the van. It was all kid stuff.

Not far from Phil's house was an old abandoned school called Mariposa Elementary. There was an urban legend that the school was haunted. And who were we not to find out? Late at night we would sneak into the school and proceed to scare the living shit out of each other. As the story goes, a kid named Scotty had died, possibly murdered, in the office of the school and was now doomed to roaming the halls as a ghost. One night a full moon cast an eerie glow over the rundown school and Ryno, Factory Phil, his brother Randy, and I decided to break in and find the poltergeist.

As we made our way tip-toeing toward the office, every little creak sent us flying. We were totally freaking out. When you got to the office you were supposed to tap on the glass and wait for Scotty to reply. Phil went up to the glass and posed a question. "Scotty, if you can hear us tap twice?" Phil asked nervously. There was a moment of silence, then we heard two taps. Have you ever heard the saying, "Like a bat out of hell"? That was us. We all took off screaming like little girls. To this day I don't know what that was, but I don't think anyone was messing with us.

TIPS FOR SMART RIDERS

No matter what line of work you're into or what hobby you devote your life to, there are tricks of the trade you can't be without. Check out these five tips to amaze your friends and make your life easier.

Drill Your Levers

Drilling small holes in your brake or clutch lever doesn't sound like a good idea until you crash. What if you go down and your clutch snaps completely off? With tiny holes drilled about halfway to the end, your levers will snap in half on impact. You'll still have to buy new ones, but at least you can finish the race.

Jeremy McGrath

Plug It

If you want to keep your bike as shiny as a factory rider's, you'll need to wash it after each outing. But an ill-placed stream of water can cause plenty of headaches. Invest a few dollars in a tailpipe plug. It prevents water from getting in your tailpipe when you're washing the rear fender. You can bet a bike won't start with a crankcase full of water.

Registration, Please

Chances are you and your buddies will spend a portion of your life riding on illegal property. This highly increases your chance of being harassed by cops. You'll need to prove your bike really belongs to you. (It does, doesn't it?) Make a copy of your bike's registration and tape it underneath your seat. If you get stopped, you can avoid those nasty theft charges. Although you might still get nailed for trespassing.

Key, Please

When you go riding with your buddies, never bring your car keys with you. You could lose them. If you lose them, you won't find them. (Just ask my dad.) Hide them in a safe place. Tell one of your pals just in case you forget. If you must ride with your keys, bring an extra set and hide those.

A Little Premix

For long rides on your two-stroke, it won't hurt to bring a small bottle of premix oil. Since regular gas just won't cut it in your two-stroke engine, you'll need to mix your oil in if you run out of gas. That is, if you can find a gas station. Here's a better idea: Don't run out of gas.

Mammouth Weekend

At the end of June, there was a pretty important local race at Mammoth in Northern California. Everyone was there: Ryan, Phil, Joel, Jeremy, everybody. The race format had each rider sign up for three classes: 125, 250, and 500. I had no experience on a 500, but I borrowed my friend Ken Faught's bike and raced the class anyway. There were three motos per class, and I ended up winning seven out of nine for the weekend. One of the motos I didn't win was because the motor on Ryan Carlisle's KX 500 (the first bike I borrowed) blew up. I had a huge twenty-second lead, but I couldn't outrun bad luck. I ended up using Ken's YZ 490 to win the 500 main.

The other moto I didn't win was a bit different. I was battling for the lead of the final 125 moto with this really fast kid named Chad Pederson. He was a top-level rider who was totally supported by Yamaha and had been a favorite to win the 125 class that weekend. Diving into a turn, Chad completely took me out with a cheap move

Jeremy McGrath

that caused both of us to slam hard on the ground. Total pandemo-nium broke out. I could hear the parents and onlookers screaming about what had just taken place. Chad then shoved me out of the way and stood on top of my bike to get to his. He picked up his bike and finished ahead of me.

After the race my dad was livid. He was yelling for me to go over to Chad and start a fight. "If you don't go over there and smack that kid . . ." I remember my dad screaming. But there was no way I was go-ing to fight anybody. He was a fully supported kid and I was just some local dirtball. If I started a fight it would have followed me around every-where. Besides, I've never been much for fighting. So I said the heck with it. Why spoil an otherwise great weekend?

That weekend at Mammoth was a huge turning point for me. My confidence soared. It proved I could be competitive in the intermediate class. Ryan had strung together a bunch of seconds and thirds that weekend, so I knew my performance wasn't a fluke. I did really well as an intermediate for the rest of the year.

But the high I was on after winning Mammoth wouldn't last long. We still didn't have the money to pay for a serious, full-fledged amatuer career. So I did the only thing I could think of. At the end of the 1988 ·season, I turned pro.

Turning pro didn't exactly mean I was a motocross god. Far from it. I was the same kid with the same mullet (don't ask) from Sun City who couldn't step out of the shadow of faster kids.

I also wasn't the only one who turned pro at the end of the '88 season. Ryan and Phil did, too. But they were too fast to stay amateur, and the idea of them soon getting factory rides wasn't that far-fetched. Jeff Emig was on the same track as well. He was destroying the comp at the nationals and was highly recruited by several manufacturers. But all eyes were on Damon Bradshaw, the Beast from the East, who made his highly anticipated pro Supercross debut in January of 1989. As soon as he turned sixteen, Yamaha signed him to its factory team and gave him a five-year, $2.5 million deal. That was unheard of at the time! Damon was only sixteen, but that contract officially ended his life as a kid. Loretta's and Ponca City were replaced with the Anaheim and Daytona Supercrosses. With the money came tremendous expectation, a glaring spot-light, and harsh critiscm that stung him hard each time he rode less than perfect. In a lot of ways it contributed to his downfall. He had more pressure than a sixteen year old should have had to deal with. But that's motocross. Meanwhile, I was struggling to get anyone to notice me and buying my race bikes with my own cash. At that time I would have given anything to be in his boots.

Even though Damon was a year younger than me, I looked up to him. He was the guy everyone said would rewrite the record books. But deep down I knew I could compete with him. I just needed the chance to prove myself.

Even so, it probably wasn't a bad time to start thinking about a ca-reer to fall back on. Something I could do for a living. One problem: I couldn't think of anything. And that wasn't good considering that grad-uation was less than five months away. I liked the idea of being a con-struction worker. That was good honest work, something I could be proud of. I looked at my dad and the way people trusted him, counted on him, to fix their cars when they brought them in. I also wanted to be someone people counted on. But who was I kidding? I wanted to race motorcycles. I wanted to race Supercross under the lights in football sta-diums and domes all over the country.

I constantly dreamed that I had a full factory ride with Team Honda, just like Rick Johnson. But being a Red Rider was just a pipe dream for a kid from dusty old Sun City. I had to buy my CR 125 my-self. I didn't even have a mechanic or matching race gear. I was a pro, yes, but at this stage the only difference from being an amateur was that you got a small purse for winning local races and that hardly cov-ered gas money and new tires. It wasn't like I had a factory ride with unlimited bikes and a six-figure salary. To tell you the truth, I didn't think that was ever going to happen. I knew I was fast, but how far could I go without the right kind of support? I came pretty close to just hanging it up for good. But then something happened that gave me hope.

Jeremy McGrath

Taste of the Big Time

In January of 1989, right after turning pro, I had a brush with the big time. In other words, the fifteen-race AMA 250 Supercross series, which is piggybacked by the 125 SX series. The 125 races are broken down into East and West divisions. Riders west of the Mississippi race the West Coast dates. It's where you find out if you've got what it takes to be among the elite and make the leap to the 250s. The Big Four bike manufacturers spend millions supporting and grooming their 125 riders in hopes of developing the next big thing. The closest the Supercross tour came to me was Anaheim and San Diego.

That's all I ever wanted to ride since I threw a leg over that chewed up RM 80 all those years ago. I had worked my whole motocross life to race in the stadiums. I knew that because I was a good jumper I would do well on those technical tracks. After all, they were all jumps and that's what I did best.

Not long before Anaheim my dad gave me his 1987 Toyota extra cab pickup. I was so glad to not have to be seen in that Datsun anymore. Right away I lowered the truck and a friend from high school sold me some stolen KMC wheels with low profile tires. Derek Natvig wired up a trick Kenwood sound system that pumped hip-hop and rock through a couple of twelves. I loaded up my CR and headed forty miles up Interstate 5 to Edison International Field, the site of the Anaheim SX. (Embarrassing side note: A few years after I got the truck, we still kept the Datsun in the driveway. One day I'm looking for something in the car and notice a tape in the deck. I pop it out and it's Lisa Lisa and the Cult Jam.)

Like every other Supercross wanna-be, I had to qualify to race at Anaheim. I wasn't worried about that at all. Even though the track was more difficult than any I had ever been on, I felt at home with all the obstacles. Jumps were my strong suit, and Anaheim was cluttered with them. I finished fourth in the main event, which was excellent for a first-timer. I was so excited about the prospect of doing this for a living. Now if somebody would just pay me!

Chicken and the Snowstorm

Two weeks later, I decided to make the trip up to Washington and try to qualify for the Seattle Supercross. This was a total privateer effort. My dad and me loaded my bike in the Toyota and drove 980 miles to Seattle. I qualified for the main in the first semi. On the gate in the main was some pretty fast talent. Hometown boy Larry Ward was a Honda support rider and a favorite that night. His CR was so clean. My bike still had dirt caked on from Reche Canyon. I looked at him and I wanted to be in his shoes. Jeff "Chicken" Matasevich had a wide-open, full-throttle style that served him well that night as he blasted his way to a first-place finish. But I wasn't in awe once the gate dropped. I turned in one of my best rides to date and finished right behind Chicken for second place and a spot on the podium. And I didn't need a factory ride to do it.

The ride back down to Sun City the next morning was treacherous. It was snowing like crazy in Seattle and in some places there was three feet of accumulation. I was in the fast lane driving cautiously due to the wet snow all over the road. Another racer, Heath Kirkland, was following us until we got to California. Everything was going steady until some jerk in a huge cargo van with a motorcycle trailer swerved from the slow lane to the fast lane. To avoid hitting him, I jammed the brakes to avoid the fishtailing van in front of me. Heath didn't see my brake lights in time and smashed into us from behind, sending both of us careening into the center divide between the highways. It's a miracle my bike didn't go flying out, but the front forks were badly bent. The snow was deep as hell and didn't want to let go of my mini truck right away. Luckily, no one was hurt. It wasn't until we got back home that I realized that my helmet flew out of the truck during the crash. It was just another setback. I had finished second in a 125 Supercross, but I was too bummed to care.

Paper or Plastic

It got to the point where my parents could no longer afford to financially support my career, but they didn't just cut me off cold turkey. My mom gave me $500, which she used to open a checking account for me, and I continued to race on the weekends while I mulled over my dwindling career options. If I raced two classes and won I could bring home $300 to $400 a weekend from the local tracks. Whatever money I earned racing would go right back in my checking account.

Competing against guys who were racing for paychecks was a whole new ballgame. They were far more aggressive than amateurs racing for fun. People needed to eat. That meant I would have to put in a lot more practice time if I was going to compete and get my little $350 a week to keep my career going. But school ate up a lot of valuable practice time. I decided that I had to get a job. The extra cash would help, but more important, seniors with jobs could leave school at noon as part of a work program. That meant more practice time when I wasn't working.

One of my best friends at Perris High, Darren Hoopengardner, got me a job at a local Vons grocery store. For five months I stood at the end of a register and bagged groceries for $6 an hour. When I wasn't bagging I chased down wayward carts in the parking lot. I wasn't crazy about it but I needed the money. There was one problem. My boss kept scheduling me the weekends, causing me to miss the races. He did this a couple times and I let it slide. After this happened a few more times I got fed up and quit.

I got another job at Raceway Honda in Perris making almost no money. I dusted bikes, recharged batteries, and sometimes worked the parts counter. Basically, I was a total peon. But I had to work to get out of school.

HOW TO CLEAN YOUR AIR FILTER

Periodic maintenance is a must if you own a motorcycle. And since your dad can't work on your bike all your life, eventually you're going to have to do it yourself. If there's only one thing you need to know how to do, it's clean your air filter. (You do know where your airbox is, right?) After time, dust and dirt will collect in your filter, robbing your bike of its ability to breathe freely. This will cause your bike to lose power. Here's how to deal with it:

1. Remove the air filter from the airbox. Put the wingnut where you know you won't lose it. Take special care not to let any dirt fall into the airbox.
2. Clean the air filter with filter cleaner. Rub in thoroughly to remove all the excess dirt.
3. Submerge filter in a bucket of warm soapy water. Squeeze filter gently (don't wring) to get out filter cleaner and any remaining dirt.
4. Squeeze out any excess water and hang the filter in a clean, dry place for about an hour or until completely dry.
5. Modestly apply filter oil to filter then gently massage in. Take care not to drown the filter in oil. The purpose of a clean filter is to allow your bike to breath.

Install the filter in the airbox. Repeat this process every three or four rides.

Now Hear This, Uh, Mr. Payton

Because I was getting more serious about racing, I needed my bike dialed in better than I could do myself. Tightening up the chain and changing flats is one thing, perfectly adjusting the suspension is another. That's something that should be left to the experts. So I did what anyone with a Honda CR 125 would do. I took my bike to Mitch Payton to fine-tune my suspension.

Jeremy McGrath

Mitch owned a race shop called Pro Circuit that specialized in aftermarket exhaust and suspension hop-ups. Because of his expertise, Mitch was one of the most revered and respected men in the industry. Plain and simple, Pro Circuit bikes were fast. Mitch had a rep for finding and cultivating promising young talent. To have him interested in me meant I was doing something right. I was stoked to have him working on my bike.

Payton had been around motorcycles all his life. He was a pretty good desert racer until a disastrous crash left him paralyzed form the waist down and confined to a wheelchair for life the day after his seventeenth birthday. Despite that, he can be a very intimidating man. He's incredibly demanding of his racers and shop employees. To a young racer looking to impress people in a position to further his career, he loomed like a giant. When Mitch speaks his word is pretty much law.

But he was also prone to moodiness. You never knew which Mitch you'd get when you walked into his shop. Sometimes he'd give me a discount on parts. Sometimes he wouldn't. It all depended on what kind of mood he was in. I'd drop by his shop to pick up a pipe "for free" and the next day we would get a bill.

Late in the spring of 1989, just a few months into my pro career, I was having huge problems with my Pro Circuit–tuned suspension. It worked so poorly I was afraid to ride my CR at any speed. At a local race at Carlsbad, a completely unforgiving legendary, rut-filled SoCal track, I thought I was going to kill myself on my bike when it began bucking wildly. Enough was enough. I decided to tell Mitch that I didn't want Pro Circuit working on my bike anymore. I would take it to White Bros., a Pro Circuit competitor, to handle the suspension chores from now on. I talked it over with my dad and decided that I would go see Mitch alone. It's not easy for a seventeen-year-old kid to tell someone who holds a lot of sway in the business that he's "going in another direction." I was extremely nervous about telling Mitch. I wasn't even a big name, so I thought he wouldn't be that bothered by it.

I gave him the news in his office at Pro Circuit. I was as professional and cordial as possible and told him that I would be getting my suspension done elsewhere. Mitch did not take the news well. He kindly proceeded to tear me a new one. He questioned everything from my riding to my manhood. "Who do you think you are, Rick Johnson?" he barked at me.

I hated him for that remark. It stung deep that he tried to use my favorite rider to put me down. I started to cry right there in his office, but that didn't faze him at all. He kept on berating me and told me to get out. He made me feel like I was nothing.

With tears in my eyes, I left. Part of the reason I reacted the way I did was because I thought that I had just erased everything I struggled for up to this point. I had it in my head that I was now going to somehow be blackballed from the sport before I really even had a chance.

But something happened to me as I left. I got in my truck and just sat there. My tears dried up and my sadness turned to vengeance. I decided right there, from that moment on, that nothing would stop me from achieving whatever I wanted to do in this sport. Something just hit me. I had felt like shit minutes earlier, but now I realized that Mitch yelling at me was the best thing that ever happened to my career. Well, I didn't actually realize it until years later, but something was definitely churning inside me that day. The whole time I had been floundering about with little direction and less money. But I decided that all of that was going to change. I'll show Mr. Payton who thinks he's Rick Johnson.

World Mini GP

In June of 1989, the entire motocross community headed to Las Vegas for the World Mini GP. It's pretty much a prelude to Loretta's and Ponca City. All my friends from Reche Canyon cleaned up in Vegas. Ryan got great starts all weekend and finished second in 125 modified pro. Jeff Emig went nuts and won four classes, further solidifying himself as one of the most decorated amateurs ever. Tommy Clowers won 80 modified and expert. Joel Albrecht rode to a respectable third in the Super Mini 80 class after a great battle with Buddy Antunez. Joel came back to beat

Buddy in the coveted Kawasaki Race of Champions, a race in which Kawasaki supplies riders with identical KX80s. But that's because Buddy ran into a little trouble in that race.

Buddy and Tommy's history of rough riding was well known going

into the Mini GP and reached a boiling point in the R.O.C. Buddy was leading when Tommy T-boned him, causing Buddy to crash out of the race. Buddy then cut the track and challenged Tommy to a fight. The two had to be restrained by track officials from tearing each other's heads off. When winning the nationals can lead to a factory ride at age sixteen the pressure to win is through the roof. And here's a little foot-note from the Mini GP: The winner of the 60cc modified class was a nine-year-old Floridian named Ricky Carmichael.

Team Green, Finally

Soon after my run-in with Mitch, I ditched my Hondas altogether when I finally got a call from the folks at Team Green saying they wanted me on the team.

The guy who ran the Team was Mark Johnson. He was in charge of handing out all of Kawasaki's amateur support. (Even though I was a "pro," everyone who isn't racing AMA Supercross or the AMA Outdoor Nationals is considered to have amateur status.) I was so stoked when he asked me to join the team. I couldn't believe it. I thought, "Finally, I made it." I started to salivate thinking about all the stuff I was going to get. Three bikes, a $500 parts allowance, a top-shelf mechanic to work on my bikes at the races. Crazy. I was *finally* getting support. No more shoestring career. The Team Green ride loosened the financial noose my racing career put around my dad's neck.

Jeremy McGrath

After signing with Team Green, I continued to race locally for the rest of the summer. Since school was out I practiced seven days a week, three or four hours a day. All I did was ride my bike. My goal was to get in top shape for Loretta Lynn's and Ponca City. Since Team Green was picking up the tab this year I was definitely going.

My parent's were equally stoked about my Team Green deal. But there was one thing about it that wasn't cool: Jose Gonzalez, who was in charge of distributing the parts to the riders. This guy was pretty much a dick to me. He played favoritism with all the riders. He loved Ryno and would always hook him up with whatever he needed. It was the same with all of the other Team Green kids, as well. I felt like I was always on the back burner. I didn't sweat it, though. It just made me ride harder.

At all of the amateur nationals, Kawasaki had three mechanics on hand to work on all the Team Green bikes. One of those mechanics was twenty-two-year-old Skip Norfolk. After graduating from college, he went to work for Team Green and operated out of their East Coast office in Atlanta.

In April of '89, he was transferred to the West Coast office and first wrenched for me at the World Mini in Vegas that year. Skip came over to my dad's pickup and introduced himself to my family. We ended up talking for a while that day and just hit it off. I had only had my new KXs for about a week and right away Skip asked how I liked to have them set up. I didn't really know. I had never done any testing in my life, but neither had Skip so we really felt like we were in the same boat together. Little did we know-what kind of ride we were in for.

A side from figuring out how I was going to pay for parts or squeeze in more track time, my senior year in high school was pretty normal. Even with racing, I was able to graduate with a B average in June of '89. My parents always kept in my ear about studying. They knew full well about my scam to secure an early work release from school, but they never really gave me any trouble about it because I proved to them I could hit the books and race without getting in any trouble. And at least I was earning money. Another good thing about my work release job at Raceway Honda was Sherrie McGloughin. She was a pretty hot girl my age who worked at the front desk. When I wasn't recharging batteries or pretending like I was sweeping up, I would flirt with Sherrie. Before long we started dating. I thought it was cool that she was a chick and worked at a motorcycle shop. We fooled around some, enough to satisfy a seventeen-year-old boy's appetite for the opposite sex, but Sherrie was just puppy love in between dusting exhaust pipes. I really had my eye on someone else.

There was a girl who who went to Perris with me named Jennifer Thomas. After I stopped seeing Sherrie, I got up the nerve to ask Jennifer out. I got all worked up for nothing, because Jennifer was so into me she said yes right away. When I wasn't riding, I was with Jennifer. She worked at a local Baskin Robbins, and I'd always go see her at work and she'd hook me up with free ice cream. She got along really well with my parents and they were great about having her over to our house and even let her regularly spend the night. A lot of times we would just stay up and talk. It was then I realized that for the first time I was in love with someone.

I could probably have stayed with Jennifer for quite a while but my life was about to change. I would have the opportunity to see what else was out in the world.

RJ On Line One . . .

Life with Team Green in 1990 was a big improvement. I was winning enough to afford a decent car payment, so I bought a brand-new box van to take to the races. The $35,000 price tag was still pretty steep, but it made my 1990 campaign feel somewhat legitimate. No more rolling up to the pits in a pickup truck with my bike in the back. I'd actually started to feel like a racer.

I raced seven of eight 125 West Supercrosses that spring, finishing second in the points standings by just seven points to Ty Davis. Buddy Antunez finished third and Jeff Emig fourth. Even though I was racing Supercrosses, I was still contracted by Team Green to race all of the amateur nationals (Loretta's, Ponca City, Las Vegas World Mini). I had a great Supercross debut, but when I raced the nationals I could rarely ever catch Ryno. And he was two years younger than me. At the World Mini GP in Vegas, I entered two classes and got two second-place finishes. Ryan came in first both times. That was followed by the GNC Nationals in Texas where Ryan got three firsts while I finished second each time.

In Ponca City that year, we each came away with two wins and a third. I ended up winning my second amateur national championship before moving on to Loretta Lynn's. As usual, Loretta's was a nightmare for me. My bikes were so worn out by then they just kept breaking down. I had problems concentrating and had a couple of nasty wrecks. In 125 modified, a huge rock got caught in my chain and tore up the cases. I was looking forward to kissing that place good-bye.

One night back at the hotel I was winding down, trying to put my rough weekend behind me when the phone rang. "Hi, this is Rick Johnson. Can I speak to Jeremy?" the voice said. Real bad joke.

"Stop joking around Phil. I can hear you laughing," I replied.

"No, seriously, this is Rick Johnson."

Quick RJ history lesson: He was one of the most colorful characters in Supercross and the sport's all-time winningest rider. He had that typical Southern California cool about him that you would expect from a motocrosser from El Cajon. Once he posed nude in "The Thinker" position in an ad for motocross gear. (Thank God he was wearing boots.) And after a race in 1987, he punched fellow rider Ron Lechien in the face after Ron had beat him to the finish line. In those days a lot of riders wore open-faced helmets. Riders like Lechien. When Ron pulled off his goggles, Rick popped him with a right hook and drew blood. And they're from the same neighborhood!

People either loved Rick Johnson or hated him. But either way, he was respected. He had won three 250 Outdoor National titles, two 250 Supercross championships, and two titles in the now defunct 500cc Outdoor Nationals. I was one of the people that loved him. I can't remember how many times I pretended to be RJ with a full factory ride while thrashing around on my first YZ.

And it actually was him on the other end. I was trying the best I

could not to flip out. We made small talk for a few minutes, he asked how I did that weekend, then he got to the point.

"How would you like to ride for Honda?" he asked.

Did you say Honda? Excuse me while I pick myself up off the floor. "Of course," I told him. I had always dreamed about being a factory Red Rider and now my idol, the best Honda guy ever, was asking me to join the team. He told me that he would talk to my parents and get their approval and that Honda was in the process of drawing up a contract. I had to see Dave Arnold as soon as we got back to California. Arnold was Factory Honda's team manager. A guy who could make big things happen for you.

A few days later in Torrance, California, I signed my first real pro contract at the Honda headquarters. I was the first 125 rider they signed for the 1991 season. My job was to race the 125 West SX series and the 125 Outdoor Nationals. I would be paid $35,000 a year.

I was totally obsessed with the idea of racing Supercross. I didn't care about outdoor motocross. Even as a kid I wasn't really interested in the outdoor series. But factory riders had to race both Supercross (from January to May) and outdoor motocross (May to September). That's just the way it was.

After signing with Honda for 1991, I finished up the 1990 season with Team Green. I decided to race one 125 AMA Outdoor National. The

At the G.F.I. SX, Jeff Ward finished 1st, I finished 2nd, and my hero Rick Johnson finished 3rd. Rick showed me how to open the champagne.

track was Hangtown in Sacramento. It also happened to be Ryan's first outdoor, as well. It did not go well for me. I ended up a lackluster fifteenth or sixteenth (out of forty), but Ryan was blazing as usual and rode to a respectable fifth in his outdoor debut.

HOW TO RIDE SAND

While riding a dirt bike off-road you will encounter all
types of different terrain and conditions. One of the most
difficult situations to traverse is sand. Loose, slippery, and
unpredictable is the best way to describe a sandy track or
trail. Here are a few tips for keeping you and your bike
upright when riding the grainy stuff.

The Right Setup

The first thing you'll want to do is equip your bike with tires
specifically designed for riding in the sand. The knobbies on
sand tires usually have a direction pattern. Run your tire
pressure the same as you would on a hard-packed track.

Turning Things Around

Keep you RPMs high. Sand slows you down pretty quickly,
so you don't want your motor bogging. Keep in mind that in
a sandy turn braking points are much later. The object is to
keep your momentum. You either want to be on the gas or
on the brakes. You'll have a lot more control than if you're
just coasting and reduce the risk of falling over.

Pick a Line

In sand, track conditions are ever changing. What was a
good line at the beginning of a race may not even exist
a few laps later. The tough thing about sand is that it's
constantly moving underneath you. A lot of riders stay to
the outside of the track because that's where lines are
smoothest and the ruts most shallow.

Jeremy McGrath

Give Me a Brake

Under normal conditions you'll rely on your front brake to give you 75% of your stopping power. For sand it's just the opposite. Sand has so much natural resistance, you'll begin to slow down once you let off the gas. Too much front brake can cause you to wash out easily. Always keep your front end light in sand.

Fatigue Factor

You find yourself moving all over the bike and constantly fighting it. The more you move, the more tired you'll become. The more tired you are, the more likely you are to crash. Don't try to blast your way around the track. Find a nice pace and stay with it. Relax. When you're nervous, your arms tend to pump up. Keep these things in mind and you should have a much easier go of it in the rough stuff.

A couple months after I signed with Honda, they threw me a curve. While the 250 team (Rick Johnson, Jeff Stanton, Jean-Michele Bayle) was run directly by Honda, the 125 effort would be run separately by Mitch Payton and his Pro Circuit shop. Honda would fund and oversee the entire effort, but Mitch was in charge of the bikes and day-to-day operations. The team was called Pro Circuit/Peak Honda. I still had a healthy fear of Mitch brought on by his tirade that day in his office and my dad was a little pissed at the arrangement. He thought we were supposed to be 100% factory Honda, and then it turns out to be a shop deal. Jack was also still a little irked at the way Mitch had laid into me three years before. Nevertheless, it was still Honda and all I had to do now was win. When I signed the contract, I remembered Mitch's infamous words, "Who do you think you are, Rick Johnson?" and I still planned to make him eat those words.

I just didn't expect it to happen at such close range.

When the season started and I began working with Mitch on a daily basis, we never talked about that day in his office. But rest assured, I never forgot it. When I signed with Honda I felt that he got the short end of the stick. He knew what he'd done to me but it didn't work. He tried to knock me down and he said I'd never make it this far. But look who made it. I was really lucky that I believed in myself or my career could have pretty much died that day in his office.

Reunited with Skip

Other than achieving a lifelong dream, signing with Honda brought another bonus: I got to have my own mechanic. There was only one person I wanted. So when I asked Skip if he would come wrench for me at Team Peak it took him all of two seconds to say yes.

When most amateur motocrossers dream of Supercross glory, at ten years old, Skip Norfolk dreamed of working on bikes. All he ever wanted to do was be a factory mechanic. As a teenager he would take his bike completely apart and put it back together just to get a better understanding of how things worked. He has always had a cerebral approach to his work. In his senior year in high school, he even wrote an English paper about his goals in life: 1) be married with children by thirty; 2) own a home by twenty-five; 3) become a factory mechanic.

Now that's commitment.

I was so excited that Skip would be wrenching for me because I knew his assets as a mechanic went beyond turning wrenches. A good mechanic is someone who can motivate the hell out of you. Get you out of bed at seven in the morning. Make you see the importance of preparation. Be a shoulder to lean on. As well as be a good pal to knock back beers with (although I wouldn't taste alcohol for another three years).

Even though Skip was five years older than I was, our interests were the same: winning races. Not to mention learning along the way. Skip had only been in California for a couple of years and was still getting over the culture shock. He wanted to try everything from surfing to wakeboarding. Plus he still loved to ride. He also had a sort of Dr. Jekyll prankster side to him that offset his Mr. Hyde seriousness.

At the time he was renting an apartment up in Mission Viejo, a twenty-seven-mile drive from where my parents now lived in Murrieta. Since we would be spending so much time together on my racing career, I asked my parents if he could move in with us. They said he could stay as long as he wanted, because they knew he was trying to save money to buy a house. It didn't make sense for him to waste money on an apartment. Back then mechanics still drove box vans from race to race as opposed to today where each team has a professional driver to man the eighteen-wheelers. It meant Skip could be on the road for six months at a time. But our 1,500-square-foot, one-level abode was already jam-packed with a family of four. So we put a bedroom set in the finished portion of our garage and Skip called it home. Where was a better place for a mechanic to live than a garage?

Follow the Leader

When I first signed with Honda, I couldn't believe how serious the race effort was. They existed to win. Honda had won an astonishing seven

Skip and me, 1991.

out of the last eight 250 Supercross titles. And they spared no expense in the process. Their domination in the last ten years was so unparalleled because they invested more money in their program than anyone. They did everything right and then some.

Prior to joining Honda, I had never really done any testing. But it is an integral part of a rider's success. Testing is a long tedious process where a rider and his mechanic try numerous suspension and motor setups at the test track in an effort to perfectly dial in the bike. It's a never-ending process that starts months before the season and continues through to the last week of the season. "There's no such thing as the perfect motorcycle," Skip likes to say.

Regardless, we looked for it. Even if you find settings that you're comfortable with, track types and conditions are ever changing so the testing goes on. It's not like NASCAR where the track never changes. A motocross track changes with every heat. New ruts, grooves, and holes are forever popping up.

Mitch built the motors on my race bikes and Pro Circuit suspension ace Jim "Bones" Bacon handled the suspension. It was a first-rate program all the way, and countless hours were logged by me, Skip, bike engineers, and other various experts employed by Honda with the expressed purpose of trying to shave a few seconds off of my lap times.

As a result, most of my time was spent at Honda's 1,000-acre, top-flight practice facility called Hondaland in Simi Valley. The only problem was that it was two hours from my parent's house in Murrieta. Even though I had just built a Supercross track at home it was worth the trip. The daily hike would wear me out, so I ended up just staying in a hotel in Simi Valley throughout the week. Hondaland had a state-of-the-art Supercross track, a grueling outdoor course, and endless acres for playriding.

Up until that time, I never had any parts that were over and above what you could modify a standard bike with. But at Honda, the trick factory parts rolled in. My bike was outfitted with factory Showa suspension and all manner of "unobtainable" aluminum and titanium parts. I had several practice bikes and never raced more than four or five races on the same bike without having everything replaced from the grips to the frame. Honda went out of their way to make sure I had everything possible to do the best job I could.

When you're that young and you get that kind of treatment you feel like a king. That feeling alone could make me go a couple seconds faster each lap. I was super stoked that someone finally cared about my racing as much as I did.

Honda's win-at-all-costs mentality matched my own desire to finish at the front of the pack. They poured twice the money into research, development, and testing than the next biggest manufacturer. Honda engineers explored every possibility of getting the motorcycle to handle smoother, deliver more power, and perform better. Their knowledge and technology is extensive to the point that the AMA's production rule, which states that factory bikes had to use the production frame, swingarm, engine cases, and body panels, could be stepped over as easily as a giant could step up a curb.

BENEFITS OF BEING A FACTORY RIDER

The bottom-line purpose of a factory team is to sell motorcycles by creating attention for a brand through winning. Think of a factory team as the ultimate marketing tool. It's every rider's goal of winning a spot on one of those factory teams. There is no greater honor than to sign with one of the major factories such as Honda, Kawasaki, Suzuki, Yamaha, or KTM. The factory team's efforts are funded directly by the manufacturer. There are many pluses to being a factory rider, like huge contracts, notoriety, and job security. Where you once paid for bikes, travel, and entry fees, you now have those things taken care of. On race days factory riders operate out of a well-appointed eighteen-wheeler instead of box vans.

Here's a quick look at team history.

Back in the sixties, when the sport was dominated by Old World manufacturers such as Husqvarna, Bultaco, BSA, and Montesa, a factory ride meant a free bike, parts, and a jersey. And little or no money. In the seventies, the Japanese bike makers pushed out European companies with better technology and more efficiently run operations. This sparked a global competition between the old guard and the new that led to warlike advancements in product development. More important, riders could now hire themselves out to the highest-bidding team.

The Japanese Big Four manufacturers came to rule motocross, snapping up most of the talented riders on factory teams that went twelve to fifteen deep in some cases. Team Honda had eighteen riders in 1978. The eighties, however, ushered in a new age of downsized, cost-effective race programs. Motorcycle sales had boomed in the seventies and early eighties, but by the mid-eighties a struggling economy slowed the sale of motorcycles slightly. Most of the Big Four began slashing their racing budgets. This meant fewer spots on factory teams. As a result, the prestige of winning a factory ride shot up. The strategy of the manufacturers was to hire the two or three best riders who would win the same amount of races as fifteen really good riders.

In an outdoor national, it is possible to have just twelve of the forty riders on the gate representing the factories. Others are support riders who ride for satellite teams (Yamaha of Troy, Moto XXX, Blackfoot, ECC Suzuki,

Jeremy McGrath

etc.), who have most of their expenses covered but make a fraction of the salary of a factory rider.

The rest of the riders are privateers, who pay for most of their own expenses, work on their own bikes, and travel to the races by their own means, usually a pickup truck or box van. Many times privateers have a small degree of support from clothing companies, MX products, and lubes, but being a privateer means being at a distinct technological disadvantage before the race even starts. Privateers have no factory engineers to work with. Practice time is slashed to one or two days a week because of long hours on the road. A factory rider's contract can be twenty pages of points regarding salary, injury clauses, testing and promotional requirements, and conduct clauses. An average 250 factory rider's contract is about $500,000 a year. This obviously varies depending on the rider and the company. Top riders often garner boot, helmet, and clothing endorsements that can push his yearly take past a million dollars. Most riders also receive bonuses for winning races and championships, as well.

Riders must sign a release giving up any claim that the manufacturer equipment is liable for any potential injury. When they aren't racing, promotion is the name of the game, as riders are required to do a number of dealer promotions and autograph signings. Failure to appear can result in fines.

Despite all of that, factory riders are not employees of the factories. They are more like independent contractors who work at the factories. They are not eligible for retirement, workmen's comp, or health insurance. So a factory team isn't really a team at all. The rider's goals are individual and it's not unusual for an older rider to help a younger rider. But that stops immediately when the younger rider beats the older one. The only real case of teamwork is when a rider who has no chance of winning the championship lets a teammate by so he can gain extra points toward the title.

The pressure on a factory rider to win is tremendous. The more the season wears on and the longer you go without a win, the more uptight and rattled you can become. You begin to start trying too hard or worrying that the team won't pick you up next year because they've got their eye on the next "can't miss" amateur hotshot.

Still want to be a factory rider? So do millions of other racers. But your chances of making the NFL (1,696 roster spots) or the NBA (465) are far greater than becoming a factory motocross racer. With only about twelve factory riders racing today, aspiring to become an astronaut is a less lofty goal.

But they told me the same thing . . .

Life with Stanton & Bayle

Probably the best thing about Hondaland was that I got to ride with Honda's 250 factory riders on a daily basis. Jeff Stanton won the Supercross title in 1989 and 1990. Jean-Michel Bayle won the championship in 1991. Every day I got to test my skills against the two best riders in the world. I soaked up whatever I could. Since I was riding 125s and they rode 250s, they often gave me advice or shared riding secrets.

Bayle's riding style was effortless. He blasted around the track so smoothly that his riding revolutionized the sport because many riders began imitating him. Jeff's blue-collar style, which emphasized stamina and strength, was the polar opposite of Jean-Michel's, who had talent in

spades. While most riders specialized on one size bike or were clearly better in one discipline than another, JMB could ride anything. Whether it was a 125, 250, 500, indoors or out, in the mud, sand, technical or super fast track, it didn't matter to Bayle.

The staple of a motocrosser's training week is riding motos at race speed to simulate competition. Everyone does them. Except Bayle. At Hondaland, while Stanton was working on his lap times, Bayle would be out play riding or practicing his jumping. He might practice particular sections of the course, but never motos. One morning when Stanton finished a couple of grueling motos at Hondaland, he noticed JMB goofing around on a hillside. He was trying to carve his initials in the side of the hill by roosting up the dirt with his back tire. He'd do a half donut for the bottom of the J, then blast up the hill to finish the letter. It took him all day but by the end of practice there was a huge "JMB" for all to see.

At the races it wasn't much different. Stanton would put in a solid practice session only to find JMB back at his box van eating candy bars and watching TV.

Off the track they were night and day, too. Bayle would rather go surfing than lift weights. He regularly blew off Honda functions and autograph signings. As a result, he became one of the most penalized riders in motocross history.

On the other hand, Jeff trained like a triathlete and was never late for anything. He was the clean-shaven, consummate professional. Jeff signed autographs until the last fan went home happy. Jean-Michel was booed often and dismissed by many fans as the "typical, rude Frenchman." Bayle had a decent grasp of the English language but was distant and aloof. He really didn't speak to other riders that much. Maybe he wasn't such a bad guy but he just never let anyone too close to him. Whatever the reason, Bayle began to play up to his bad-boy image, telling himself he was only concerned with winning races, not fans. But if he had tossed his goggles into the crowd occasionally or treated the fans to some style over the triples, he would have made things a lot easier for himself.

Jeff was often annoyed by Jean-Michel's disregard for protocol and sometimes their differences came out on the track. They weren't afraid to cut over on one another on the start straight or stuff each other in the corners.

In their three years together on Team Honda ('90–'92), Bayle and Stanton never finished lower than third in the points, won a combined six 250 titles, and rarely ever spoke to one another. Even their mechanics didn't get along. During the '91 season, Jean-Michel's antics ate away at Jeff, preventing him from focusing all of his energy on winning the championship.

In the 1991 250 nationals, Stanton won four races. Bayle won zero, yet he earned the championship by finishing on the podium in every race. It was all about consistency, a lesson that Stanton would take to heart in his quest to win both 250 titles the following year.

Bayle's plan was to come to America and test his skills against the world's best, to show everyone he could compete at the highest level. And that's exactly what he did. Even with all his goofing off and lack of commitment, Bayle rode his way to probably the greatest single season any rider ever had. In 1991, he won the 250 and 500 outdoor national titles and the 250 Supercross title, becoming the only rider ever to win three AMA championships in one year.

I took mental notes of the tactics Stanton and Bayle used on each other. I watched their practice habits closely, as well as the way they rode the track. I was getting valuable experience in the 125 Western Region Supercross series, but having a twenty-four-hour front-row seat to a head-to-head matchup of two motocross legends was something I never expected.

Ain't That a Mitch

Despite the fact that I was living a dream by riding for Honda, it was still a little hard to shake the feelings I had toward Mitch as a result of our confrontation in his office at Pro Circuit a few years back. It was a little hard for me to relax around him because he was an authority figure and I was a kid still trying to impress. But early in the '92 season, my second with Honda, I began to get a different picture of Mitch. On race days he was as hard as a stone wall. He was so serious about winning he projected this image that nothing else mattered but doing your job right and finishing first. Only it wasn't an image. That's who he was and he ripped you if you didn't have your shit together. If you were working for Mitch it was because you did. But the more time I spent around him, I began to see cracks in that serious facade. Mitch had a playful side that he couldn't hide. At the end of the night when you closed shop it seemed like he would become a different person.

He liked to party like anyone else. He liked to knock back a few cold ones. And he really liked to get into *Jackass*-style mischief. Well, he liked us to. Then he'd laugh his ass off when something would go awry. I began to feel like I could relate to Mitch and that I could ease up around him. At the Seattle Supercross in February, Mitch and I went with a bunch of riders exploring in downtown Seattle. We ended up at the downtown wharf, which is a popular tourist destination. We strolled out on a short dock where a couple of fisherman were finishing up for the day. One of them had left a cooler filled with tons of bait and even a couple of fish they had caught that day. The fisherman were using anchovies to fish with and they smelled terrible. Someone get the bright idea that they would smell even better in somebody's hair. The next thing you know five motocross riders and a team manager in a wheelchair were engaged in full-scale hand-to-fish combat. Everybody is smearing anchovies on each other's faces and smashing fish over our heads with fish guts exploding everywhere. A couple of us pinned down 125 rider Steve Lamson, ripped his clothes off, and poured anchovies down his underwear. He took off running for the hotel, which was a couple of blocks away, and had to make his way through the crowded lobby holding his privates.

After about 15 minutes, Mitch had gotten the least of the attack. I think we were a little afraid to go after him, but he was laughing a bit too loud when we got a handful of fish guts smooshed in our hair. That's when I grabbed a container of anchovies and went straight for Mitch. He tried in vain to wheel away but I dumped it, nasty fish juice and all, down the back of his shirt. He was pissed but laughing too hard to care.

The Great Outdoors

When the 125 outdoor season started on March 3 in Gainesville, my focus wasn't to win the series. I know that sounds funny but I just wanted to compete and see how well I could do. Back then the outdoor season started before the Supercross season ended. Gainesville was the lone outdoor race smack in the middle of the Supercross schedule. It was a pain in everyone's ass and industry critics dubbed it the Orphan National. Round 2 of the outdoor nationals was almost two months later, after eight more rounds of Supercross.

So my mind, like most riders, was still fixed on racing indoors, where I was atop the 125 West SX points standings. I wasn't as good outdoors as I was in the stadiums, so I just wanted to spend this season learning. Everyone always says I don't like outdoor racing but that's not true. The fact is I enjoy it a lot. I just happen to like Supercross better.

Outdoor motocross is a different animal altogether. The action is a lot more wide open and things happen at higher speeds. In Supercross, it pays to be smooth, consistent, and highly skilled at the technical aspects of jumping, cornering, braking, and shifting. Motocross is full of long straightaways, high-speed downhills, and mountain-like uphills. The tracks are choppy and super rough with dozens of lines in any given corner. Normally there are about two or three good lines in a Supercross turn. It's debatable which discipline you have to have better conditioning. I always got more tired racing motocross, so I just kind of struggled with it all year.

For the first couple of nationals, Gainesville and Hangtown, I rode to semi-decent fifth or sixth place finishes. I hadn't helped my outdoor confidence but I didn't hurt it either. The third stop on the outdoor circuit was Mt. Morris in Pennsylvania.

Mt. Morris' loamy dirt and fast hills make it a favorite among the riders. I felt really confident that day and finished third in the first of two motos. It was my best moto finish of the young season. I was really pumped since a third or higher meant I'd have a great chance at the overall. I picked out my spot on the starting gate for the second moto next to my former Team Green mate and 125 West SX rival, Yamaha's Jeff Emig.

Jeff had a rep for getting great starts, but my confidence was high and I swore that nobody was going to beat me to the first corner that day. The gate dropped and we rocketed off the line. I didn't get the holeshot but I got a great start and was running in third after a couple laps. I was in a smooth rhythm when things started to go wrong. My bike sputtered and cut in and out like a lightbulb that's not properly screwed in. I figured there was something wacky going on with the ignition and I should just try to finish the race. Meanwhile, riders were picking me off one by one as my bike choked and wheezed.

When I hit the gas to jump a massive sixty-foot downhill double, the bike died. Perfect. My CR 125 lost momentum, but I kept going. I endoed down the hill and over the bars until my body slammed headfirst into the track. Mt. Morris had good, soft dirt, but I swear it felt like concrete. I slammed hard enough to knock myself out cold. I broke my right leg and severely separated my right shoulder. The next foggy memories I have were of a hospital room with doctors and nurses hustling about. I checked out a few days later but the concussion I suffered gave me double vision and headaches for the next six weeks.

It's All Fun and Games Until Your Van Blows Up

One of the fun things about traveling all over the country to race was driving the rental cars. We treated them like our own personal bumper cars. The cars were never the same when we returned them, even if we only rented them for a few days. In Seattle, where it had been raining like crazy, the rainfall had left huge puddles all over the city, but that didn't stop us from living out our car chase fantasies. Skip and I were peeling wheel through the streets with Mitch and Jim "Bones" Bacon of

Celebrating SX win, 1991.

Jeremy McGrath

Pro Circuit tailing us in a minivan. We would bump each other at stoplights and pull the emergency break when they followed too close.

We lit a piece of paper on fire and tossed it out of the window. The burning paper landed on the street and Bones drove over it. The next thing you know, the bottom of their van catches on fire. Only they didn't notice it right away. "You're on fire! Don't stop!" I screamed when they pulled up next to us at a light. Bones frantically pulled down a side street and drove through the biggest puddles he could find at fifty miles an hour. The van hydoplaned and water splashed twenty feet in the air, but the fire just wouldn't go out.

Mitch and Bones were screaming and starting to really get scared. They were afraid to stop for fear that the fire would ignite the gas tank. Bones blew countless stop signs and red lights. But when they drove fast it only fanned the flames and spread the fire. All the fun and games of rental bumper cars was replaced by the fear of a potential disaster. Finally, they hit three huge puddles in a row and the flames went out.

Do You Know the Way . . .

Twenty-one days later, the second to last Supercross was in San Jose at Spartan Stadium on the campus of San Jose State University. My shoulder had healed nicely but my leg was still broken. I called on a doctor that I knew to rig me up a special air cast that would protect my lower leg and ankle. It was a seriously risky move to race with my leg in that condition. If I bailed off a jump and landed hard enough on the leg it would shatter like a twig, but my goal was to win the title in San Jose so I wouldn't have to race the following week at the finale in Los Angeles. Going into San Jose, Jeff Emig had 126 points. I had 167. I had to get tenth or better to wrap up my first 125 SX title. I was on the cusp of a dream. I wasn't going to let a little pain get in the way. Or . . . a lot of pain for that matter.

Because of the cast, my boot was way too tight and my leg was throbbing like crazy. Most of the time I kept it elevated to help circulation. But there was nothing I could do about it when I was on my bike. When the gate dropped, Jeff shot off the line and snagged the holeshot. I got a terrible start that night and ended up mid-pack. I dreaded putting my foot down in the corners for fear that I might twist it or something. Every so often I would drag my boot or catch it on a bump that would send me screaming.

Jeff won the race but I finished ninth and won my first 125 West Supercross title. Usually when riders win a race or wrap up the championship they throw some serious style over the finish-line jump, but I rode over the finish line with no flair, both wheels on the ground, stoked that I was the champion. And ready as hell to take my boot off.

I won the championship over Jeff by three points, the second closest 125 Supercross battle ever.

. . . Rochester?

With the Supercross title wrapped up and the nationals in full swing, on August 9, 1991, I jumped on a flight headed for Rochester, Minnesota, for the Millville National. The flight seemed rather long but I didn't pay it much attention. When I got to Rochester, I picked up my bags at baggage claim and headed to the rental car counter to pick up my car.

"I'm sorry sir, we don't seem to have a reservation for you," the clerk said.

"Can you check that? I'm positive I made a reservation," I replied. The woman tapped some more keys and a puzzled looked crossed her face.

"I'm not showing anything," she responded.

Luckily, they had cars available. I then gave her the phone number to the hotel I was staying at so she could call for directions. But the lady at the rental car counter wasn't familiar with any of the streets the hotel receptionist was naming. Not a single one. Something was definitely not right.

"Where did you say you were located?" the rental lady asked the receptionist.

"Rochester," the receptionist replied. "Rochester, Minnesota."

"That explains it," said the rental car lady. "This is Rochester, New York."

I had flown to the wrong Rochester. I was so upset thinking about how I would have to explain myself I just started to cry as I drove away from the rental car lot. I was twenty years old but I felt like a junior high screwup. I had to stay overnight in New York before flying out to Minnesota first thing Saturday. When I got to the race I was pretty much the joke of the pits.

I didn't win a national that season but I finished fifth overall in the points, which I was really satisfied with. Jeff Emig ended up third overall.

Please Remove Your Alpinestars from Your Mouth

Winning the 1991 125 West SX championship kicked in a clause in my contract that upped my salary to $55,000 for 1992. To me that was big money, especially since I was still living at home with my parents. But I rarely had time to buy much since I was so busy racing.

The '92 season opened up with the East vs. West 125 SX shootout in Houston, where I finished a close second to my former Pro Circuit/Peak teammate, Brian Swink, who now rode for Suzuki. On one of the last laps I bobbled as I was about to make a move on Brian. I had been putting in so much time at Hondaland that I could tell my confidence was higher than any other rider on the track. But the fortunes of any racer can be dashed by the smallest obstacle on the course. You can be riding better than anybody and your race can end in two seconds.

I shook off my second at Houston and went on a three-race tear, winning Anaheim, Seattle, and San Diego in dominating fashion.

It's not uncommon for a factory to let a 125 rider race an occasional

250 race during his 125 campaign just to get him a taste of what life is like with the big boys. After the February 8 San Diego race, the tour didn't come back west until the Las Vegas SX on April 25. That's about two and a half months the West 125 guys had to go without racing. It was decided by Dave Arnold, Honda's team manager, that I would race my first 250 race at the Tampa SX on March 28.

After my win in San Diego on February 8, I got a little swept up in the moment during my post-race interview. "I'm racing Tampa next week so all you 250 guys better watch out," I declared, not realizing my arrogance. The other 125 riders that were in earshot looked at me like I was crazy. I can still remember the stunned look on my pal and fellow 125 racer Jimmy Button's face. "We all thought you were crazy," Button said to me afterward.

Even the slightest amount of arrogance from younger riders is not tolerated by the vets. And you don't want enemies on a race-track.

When the race came around there was pressure on me to do something when there shouldn't have been any pressure at all. No 125 rider had ever won a 250 main, but that didn't stop me from dreaming. I was more excited than anything. In the first heat race I lined up on the gate next to Jeff Stanton and Jean-Michel Bayle and actually led for a few laps. I rode the entire race in the top five and finished fourth, which gave my already soaring confidence yet another boost. The little guy had made good on his big claim.

San Jose SX

One of my greatest races came at the San Jose SX in 1992. San Jose had been good to me. That's where I wrapped up the title a year earlier, broken leg and all. As fate would have it, I could again clinch the 125 West championship in San Jose. This year I was healthy but not out of the reach of bad luck. Just after the start there was a huge pileup in the first turn. Bodies and bikes were everywhere. Riders scrambled to get back on their bikes so as not to lose too much valuable ground. I got up woozy but I couldn't find my bike in the carnage. It was on the bottom of the pile, so I had to drag a few other bikes off the pile to get to my Honda. When I finally got my bike up, I was dead last. So I began

Another win, 1991.

a charge back to the front that would define my 125 career. Within a lap I moved into nineteenth place. The next lap I was in eighteenth. I shook out the cobwebs and quickly got into a rhythm. I sailed off the triple and rocketed out of the corners, passing two and three guys at a time.

I could hear the fans going mental. Since I had been dead last everyone was cheering for me to win. By lap ten, I snaked past Buddy Antunez and set my sights on Damon Huffman, who rode for Suzuki. Damon was riding great that night but he started to get sketchy when he heard my footsteps. On the twelfth lap, I swooped by him for the lead. I had come back from last place to take the win.

After winning my second straight 125 West title there wasn't much left for me to do in the 125 SX ranks. San Jose, my thirteenth win, also made me the winningest rider in 125 Supercross history.

The Good, the Bad, and the Musical Fruit of Southwick

I was riding a lot better outdoors thanks to my much improved confidence. The second round of the 1992 nationals was at Southwick in Massachusetts. Southwick was a super rough sand track. It's really fun to ride and one of my favorites. I remember Southwick in '92 because it was the site of my first national moto win. It was a great moment for me because I had to work a lot harder at motocross. But that's not why it stands out in my mind. Usually we got into town on a Thursday night, practiced Friday, had Saturday off, and raced Sunday. Saturday night a bunch of 125 riders went to this Mexican restaurant called Chi-Chi's. I have an iron gut and I can usually eat pretty much anything. And that night I did. Burritos. Quesadillas. Tortillas. Whatever. Nothing unusual about it.

The next day was race day. It was a blazing hot Sunday afternoon. A lot of riders cut airholes in their jerseys to try and beat the heat. The first moto had all of the usual suspects: Jeff Emig, Buddy Antunez, Ryno, and the legendary Guy Cooper. Early in the race I was only running about sixth, but I got a great rhythm going. It almost felt easy. I darted through the pack and picked off Cooper, Emig, and a few others to take the lead. It was like I was just walking past them on the street and saying, "Good-bye." I pulled away from the pack and won by about ten seconds.

Over the finish-line jump I threw a nac-nac to the delight of the Southwick faithful. But after the moto I was exhausted. More so than usual. My arms were rubber and my jersey was soaked with sweat. I left everything out on the track. Well, almost everything. I started getting a really bad stomachache. Man, it killed. I didn't like where this was going. Between motos you normally just relaxed, showered, and got your mind ready for the second moto. But my stomach was pounding me and I felt like I was about to poop right there in my pants.

I rushed to the outhouse as fast as I could. As soon as I got in there it was like Jeff Daniels in *Dumb and Dumber*. Damn, did somebody slip me a laxative? I went back to the truck and felt it coming on again, so

I quickly ran back to the Porta Potti. On my way back to the truck a second time, I felt the rumbling again. I went back and forth to the bathroom no less than twelve times during the motos.

I had just won my first national moto and I was stuck in the outhouse. When they blew the horn signaling that the 125 riders should make their way to the starting line for the second moto, I was still in the outhouse. Skip was freaking. "What are you doing in there? What the hell's wrong with you?" he kept asking.

As I headed for the gate I felt another rumbling and I tried to suppress it. I almost lost it on the starting line. That would not have been pretty. I guess I would just have to tell everybody that it was just dirt if I had an accident. I ended up getting third overall. But it was a victory that I didn't crap my pants.

To this day I've never eaten beans within two days of a race.

Just as quickly as Jean-Michel Bayle burst onto the American motocross scene and took it by storm, he was gone. After his record-breaking season in 1991, the reclusive Frenchman was a ghost. Bayle retired at the end of the '92 season to race road bikes for Chesterfield Aprilia in Europe. He was one of the few people in this sport who accomplished what he set out to do. He proved that he was the best in the world for at least one magical season.

Bayle's departure opened up a spot for me on Honda's 250 team.

At the conclusion of the 1992 season, my initial Honda contract was up. There was no question about what I wanted to do, so negotiations were short. They offered me $100,000 to ride 250s for 1993. I was twenty-two years old and now a full-on 250 factory rider. Me, the little kid from Hawthorne Street, who got started on a washed-out Briggs & Stratton that my dad bought for fifty bucks. The funny thing was that I didn't dwell on my new success for too long. There were bigger things that I was out to accomplish.

Honda's 250 factory team was now made up of Jeff Stanton, Steve Lamson, and myself. I was on Stanton's turf now. He was the champion, but I wasn't afraid to compete with him at the races because of the way I rode at Hondaland. I think he could sense the winds of change were beginning to kick up. Out at Hondaland during my two 125 years, I was jumping everything that Stanton did on a more powerful 250. I was turning better lap times in practice and never backed down from him or Bayle. I was professional about it, though. Never cocky or arrogant. Jeff and I would do motos together and I'd watch him carefully. I studied how he did the rhythm sections or how he made time up in the whoops. It was just me and the three-time Supercross champ on most days. Jeff was such a tremendous worker, his stamina was unequaled on the circuit, and he put a lot of emphasis on preparation. I knew his formula worked. I saw it pay off for him right in front of my eyes. But I didn't waste time being a wide-eyed kid. I continued to soak up everything I could.

In interviews, Jeff would tell everybody that I was going to be the next "guy." But I still didn't think he or Honda team manager Dave Arnold really considered me much of a threat my rookie year. Simply being fast doesn't guarantee you a championship. You've got to be mentally bulletproof, consistent, injury free, smart, and sometimes even lucky. Rookies are usually none of the above.

Tread Lightly, Young Man

It didn't take me long to get used to my 250. I raced several East Coast 250 Supercrosses the year before and I practiced on the bike quite a bit, but the '93 Hondas were all new so they had to start from scratch to build the race bikes. After we worked out some holeshot and handling quirks, the bike felt incredible.

My bike had one of the most broad and usable powerbands I had ever felt. The handling was so forgiving you didn't have to be flawless to get good results. Skip and I had it dialed in perfectly. Honda spent millions on improving rider's sensitivity to the bike through hours of testing and we gladly took advantage of it. The better a rider can understand the information the bike is giving him, the more accurately he can tell his mechanic how he needs the bike set up. I began to truly understand the importance of preparation and became committed to the process of testing the motorcycle.

With such a great bike, my confidence was sky high before I ever lined up on the gate. But going into the season everyone focused on one thing: Bradshaw vs. Stanton. Could Damon finally win a championship? Would Stanton's rock-solid style deliver Honda another championship? No and no. I wasn't predicting I was going to win the series but the element of surprise was definitely on my side. Nobody really expected me to do that much. Including me.

The series started in Orlando back then. My goal, believe it or not, wasn't to go there and win. I wanted to use Orlando to gain the respect of the other riders and get a sense of how tough this was actually going to be. Riding 250s is a whole new ball game and I just wanted to get my feet wet without creating any enemies. There is an unwritten code of ethics that says a rookie should know his place. He shouldn't push a seasoned veteran or mix it up in the turns.

This is a very fine line young riders have to walk. You're paid to go out and compete. To win. But if you get overly aggressive and force the action on the established veterans, it's a sign of disrespect. Block passing or stuffing a vet is a surefire way to get the silent treatment in the pits. Not to mention you'll have riders looking to take you out in the next race.

Plus you never know who is going to be your teammate next year. Or what riders will retire and become team managers. The same guy you stuff over the hay bales today could be a guy in a position to hire you a couple years from now. The point is, don't burn any bridges. There are only so many in this sport. Burning even one could signifigantly reduce your future employment options.

The opportunity to mix it up in Orlando never came. That just made me more nervous for when I would actually be faced with that moment. It was even more of a thorny issue for me because my teammate just happened to be the reigning champ, a guy I really looked up to and respected. And make no mistake, Jeff Stanton was the favorite again this year.

Supercross History, Stadium Security, and Chicken's Mom

All the while I was secretly waiting for the third stop on the circuit: Anaheim. Smack in the middle of motocross country, Anaheim is the marquee event of the year and the place I considered my home track. There is just an unbelievable aura that goes with Anaheim. The fans are super knowledgeable, the girls are hot, and the racing is balls out.

My practice sessions at Hondaland the week leading up to Anaheim were flawless. My CR 250 was running great, so Skip didn't need to make many changes. I just wanted Saturday to hurry up and arrive.

On the Friday before the races there were several practice sessions at the stadium that let riders become familiar with the track and make last minute adjustments. I was extra flashy that weekend, showing off at every chance.

Finally, it was Saturday and my heat race couldn't come fast enough. I was blazing. Stanton won his heat, too. For some reason I could tell he knew something was different about me this weekend. I didn't act any differently toward him but I just think he could sense it.

On the starting gate during pre-race staging for the main I remember feeling calm. My head was so clear that night. I just felt like there was something I had to do. As usual Skip was standing next to me cracking the throttle and telling me to keep my focus. I don't think I heard a word he said.

When the gate dropped, I snapped off the line like a rubber band. My bike had been so quick coming off the line that whole week. And now when it counted, it pulled just as hard. As I was about to dive into the first turn, someone entered my sights to the left of me and stole the holeshot. Stanton wasn't quite ready to be put out to pasture by a rookie. I held on and followed Jeff into the turn in second place. Me and the

champ were running away from the pack after a couple laps, going 1-2 just like this was any old day at Hondaland.

I was a little bit in shock. What was I doing at the front of the pack? I remember riding behind him for a few laps wondering whether or not I should make a move. Do I make a move and risk having my own teammate resent me for the rest of the season? Can you imagine us in the Honda box van not speaking?

But the opportunity kept presenting itself. He was leaving the door wide open and I wasn't doing anything about it.

Then it just hit me. This was my time.

I didn't bust my ass for the last ten years to ride behind someone, defending champ or not, just because I didn't want to hurt his feelings. My parents didn't make sacrifices all my life with hopes that I would one day watch opportunity pass me by.

There was a little tabletop followed by a flat left-hand corner that led to a triple. Jeff jumped the tabletop on the right with a line way to the outside going into the flat corner. I guess his idea was to stay outside in the turn to get enough speed built up to clear the triple. But that left tons of room on the inside. I thought, "Why is he leaving so much room?" You don't have to be so far outside to jump the triple. You can jump it from the inside just as easily. I know, I did it in practice. I had watched him take this same line for nine laps.

I felt so good out there it was like I wasn't even trying. I had plenty of time to think about making a move and the consequences that came with it.

On the tenth lap he did the same thing, took that unnecessary outside line. This time I jumped the tabletop to the left and landed on the flat inside part of the corner just ahead of him. I keep it tight, grabbed a handful of throttle, and cleared the triple with ease. I was leading a 250 main! I didn't waste time looking back at Jeff. I was gone. I started to pull further and further away from Stanton. It was like he conceded or something. Like he knew a new era had begun in that flat left-handed corner. The crowd didn't exactly know what to think. Who was Jeremy McGrath? Before I know it, I was whipped out, sailing past the checkers for my first 250 win ever. I threw my fist in the air in a moment of celebration that was almost surreal. I couldn't believe it. I had arrived. This was the greatest moment of my life.

While I was taking my parade lap my dad was going nuts in the stands. My mom and my sister could barely see me through their tears. Skip hugged me so hard I nearly fell of my bike. We all worked our whole lives for this moment and now it was here. My dad immediately rushed to the podium to celebrate with me. But he didn't make it very

far. The seating for riders' families was in the lower section just behind the start area. The podium was set up on the infield just off to the right of the family seating. To get to the podium, family members had to walk back up several levels, go down to the parking lot, and reenter the stadium through the pit entrance. Or they

One of my 1993 SX wins.

Jeremy McGrath

could hop the fence and walk ten feet to the podium. My dad was so excited there was no way he was going all the way back to the pits. So he just hopped the fence. All 260 pounds of him. Right away two rambo security types rushed him and screamed for him to get off the field. They thought my dad was just some drunk fan. He tried to show them he had the proper credentials, but the belligerent security guards wouldn't have it. The first guard came at my dad full speed when Jack lowballed him and took his legs out, flipping him over his shoulder. The other guard collared my dad by his neck and started to choke him out. The first guard regained his composure, grabbed my dad's arm, and pinned it behind his back. The whole time he had his credentials around his neck, but that didn't stop those two commandos from choking him and nearly breaking his arm. Chicken Matiasevich's mom saw what was going on and was none too happy. She started launching rocks at the guards and screaming a blue streak. Next thing you know Chicken's mom jumped the fence and darted toward the guards. While one guard dealt with Chicken's mom, the other took Big Jack deep below Anaheim Stadium, hogtied him with zip ties, and locked him in a chain-link holding cell.

Before long they tossed Chicken's mom in the tank, too. A sergeant came in and my dad worked himself into a lather. "What the fuck are you guys doing?" he screamed. "I'm Jack McGrath! My son just won his first race! Let me the fuck out of here." The sergeant looked at my dad's credentials and immediately untied him and let him out. "And take your wife with you," the sergeant said.

After being freed, they ran into more trouble. The guards had taken them so far beneath the stadium they couldn't find their way back. Eventually they made it to field level and just about all the fans were gone. The whole time I had no idea what happened. I just finished my post-race interview when my dad rushed the stage and gave me a big hug and kiss. We had worked our whole lives to get to this point. It just took my dad a little longer.

After the race, back in the Honda pits, Jeff congratulated me on my win. I could see in his eyes that he was burning up about it. Jeff was always so serious and here was this young kid full of energy making him look old. It had to be hard for him. I liked Jeff a lot and I respected him like crazy but he was not happy about me winning.

After Anaheim, Jeff basically stopped talking to me. He didn't completely shut me out, but he barely said a word. To him, I was now a competitor, not a teammate or a rookie. He hid behind his "all work and no play exterior." That kind of sucked because I wanted to be friends with him. It wouldn't have been so bad if I was on a different team, but we practiced together every day. We worked out of the same pits and signed autographs together. He put on this serious facade and wouldn't budge. It must have been grueling for him.

Once I passed Stanton, everything steamrolled. I knew now that I could win. I went to races not to feel my way around and fit it, but to win. And win every week.

After Anaheim my confidence was at an all-time high. I got the holeshot and won wire-to-wire in Seattle, San Diego, and Tampa. I was now in rare company. Only Rick Johnson, Bob Hannah, and Damon Bradshaw had ever won four straight races.

GREAT MOMENTS IN SUPERCROSS—RICK RYAN WINS DAYTONA IN '87

Many people considered my win at Anaheim the biggest upset since privateer Rick Ryan won at Daytona six years earlier. The fact that it would be his only win made it that much more memorable. Daytona was already a hard enough track to ride under optimal conditions, but thanks to the unexpected torrential rains over the state of Florida back in the spring of 1987, the world's gnarliest track was now primed to swallow even the best factory riders whole. Good thing for Rick Ryan that he was a struggling privateer.

Jeremy McGrath

With rain, mud, and a little luck, Ryan struck a mighty blow for the little guys who pay their own way by beating the factories and becoming the first privateer ever to win a 250 Supercross.

He wasn't even supposed to race that day. Six days earlier at the Gainesville National he tore a ligament in his left knee and could barely walk. He came up with the idea to drill a hole in his Fox boot and attach a bolt to his knee brace to keep it from twisting in his boot.

So when the rains came and wouldn't leave it was a surprise that one of the few riders who was ready to race was Ryan. Many factory team managers wanted the race to be postponed until the next day. But Ryan and his fellow privateers simply couldn't afford it. The money already paid for a nonrefundable plane ticket back to San Diego would be washed right down the drain if the race were postponed.

Team managers were concerned that if a title chaser fell in the mud (which was a good bet to happen), championship hopes might be unnecessarily dashed. At 12:30 that Sunday afternoon, the clouds finally stopped crying. The AMA announced that the race would start at 3:30.

Off the starting gate, Factory Kawasaki riders Jeff Ward and Ron Lechien were neck and neck going into the first turn. But disaster struck when Lechien's front wheel stuck like a knife in the mud, causing him to flip over his handlebars. Following right behind him was defending champion Ricky Johnson. The slick-as-ice mud gave RJ no time to swerve out of the way and he face-planted himself in the slop right behind Lechien.

Johnson's momentum carried him headfirst between

WIDE OPEN

the fender and spinning rear wheel of Lechien's KX. RJ's Bell Moto-4 saved him from having to shop for a new head, as the visor was ripped clean off.

As a result of the Lechien/Johnson fiasco, Rick Ryan snaked through a hole and snagged the holeshot. Factory Yamaha big shot Keith Bowen and Ward closely tailed Ryan down the first straight. By the third turn Bowen powered by Ryan and Wardy was closing fast. Just as he was about to make a move, Ward threw a chain and was out of the race.

Meanwhile, the aptly nicknamed Bob "Hurricane" Hannah was running a strong fourth until he bit the face of a double and had his RM 250 smashed down on top of him.

The next victim would be the leader Bowen, whose massive endo gave him a facemask full of Florida mud and Ryan the lead. Bowen miraculously came charging back a few laps later but punched the clock for good on the second to last lap when a rock got stuck in his chain.

Ryan sailed by for the lead and managed to stay upright until he rolled the finish-line jump. A privateer had just won the most prestigious Supercross race in the world and for his trouble pocketed $5,000. While Goliath after Goliath drowned in the Daytona mud, Rick Ryan had one special day in the sun.

Elevation

I think one reason I caught most 250 vets off guard was the way I rode. I didn't ride like they did. I tried to invent a new style all my own. Not for style's sake, but with the purpose of getting around a Supercross course faster than anyone ever had.

I began to look at jump combinations no one else had ever

Jeremy McGrath

dreamed of. I stayed true to my BMX roots and the rules about staying low to the ground. The more time you spend in the air, the more time you lose. When you're on the gas you're making up time. Over the triples, I figured out how to jump six to eight feet lower than anyone else. The lower I went, the quicker I was back on the ground and back on the gas. If it saved me two-tenths of a second per lap, it gave me a tremendous advantage. Say a track has two sets of huge triples. Multiply four-tenths of a second by twenty laps. All things being equal, that's an eight-second lead, an eternity in Supercross.

I started to look for any little thing on a Supercross track to give me an advantage. I noticed that most people used the same line through just about every berm: high and outside. I found that I could use the inside of a turn, which looks slower, and still clear the next obstacle by using finely-tuned suspension to basically bunny-hop (like on a BMX bike) the distance. I could calculate the amount of throttle or hop I needed three or four obstacles in advance. I learned how to use momentum from the backside of a jump to clear the next obstacle instead of just jumping one at a time.

To me, Supercross was as much of a thinking man's game as it was one of horsepower and physical stamina. There would be days at Hondaland when Jean-Michel Bayle and I would be horsing around on the track looking for ways to clear obstacles that no one ever thought about. Jean-Michel had a unique style of skimming across the top of the whoops, barely touching each mogul with his tires.

I paid attention, applied what I saw, and tried to improve on it. At the end of the whoops at Hondaland there was a seven-or eight-foot gap before a pretty big jump. Normally, you'd go through the whoops then hit the jump. We decided if we hit the last whoop just right, we could clear the gap and land down the back side of the jump, saving valuable tenths of a second on our lap time. It was a sketchy deal, but I couldn't stop thinking about it.

"I hope he doesn't try it, because I'll be forced to," Jean-Michel told Skip one day. Well, I tried it and somehow made it. We all kind of freaked out because we knew things had just changed.

Earning Respect in the Sunshine State

In March, I boosted my confidence yet again by winning my first 125 outdoor national in Gainesville, Florida. Shortly after, when the Daytona SX rolled around, it was Stanton's plan to steal back a little respect. A win for me would mean five in a row and serve a psychologically crushing blow to the rest of the field. Daytona was almost as celebrated as Anaheim. The purses for Anaheim and Daytona were $10,000, as opposed to the normal $5,000. The race is part of the week-long Daytona Bike Week that includes the Daytona 200 superbike road race and countless industry shindigs.

It is arguable that Daytona isn't really a Supercross at all. The track was designed by Gary Bailey, legendary motocross instructor and father of former SX champ David Bailey. It's more similar to an outdoor track with several different types of terrain—huge ruts, sand, and bumped-out straightaways. The track deteriorates really fast, making it a nightmare to set your bike up for the race. Jeff had won the circuit's most brutal race an incredible four years in a row. His strength and stamina seemed to set him apart, and he took pride in the fact that he could conquer Daytona. I treated Daytona like an outdoor race because it's run on the infield of the Daytona International Speedway. All I wanted to do was keep my head above water and not get hurt. I shocked myself big-time by finishing second.

Celebrating another win, 1993.

Jeremy McGrath

Movin' On Out

My parents came to just about every Supercross. They would usually fly out the day before the race. We'd have dinner after Friday practice or just hang out. They were still my biggest fans and never failed to show their support. Win or lose. They came to selected nationals, as well. Early on, they were on the scene a lot but pretty much let me grow up and be a man. They knew I had to get out on my own eventually. It was a little weird because now I was making more money than my parents. But that didn't bother them. They handled my money, put it in the bank, hired an accountant so I wouldn't have to worry about that stuff. They raised my sister and I appreciated whatever we had and was thankful for it.

I always operated with the idea that this wasn't going to last forever. Even as a rookie I thought like that. I never really splurged like you see a lot of young riders these days. An eighteen-year-old with six cars doesn't make a whole lot of sense, but that's what a lot of young guys want to do. In 1992, I bought a Chevy 1500 pickup and that's all I had. Shortly before the '93 season I bought my first house. It was a bank foreclosure in Murrieta, five minutes from Menifee. I paid $120,000 and that was a lot for me. The paperwork was like two inches thick. I was only twenty and I started to flip out right after I did it. I didn't know if it was the right move. Could I afford to buy a house?

Despite the price tag, the Murrieta house wasn't that big. Three bedrooms crammed into about 1,400 square feet. The day I got it I just up and moved out of my parents' house. They were really caught off guard. They were like, "You didn't even say anything, where are you going?" I mean, they knew I was buying a house but they didn't know that it was ready to move in to.

My parents' feelings were really hurt by my sudden departure. They were not happy about it at all. It made me really think about what I was leaving. My dad was like my best friend and my mom was just as close. My sister Tracy was always behind me 150 percent. Because of my riding career, a lot of what my sister wanted to do was put on the back burner. She really sacrificed for a long time so the family could concentrate on

racing. And now I was leaving. I was so happy to be stepping out in the world, but at the same time it hurt to leave the people I loved like that.

My dad's parents never owned a house. It was his dream to see me be able to buy one on my own. He just didn't think it would be so soon.

My family situation was really a good one when I was at home. Even though I was a pro motocrosser, I still had chores. Tracy and I split the vacuuming, garbage, and dishes ever since we were little kids, so chores were normal to me. Tracy was cool about handling my chores when I wasn't there. Which was pretty often. If I wasn't at the races I was up in Reche Canyon or sleeping over at Ryan's house. My parents never really put a lot of house rules on me either. I actually had a pretty cool setup at my parent's house. Now that I look back, I really didn't need my own house, but the papers were already signed.

My friend Lawrence Lewis came over and helped me move my stuff out that night. Lew was a professional skier from Big Bear and occasionally rode with us. One day he came over to my house to ride my Supercross track. He just showed up. I didn't even know that he knew where I lived. But he was a cool guy my age with a great sense of humor and was into the same things as me. That was pretty much girls and motocross.

Jeremy McGrath

When Lew was working a construction job one summer, he was chipping rocks when a piece shot off and hit him in the eye. Despite a few operations he lost the use of his eye. But he still rode with us and was pretty good. Even with depth perception problems he was a pretty good jumper. At the time he was going to Cal State Northridge, but he decided to take some time off and moved in with me.

It would turn out to be an arrangement that caused my parents much grief.

Cribs

Me and Lew had the pad set up just the way we liked it. There was a punching bag hanging in the living room. The garage was super trick, too. The floor had a clear coat and there were cabinets for various MX accessories. When I was seventeen I bought a bedroom set for my parents that I ended up taking with me to my new house. I actually still have that bedroom set today in my new house in Encinitas.

We put a couple of single beds in the spare bedroom because riders were always dropping by. We never really threw out-of-control parties, but there seemed to be girls over there all the time. Jennifer Thomas and I had broken up and I was at the age where entertaining girls was pretty much all I was interested in. I cared a lot for her but also wanted to see what was out there, so it was best if we were apart.

Lew and I were hanging out a lot, too. When I wasn't riding during the day I was mostly at home doing nothing. When you have a job like mine and everyone else has a day job, you suddenly find yourself alone. Since Lew was taking a break from school and I needed a partner to train with, I paid him a couple hundred bucks a week to work out with me. Some people looked down on that. They thought I was paying my friend to hang out with me. Well, I needed someone around when I went riding just in case I got hurt. Having Lew train with me was a lot more fun, too.

Still, my parents, ever watchful, kept an eye on Lew because they didn't want anyone living off my name. Or my money.

Hater's Ball

It seemed as the season wore on, the more I won, the more doubters would come out of the woodwork. They said Anaheim was a fluke. That Daytona would eat me alive. That I could only win when I got the holeshot. It was always something. I knew I could win if I didn't come off the gate first, but I wasn't going to sacrifice a good start to prove it. In Charlotte, I didn't have to. I got a horrible start and came out of the first turn thirteenth. I managed to move up to fifth by the end of the first lap. By the end of the seventh lap, I passed Bradshaw for first place and held on to win.

Coming from behind is the most satisfying way to win, but I'd rather get the holeshot any day. What would the critics say next?

My First 250 Championship

It seems like whenever you set out to do something in life it never quite goes the way you want it to. But that couldn't be said for my career the past two years. I wanted to ride for Honda. Check. I wanted to move up to 250s. Did that. I wanted to win Anaheim. No prob. And I wanted to be 250 champion. Check. When I won the Pasadena Supercross, my ninth win of the year, I clinched my first 250 Supercross title. The Holy Grail of motocross was mine.

Everything was going so according to plan it felt easy after I won the title. It was anything but; it just felt that way. It was too perfect. No one had ever won the title in their rookie year. No one had ever won ten Supercrosses in a single season. The $100,000 bonus I got from Honda wasn't bad either. I had to stop and ask myself, "How is this happening?"

On the other hand, Jeff Stanton's confidence was further deteriorating. I suspect he was losing a little enthusiasm, too. The previous year he had ridden thirty-one races in the United States and about twelve overseas. The thought of having to fend off an upstart like me was too much for him.

At the season finale, Jeff got a small piece of revenge by winning the Las Vegas SX. But it didn't bother me that much since I had already won the championship. And besides, it would be the last Supercross race he would ever win.

Pra-ta-Tae

Jeff Emig and I had been developing a healthy distaste for one another on the racetrack. I always thought his etiquette during a race was suspect at best. At Glen Helen that year the AMA decide to experiment with a one moto winner-take-all format instead of the usual two motos. It was a sweltering 110 degrees, so not many people minded.

I lined up on the gate alongside Jeff. I knew Jeff was such a cagey rider that I had to keep an eye on him at all times. Sure enough, when the gate dropped he cut over on me down the start straight—it was one of his best tricks. As a result, I got a terrible start and Jeff got the holeshot. He raced out to a huge lead while I was stuck at the back of the pack. So I started riding like crazy until I caught all the way up to Jeff on the last lap.

Jeff had the win wrapped up when three corners from the finish line his bike broke down. He was kick-starting his bike frantically, with riders passing him, until it finally cranked up. He headed for the finish line with me square on his tail. After we crossed the finish line, I was still pissed about what he did on the start. We had to ride by the grandstands to get back to the pits. I caught up to him and just started flipping him off and trying to grab his front brake so he would crash. Back in the pits, he threw his bike down and lunged after me. I stiff-armed him in the facemask and we both flailed around trying to connect a wild blow until our mechanics stepped in.

We would definetly meet again.

Style, Bayee!

When I was growing up, with the exception of RJ, the champions of our sport were sort of bland. No one had any kind of real image. Jeff Ward, Jeff Stanton, and Jean-Michel Bayle didn't give the sport much in the

way of style. That's one thing Emig and I brought to the race scene. Jeff loved shiny suits and his sunglasses were ever present. It seemed like whatever I did concerning my looks, it always got a lot of attention. I never tried to do it on purpose. I liked to change my hairstyle about once a month. Sometimes I had shoulder-length hair, other times it was shaved pretty close. I would dye it platinum or blue or black depending on how I felt.

Another one of my favorites was to regularly change my goatee and sideburns. Trying new looks was almost like setting up your suspension or tuning your motor. I liked to try different things so I didn't get bored. Still do. But I guess I've grown a bit more conservative and I pretty much stick to black dye, blond highlights, or my natural brown. I've always admired Andre Agassi and the fact that he wasn't afraid to express himself through his personal style. Up to this point, people in the sport just didn't care about personal style.

But I got a little carried away when I got both my nipples pierced. Looking back, it was a dumb thing to do. A couple of my friends had it done so I went along with the crowd. I never wanted my dad to find out because I knew he wouldn't like it. I could never admit to him that I pierced my nipples and it took me a long time to get the balls to tell him. Actually, I didn't even plan on telling him, but after a moto at national he found out. I used to tape the rings down on my chest so they wouldn't get caught on anything if I crashed. After the moto he saw the tape when I took off my shirt. He knew what it was right away. He just laughed a really disgusted parent's laugh like I was a total idiot. I didn't keep them in much longer after that.

Motocross Des Nations

After the nationals, I was selected to ride for the American Motocross des Nations team. The des Nations is basically the Olympics of motocross, which was being held in Austria. It was a tremendous honor to be selected, but I was a little confused. I was picked as the 250 rider even though I had yet to race a single 250 outdoor national. Jeff Emig handled the 125 duties and Kawasaki's Mike Kiedrowski, the former Open Class champion, was the 500 rider. (The 500 class had been long defunct in the United States.)

Late in September, we headed for Austria. When we first got to the track, local kids were swarming everywhere. Motocross is huge over there and we were like rock stars to them. When I actually got a chance to check out the track, I started to get a little worried. It had a very European feel to it, fast and rough with few jumps, which didn't suit me that well. There were like two jumps. I knew that things would be tough for me before I even suited up.

My strategy was to get great starts, go as fast as I could, and see what happened. The des Nations had a six-moto format (125, 250, and 500 each run twice) and the team with the lowest combined score out of four possible motos wins. (They drop the two worst motos.)

In the first moto, I was running third for the entire race when the Austrian Kurt Nichol passed me on the last lap. I was so pissed at him because he totally roughhoused me. It's a good thing I didn't punch him out or anything because now he's my boss at KTM. But I was really bummed about finishing fourth.

It went from bad to worse. The second moto I crashed in the first corner. I struggled to my feet, got back in the race, and finished ninth. Meanwhile, Emig was on fire winning both motos. He was an excellent outdoor racer and this track suited him really well. Kiedrowski also rode

great. They ended up dropping both of my motos. I felt terrible because I thought I was going to be the reason the United States lost the des Nations for the first time in twelve years.

Luckily we had enough to take the overall win despite my efforts. I was the weak link for sure. That was a really scary experience. The Des Nations is such a high pressure event. The eyes of the world are on you and everyone expects you to bring home the championship. Second place is considered a failure.

Jeremy-San Representin' in the Orient

After the outdoor national season ends, there are a series of exhibitions Supercrosses in Europe and Asia. Because American riders are offered decent start money it pays to hit a few of them in the off season, which runs from September to December. The races are useful if you want to stay sharp without a ton of pressure heaped on you.

In November, I took my first trip to Japan to race the first annual Fukuoka Supercross, which had the biggest purse of any Supercross race in history. The prize for winning was $50,000 or a Porsche convertible, for which the promoters paid $100,000. The Fukuoka event was a first-class operation all the way. Promoters sent shipping crates to America to send our bikes over and offered to pay the return shipping costs, as well. At most overseas events, riders just use stock bikes provided by a local dealer. No one really cares how well they do overseas, it's just a way to get paid. But with such a huge purse this was an event everyone wanted to win. Airfare, hotels, and meals were also taken care of. Our hotel rooms were actually condos that sold for around $500,000.

The state-of-the-art 47,000-seat Fukuoka Dome was located on Kyushu Island, Japan's southernmost. The dome's huge retractable roof used $10,000 worth of electricity every time it opened and closed.

For some reason, I was still being doubted despite winning the Supercross title. Going into Fukuoka, many people picked Jeff Stanton to win (Bradshaw turned down the invitation). Jeff looked fast in practice but you can't win a race in practice. The track was pretty tough, with two gnarly whoop sections and back-to-back triples.

Coming off the gate in the main, I narrowly avoided a pileup that sent Mike Kiedrowski cartwheeling off the track. I took the holeshot and felt a little heat from my other 250 teammate Steve Lamson and Suzuki's Brian Swink. Stanton got a horrible seventh-place start and worked his way back up to third before Lamson took him out over the triple. I built up enough of a lead to throw heel clickers and no-footers over the triples. The Japanese fans had a blast and I crossed the finish line forty-five seconds ahead of Stanton.

When I won the race, I decided to take the fifty grand over the Porsche. I already had a truck and selling the Porsche wasn't worth the trouble. Besides, I already had an Acura NSX.

Not a bad way to end my first year as the king of Supercross.

As far as my '93 Supercross title was concerned, a lot of insiders were throwing around the F-word. Fluke. After one great season there is a natural tendency for people to do that until you show some staying power. No one wanted to accept that my record ten wins was something that could happen again. If it wasn't one thing it was another. They said I could only win if I got the holeshot. That rough tracks would do me in. Or my conditioning was subpar. I didn't mind the naysayers, though, because it only added to my desire to win.

I won the first five rounds of the 1994 Supercross series, which included Orlando, Houston, Anaheim, San Diego, and Tampa, with relative ease. I had so much confidence I expected to win each time I lined up on the gate. In Orlando, I started second behind Larry Ward. On the fifth lap I passed him over the finish-line jump and led the rest of the way to the checkers.

The Houston track was awesome but I got a horrible start, thirteenth. On my charge to the front of the pack, I collided with Suzuki's Brian Swink over a jump, sending him crashing to the ground. It wasn't a dirty move, just something that happens.

By the fourth lap, I had worked my way back to fourth place. It took me two more laps to catch up to the leader, Jeff Emig. Because of the way he uses the whole track when he rides, Emig is regarded as one of the toughest riders in the sport to pass. But he often rides on the ragged edge by jumping across the face of jumps and stuffing riders in turns. Jeff was already beginning to fade, and I shot by him through the whoops on the eighth lap.

At round four in San Diego, I was battling a serious case of the flu. My body was dehydrated and I barely had enough energy to put my boots on. I got a fifth-place start and even in my tired state was still able to gain the lead by lap twelve. But I was hanging on by a thread. I couldn't wait for this race to end. It was a good thing that my competition were busy taking each other out. About the tenth lap, tough guy Mike LaRocco was charging hard on Emig when he tried to squeak by him on the inside of a hairpin turn. There wasn't enough room and both riders slammed hard. Emig quickly got up and kicked LaRocco in the back soccer-style. LaRocco wasn't wearing any upper-body protection, so getting a steel-tipped motocross boot to the spine probably did not feel too good. The AMA fined Emig $1,000 and gave LaRocco a rough-riding warning. I managed to hold on for the win and was met by paramedics immediately after the race and administered oxygen.

I was in a zone at Anaheim and led wire to wire. One cool thing about Anaheim was the return of motocross legend Ron Lechien. Nicknamed the Dogger, Ron had put together one of the most notorious racing careers ever. He was one of the all-time great talents but never won a 250 championship. He probably finished second and third (usually to Rick Johnson) more than anybody. In the main at Anaheim, he crashed in the first turn and, true to his hard-charging style, fought his way back to a respectable thirteenth. Not bad for a twenty-seven-year-old guy who hadn't raced in five years.

Jeremy McGrath

THE LEGEND
OF RON LECHIEN

Very few motocross riders are ever blessed with the ability to navigate a motocross course like Ron Lechien. His combination of speed, grace, and aggression mixed with all-out ease put him in a class by himself. But unfortunately Lechien's gift came with a curse that led to the premature end of his motocross dreams. One opponent Lechien could never beat was his alcohol and drug addiction.

In the early eighties, El Cajon, California, produced motocross prodigies by the truckload. Former MX Champs Ricky Johnson, Broc Glover, and Marty Smith honed their skills in the El Cajon Zone but few could match the explosiveness of Lechien. After traveling the country with his father, Dick, the owner of Maxima Oil (a popular oil company), and dominating the amateur nationals in Ponca City and Loretta Lynn's, Lechien turned his sights to the 1983 125 nationals. That year, arguably the most competitive ever, he matched wits and banged fenders with the likes of Johnny O'Mara, Mark Barnett, and Jeff Ward.

Ronnie's balls-to-the-wall style earned him three wins and fourth place in the final standings. The next year, the Dogger, as he was affectionately nicknamed, made a premature jump to the big bikes for the 250 nationals. Only seventeen, he matched Rick Johnson with four wins apiece. The title came down to the last moto of the last race. The picturesque Washougal track was the setting, but Johnson's conditioning proved to be too much for Lechien to overcome.

Lechien was never fond of training. He had missed so much of his youth racing and practicing that he turned to drugs when the pressure to win became too overwhelming. He started drinking beer, smoking pot, and partying to all hours of the morning. Even with a hangover, Lechien's talent would carry him through. In the rough and tumble 1985 250 SX series, against luminaries such as David Bailey, Bob Hannah, Ward, and Johnson, Lechien earned three wins and third place for the series.

He dominated the 125 nationals to win the only championship of his career. The more he won, the more he partied, graduating to heavier drugs like crystal meth and cocaine. Kawasaki put drug clauses in his contract and the fines piled high as he routinely skipped mandatory drug tests. For the first time in his career, his results began to slide. He raced three classes in 1986 but failed to win a single race.

In 1987, he entered rehab at the urging of his loved ones and sponsors. His hiatus from drugs resulted in his best season to date in 1988: second in 250 SX and 500 nationals, third in 250 nationals. It wouldn't last. Later that year, Ron was arrested for his third DUI and sentenced to one year in jail with no bail.

Ron's once bright racing career gave way to his craving for illegal substances. Over the next few years he was arrested for DUI, hit and run, driving with a suspended license, and brandishing a firearm. He was doing drugs every day. If he wasn't using, he was plotting the next score. For a couple years he was on the lamb for violating his parole. During his most recent lockup in 1999, he lost his house to foreclosure.

Lechien's family and close friends never lost hope and still saw the kid who could turn the world on with his smile. They were adamant that Ron would kick his habit and pick up his life where he left off. For the last four years Ron has been riding on the straight and narrow. He works side by side with his father at Maxima Oils.

He still loves to ride and some say he's even got a touch of the old magic left in his throttle hand.

Jeremy McGrath

Pro, Old Flames, and Hard Feelings

The 1994 Supercross season marked the rebirth of my rivalry with Jeff Emig. We were both in California's hotly contested amateur GMC State Series in the winter of 1988, but there were too many guys in that class to consider it a rivalry. We also battled on 125s outdoors in '91 and '92, but I was never really a title contender. And the previous year Jeff was a nonfactor in his first season as a 250 Supercross rider. The rivalry intesified in '94, but the bad blood between us went back a few years.

I met a girl named Jennifer Carter at the Vegas SX. She was a cute blonde whose grandmother lived by my dad's shop in Sun City. We hit it off and started seeing each other regularly. Before you knew it, we were dating. It went well for about a year before I decided that I didn't really want to be tied down with a full-time girlfriend, so we broke up. I was young and traveling a lot and a girlfriend wasn't the best thing for me. The split was pretty amicable and we remained friends. A few months later Jeff met her and they ended up dating pretty seriously.

Jeff hated the fact that Jennifer and I used to go out. He couldn't stand the thought of it. I knew that so I used it against him. I'd tell him that Jennifer and I were still seeing each other just to mess with him. He would confront her and she'd deny everything.

Most of our rivalry was really based on our cutthroat competitive nature on the track and it often spelled trouble. We just couldn't get along. That was unfortunate because we traveled in the same circles, knew the same people, and liked to do the same things. We both loved to go to Lake Havasu, a hot spot for the MX crowd. We both had boats we'd take up there. He'd have his friends with him and I'd have mine. Everyone knew each other so it was impossible for us to avoid each other.

Jeff was not one that could ever just hang out. A lot of people thought he was too busy trying to be a rock star. That's just something I could never understand about Jeff.

I've always felt that no matter how successful I am or how much money I have, I still treat all my friends like they are the same as me. I come from humble beginnings, so just because I have a bigger bank account and can ride a motorcycle, it doesn't make me better than you. It's just the wrong approach on how to treat other people. But I still tried to give him a chance.

One summer I threw a party for one of the Mike Tyson pay-per-view fights. We had tons of food: pizza, pretzels, beer, everything. The fight was scheduled to start at seven and Jeff and a few others showed up around four. Jeff was already lit out of his mind. After the fight, he passed out on the floor and people were just stepping over him. When he came to a while later, he wanted to go home. My dad took his keys and told him to lay his ass back down. He put his keys on a bookshelf

and Jeff went to sleep on the fireplace. About twenty minutes later we checked on him and he and his keys were gone. Back then I wouldn't have called him to go play golf and he wouldn't call me either. But we were able to coexist. These days we get along fine. We no longer race against each other and we're both married (he married Jennifer in November of 2002). Every now and again we even go riding together, and when we see each other at the lake, neither one of us is above swapping a race memory or two.

Prelude to the X Games

One day my BMX pal, Eric Carter, and I were at my practice track screwing around on our motorcycles. I was a little tired of doing the

Jeremy McGrath

same jumps, so we tried to figure out something that would challenge us a little bit more. "Why don't you try a nac-nac?" asked Eric. I had never even thought about that. A nac-nac is when you take your right foot off the peg in midair and swing it over behind you as if you were getting off the bike. At the last second you kick your leg back around and get back on the bike. It was a fairly new BMX trick that a lot of guys were doing on bicycles. I tried it a couple of times and started to get more confidence each time. At the end of the day I was wrapping my leg around pretty far.

Over the following weeks I began to get more and more comfortable with the nac-nac. The fans at the races got a huge kick out of it and demanded it wherever I went. The nac-nac was a pretty basic trick but nothing like that had ever really been done on a motorcycle. A lot of other riders picked up on it and began doing different varieties of tricks like heel clickers, nothings, and can-cans. It was the humble beginnings of what would come to be known as freestyle motocross. It was the basis for ultra-hyped racing alternative events like the X Games and the Gravity Games.

Another trick that would serve as the building block for nearly two dozen of today's best tricks was the Superman, which I was kind of doing on accident. I had an off weekend in my schedule and I planned to spend it at Lake Havasu where everyone else was going to be. But Honda demanded that I go to a photo shoot at Castaic Lake an hour northeast of L.A. There was no way I felt like doing that. I told Honda that the only way I was going to do that was if they got a helicopter and flew me to LAX right after the shoot so I could fly to Havasu. They agreed, so I went to the shoot. When I look back, I can't believe how bold I was.

Even when I got there I still wasn't that into it. They had me doing a few jumps, so I just starting clowning around. I was doing some basic no-footers when it happened. I extended my legs straight out behind me while hoisting my body up above the bars. My first Superman. Actually, it looked like a super squirrel compared to the way today's freestylers hang it out.

LCQ

When I won after getting holeshots, they said that's all I could do. Then I showed I could win with a bad start. But on April 9, 1994, at Pontiac, I won in a fashion that no one ever had before. Or since. I became the first rider in Supercross history to win a main event after qualifying through the Last Chance Qualifier. In my heat race I got a bad start and couldn't make up the ground, so it was off to the semifinal. That was just a repeat of the first heat. In the LCQ, which is mostly struggling privateers and out-of-their-league local pros, I won easily. In the main event, I didn't get the holeshot but took the lead by the second turn and held on for the win.

I didn't match last year's win total of ten, but I proved that it was no fluke by winning nine Supercrosses for the season and my second straight 250 Supercross title. For winning the championship I recived another $100,000 bonus from Honda.

After the season, my contract expired and I again re-upped with Honda. I signed a two-year deal worth $500,000, one of the richest motocross contracts ever. They also hooked me up with a couple Acura Legends and Goldwing touring bikes for my dad. When you're taking care of business for Honda there are a lot of perks that come with the job.

Caddyshack

I moved up to 250s for the outdoor nationals in the summer of 1994. The entire outdoor series that year was a learning experience for me. I was still feeling my way around on the outdoor circuit. I didn't win a race all summer, but I rode strong enough to finish third overall in the final points standings. But outside of motocross there was something else that I was trying to get the hang of as well. Golf.

It was a fun way for me to go out and relax, and at the same time challenging enough so I didn't get bored. The development of my game probably would have come quicker if I hadn't spent so much time goofing around in the golf carts. But that was part of the fun of playing golf.

That summer at the Murrieta Hot Springs Golf Course about fifteen minutes from my house, Lawrence Lewis and I spent most of our time learning the finer points of golf-cart derby. We quickly learned that we could easily access the carburetor on the golf carts by popping up the seat. The carburetors had a limiter that would only allow the carts to go about ten miles an hour. But we would stick a golf tee in the carburetor, which would allow more fuel to flow through and the cart to go faster. With a tee jammed in there I could get the cart up to a good forty miles an hour.

Hot Springs had a ton of rolling hills that were ripe for sailing off. On the twelfth hole there was about a ten-foot hill that was almost vertical near the top. My plan was to jump up the hill and land on the plateau atop the hill. I got the cart up to about thirty miles an hour with the runway I had and hit the hill clean.

The cart got about five feet of air and shot straight up like we were launching the space shuttle. The golf bags flew out of the cart and the clubs and golf balls went everywhere. I knew we were in for one hell of a rough landing. We would have been good if not for those safety bars they put on the sides of carts to prevent you from falling out. When we landed, my tailbone came down square on the bar and it felt like I had jumped out of a two-story window. I thought I broke it but it was just badly bruised. It would have been tough explaining that one to Honda. When we returned the cart the roof was bent, the wheels wobbled, and strange noises were coming from everywhere.

That was the last summer Murrieta Hot Springs used gas-powered golf carts.

Bercy, Me

When the outdoor national season ends the first week of September, riders use the next four months to rest, recuperate, and start gearing up for the following Supercross season, which begins in January. Those four months also represent a great opportunity to travel the world and make easy money at the exhibition Supercrosses in Europe and Asia. But the real fun starts at the post-race parties when you hit the town.

That year I raced the Bercy SX in Paris and picked up $25,000 for my trouble. After the race we went out drinking that night and got hammered. We came back to the hotel where the American riders were staying and the English rider James Dobb introduced me to a girl named Emma. I ended up going back to Emma's room and drinking some more, then eventually passing out with her. The next morning our flight was at nine and Skip came knocking on my door about seven. Of course, I was nowhere to be found. They waited as long as they could before Skip, Jeff Stanton, Steve Lamson, and their mechanics left for the airport and boarded the plane for Japan.

At two o'clock I finally woke up. I had a headache so bad I thought my head was going to explode. I was in deep shit. It was officially time to be scared. Forget that I was supposed to be in Japan for the Tokyo Supercross, but we were going to the Honda factory to test. It's a big thing for the factory riders to go to Japan and test. You meet all of the Honda bigwigs who are making all of this possible. As riders, it's in our best interest to put our best foot forward with regards to professionalism. But I was stuck back in France without a clue as to what to do.

When Skip and company arrived in Japan the Honda bigwigs were puzzled.

"Where is Jeremy-san?" they asked.

Jeremy-san was trying to figure out how the hell he was going to get out of France!

I took a shower, got my things ready, and went down to the lobby. All of the race promoters were in the hotel restaurant eating breakfast. I cruised over to them and sat down. "Where were you?" they begged. They put me on a flight that left Paris at six P.M. How was I going to explain this one?

Next Stop, Barcelona, Pain

A few weeks later there was another exhibition race in Spain. Afterward, a bunch of us decided to paint the town. Well, I actually didn't go out this time. I always had trouble sleeping in other countries due to the time difference. The night before I barely caught a wink, so I was too zombied out for another night of partying. About four in the morning, Skip, Ryno, Lew, Mike Craig, Alley Semar (125 rider Kevin Windham's mechanic), and Factory Phil came back to the hotel all banged up and bloodied and hyped up after getting into a major bar fight.

After hours of pounding anything that the bartender put on the counter, pretty much anything can take place. It started out innocently enough. Alley slapped Skip from behind, I mean really cracked him, but Skip didn't see who did it. Skip turned around and popped some Spanish guy standing next to him. The Spanish dude was pretty liquored up but retaliated by coming right at Skip with arms swinging. Ryno and Alley jumped in, as do the Spanish guy's pals. Instant bar fight. Bodies, fists, and barstools flew everywhere. On one hand are these American MX guys, on the other are the Spanish locals duking it out for supremacy.

Unfortunately for the MXers, they were outnumbered two to one.

Somewhere in the fray Ryno ended up getting a broken jaw. People were getting bottles smashed over their heads like in the movies. Except in real life it hurts a hell of a lot more. The Americans pretty much got their asses kicked and had to make a getaway.

In Spain, scooters are one of the most common forms of transportation. Most of the people in the bar that night rode scooters and had them all parked in a row. On his way out of the bar, Lew went Clint Eastwood on the scooters and knocked them over like dominos. There must have been thirty scooters tipped over in the parking lot. He finished the job by stomping on cars, running roof to roof.

They got back to the hotel and half the guys were missing shirts. Everyone had some kind of wound to prove they were there. It was a complete mess and I was glad I didn't go out that night.

Stanton and the Beast Call It Quits

Even though I had won two straight 250 titles, I didn't let my focus waiver for one day. I couldn't wait for the '95 season to start in January. But Jeff Stanton had had enough. After winning six championships, Jeff retired from competitive racing. During the '94 season he just wasn't into it. He had the worst Supercross season of his career (sixth overall) and his outdoor campaign was even worse. He broke a vertebrae in a nasty crash at Hangtown. He toughed it out and actually raced the next week at Budds Creek only to slam hard yet again.

He had taken over for Rick Johnson in '89, weathered Bayle's dominance in '91, and won back both the Supercross and outdoor national championships in '92. But in fairness to Jeff, he was really losing his love for riding and no longer had his competitive edge. I was the obstacle he couldn't get over.

I was sad to see Jeff go. He had been there from day one of my Team Honda experience. But in a way I think I helped end his career. He was no longer the big dog on the porch as far as Honda was concerned. Jeff couldn't beat me anymore and I got the lion's share of the attention. I

Jeremy McGrath

broke him. I broke his spirit. As quickly as he rose to the top of the sport, he faded. He could tell that it was time for a new generation to take center stage.

At twenty-six Jeff Stanton's career was over.

When I first met Jeff, I was actually kind of scared of him. He was always so serious, so businesslike. He rarely went out after the races and he never drank. I wanted his respect and I never knew how to act around him. He never let loose, but I think in this sport you have to. You can't overwhelm yourself with the seriousness of it all. It's supposed to be fun. Then I took his title away in '93 and things were cold between us. Eventually we warmed back up to each other and remain friends to this day.

In a way, Jeff Stanton was reflective of the era he grew up in. He was a middle-class guy from Sherwood, Michigan, with simple values, and you can't knock that.

At the end of '94, another one of my idols was packing it in as well. Damon Bradshaw's motocross career had come to a premature end. The rumors were widespread as to why Damon quit: He was burnt out. Girls. He was more interested in his ranch. He didn't care anymore. He'd rather be flying his planes. Whatever the reason was, he was through. When he was fourteen years old, Damon said he wanted to win the 125, 250, 500, and Supercross championships. He missed at every one of those goals. The most hyped mini rider of all time failed to win a single pro championship.

Good-bye Murrieta, Hello Canyon Lake

By 1995, I had outgrown my first house I shared with Lew in Murrieta and moved to a house that sat on the water in Canyon Lake, fifteen minutes away. Built in a cove, the house had 200 feet of lake-front property, a pool with a rock waterfall, and a jacuzzi. I would come home the Sunday after a race and the raging would begin. The lake would be bumper to bumper with boats and Jet Skis. Everyone was drinking and girls would be dancing everywhere. The lake was a scene right out of *Girls Gone Wild*. It was so crowded sometimes that I wouldn't even have to leave my dock to join the party.

Just about every weekend a ton of people would come over to my house and we'd take my boat and go wakeboarding or just clown around on the water, then come back to the house and relax in the pool. One afternoon we had spent several hours on the water and were pretty pooped when we got back to the house. Everyone was dying of hunger, so we fired up the barbecue on my deck and then stepped just inside the

screen door to pop back a few beers in the rec room. One thing about wakeboarding—it makes you tired as hell. After about fifteen minutes of lounging around, everyone nodded off to sleep. We would have slept for a while if it hadn't been for the screams. On any given Sunday the lake is crawling with people wakeboarding, Jet Skiing, and just having a good time. Everything came to a standstill as people pointed at my deck and shouted for us to come out.

This barbecue was engulfed in flames. Searing hot tongues of fire were shooting ten feet in the air threatening to capture the ceiling of my deck. I ran outside and quickly grabbed the hose and trained it on the flaming grill. Lew turned the knob and I sprayed the fire. Huge mistake. Never try to put out a grease fire with water. It only makes it worse. I knew that, but water was all I had. I just keep spraying it down and eventually it went out.

I had a huge black, sooty reminder on the ceiling of my deck that told me never to fall asleep with the barbecue on. Luckily, the deck was made of stucco. If it had been made of wood, my house would have burned down.

Somebody Stop Me!

If anyone was going to challenge my crown in 1995, it didn't happen at the season opener in Orlando. No one could stay on their bikes. Jeff Emig grabbed the holeshot but sampled the soil in the first turn, igniting a major pileup. After getting jacked up, he rode hard to finish ninth but was never a factor. LaRocco went down on lap four and never really recovered. And what of Greg Albertyn, DeCoster's new hope? He didn't even make it to the main. The rookie crashed twice in his heat race—the finish-line tabletop and the whoops section were more than he could handle. He left the arena in an ambulance. But that's what the pressure to win can do to a guy. After taking the lead from Noleen Yamaha's Kyle Lewis, I never looked back.

At round two in Minneapolis, it was six degrees outside with a wind-chill factor of ten below. That didn't stop 55,723 fans from braving the arctic-like winds outside the Metrodome to see their favorite riders. The year before was the first ever SX in Minneapolis and one of the best crowds all year. I hoped they weren't looking for a close race because I holeshot the main, led for twenty laps, and took the checkers. Even though LaRocco finally got a decent start (second), I lost him after two laps. I was turning 57.13-second laps and lapped all but five riders.

For round three, it was back home at my favorite track: Anaheim. I felt as good as I normally did at the site of my first ever 250 win, but unfortunately I got a bad start and had to fight my way to the front from mid-pack. Due to heavy rain all week, the track was soupy and rutted out pretty quickly. That weekend Mike LaRocco was fined $250 by the AMA when he slapped KTM's Jeff Dement in the helmet after both riders had crashed in a turn. By lap thirteen, I got by Team Noleen Yamaha's Larry Ward, who was having a sensational year with three straight podiums. Ward hung tight and piggybacked me all the way to the finish.

The next week in Seattle, I felt that I was in as good a groove as I'd ever been in. I got my second holeshot of the season and led the race wire to wire for the win. (The year before I got second at Seattle with a flat tire.) With two pumped-up Dunlops no one else had a chance. Round five was at Jack Murphy Stadium in San Diego. With a win I would tie Rick Johnson's record of five straight wins to start a season. Once again, I ripped to the front of the pack for the holeshot. My CR pulled so great off the line it felt like I really didn't have to work too hard. It definitely boosts your confidence when you know you've got the best machinery.

On the first lap, I received some surprise pressure from Honda of Troy's Mike Craig, who snuck by me and led until the second lap. But I quickly settled in and reeled him in over the whoops to assume ultimate control of the race. Hats off to Mike, however. He was racing with a broken shoulder blade as a result of a major body slam two rounds ago in Minny. Regardless, I was five for five and didn't plan on slowing down any time soon.

Like a Fox

One of the most important decisions a rider will make in his career is deciding which brand of motocross gear he'll wear. Gear companies like Fox, No Fear, Thor, Shift, Sinasalo, and O'Neal hand top riders six-figure deals to endorse their MX gear and casual wear. For the first two years of my 250 career I wore Sinasalo. But before the '95 campaign I signed a three-year deal with Fox, which was the largest clothing company in the business. Their roster already had my Honda teammates Doug Henry and Steve Lamson, up-and-comers Robbie Reynard and Kevin Windham, and fourteen-year-old minicycle champion Ricky Carmichael.

Riding for Fox was a great experience at first. They made really

Jeremy McGrath

cool gear and whenever you called to order something, they would send a ton of product. They treated their riders well and I really liked how I looked in their gear. Things were always good with them when I was winning.

But that was soon to change.

LIFE OF A PRIVATEER

You want to race Supercross. You're good enough to qualify for main events but can't come anywhere near the top ten. Which means you can't get that long-desired factory ride.

You are a privateer.

Many of the riders who make up the heat races and attempt to qualify for the main are privateers, riders without the financial backing of a factory or major sponsorship. They cover most of their expenses out of their own pockets, travel to races by themselves, and usually hire a friend to work on their bikes.

Many privateers have some sort of deal with their local bike shop to get them a couple of bikes while securing free lube and other parts.

Without the benefit of factory testing and the knowledge of experienced mechanics and engineers, privateers are at a serious technological disadvantage. Oftentimes their bikes are less powerful and not nearly as well suspended. And if the bike experiences a major mechanical breakdown the weekend of a race, he is pretty much done. But there is no mechanical problem that a factory team can't overcome.

On the track, lining up against the factory boys can be an intimidating prospect. Not only will they be more talented than you, but they've had the benefit of practicing all week on their personal Supercross tracks that are well maintained and give them a sense of the real thing.

While factory guys are practicing, privateers are driving their pickups or box vans to next week's race. The top-level stars are well rested because they've been at home all week before flying out two days before the race.

On the track, privateers rarely finish ahead of factory riders. If a privateer finishes somewhere out of the top ten, he can expect a few hundred dollars. Just enough to pay for his travel expenses.

It's not all bleak, though. The motivation is that every week you are auditioning for a factory or high-level support team. Or even an extra sponsor to help lighten the load. If you do well, the entire industry will know it.

With consistently strong finishes, you might get a call from someone asking if you want a ride next season. Just try not to faint.

Honda's New Management

The winds of change were blowing through Camp Honda during the 1995 season. The highly respected Roger DeCoster left his post as team consultant. Then DeCoster's handpicked successor, Dave Arnold, departed due to internal politics. I was sad to see Dave go. He's one of the guys who made racing fun. He didn't care for the politics or bureaucracy from the higher-ups at Honda. All he wanted to do was race because racing flowed through his veins. J.C. Waterhouse was pegged to fill Arnold's shoes but that didn't exactly work out. J.C. was a longtime Honda guy who handled parts supply, ran the race shop, and dealt with the day-to-day affairs of team management. He was fired just a week before the Supercross season started.

That left Honda bigwigs scrambling for a skipper. They hastily chose Wes McCoy, who had been in charge of Honda's long defunct three-wheeler race team. (Production of three-wheelers was banned by government legislation in 1987 due to a high accident rate.) Wes was not a popular choice with, oh, just about everybody. In fact, he was so immediately unpopular that rumors by outsiders began to fly that Dave was called back in to smooth things out between him and the riders.

Wes took his new power seriously enough that it changed the entire mood around the Honda pits. Honda had always had a reputation for being one of the freindliest, most efficiently run pits when Roger DeCoster was there. McCoy was able to turn the Honda camp into a closely guarded, security intense fortress in no time flat. People called it a prison. A huge tent was put up around the pits and the box vans were parked so close to each other that no one could even get back there.

Closing the pits off to the public is such a bad idea. Look at it like this. Say you're from Phoenix and you come out to the Supercross. This is your one chance a year to see a race. Miss it and you wait a whole year. You want to catch a glimpse or perhaps get an autograph of your favorite rider. If you don't regularly attend races this may be your only chance to meet them.

Why close off the pits? Not a great way to create brand loyalty. Let's face it, the purpose of a manufacturer is to sell bikes. That's it. When a fan doesn't come away with a favorable impression of a manufacturer it's going to be reflected in their decision making when they walk into a showroom with a wad of cash.

Everyone within earshot of the Honda pits was questioned or tossed out. Someone even asked my dad to leave at one point. No one was safe. Media, industry folks, photographers, parents, friends, and track personnel were all shooed away by Honda's new iron-fist approach.

After the races, crowds of autograph seekers swell around the box vans. Sometimes it's hundreds of people. They don't mesh well with a closed door policy. After one race, my dad and I had to walk over to Team SplitFire Kawasaki's pits to sign autographs.

Wes just got off on the wrong foot. But once I got to know him he was a pretty funny guy. It was tough for Wes to follow Dave Arnold. I hated to see Dave leave. He was the guy who hired me in '91. He was just so excited to go racing week in and week out he never paid much attention to the word "budget," and everybody got along with him because of his easygoing personality. It took people a while to get used to Wes' tell-it-like-it-is leadership. The Honda pits had turned into a dictatorship.

'93 Was a Very Good Year

There was one thing that I did that Honda wasn't too excited about. In each of my first three years riding 250s for Honda ('93–'95,) I used the chassis from a '93 CR. This was something that Wes and many higher-ups had a problem with, though they couldn't complain too loud because I was winning on their brand. In '93, I got out to a great start and didn't feel it was necessary to make radical changes. The bike had great geometry and I got great starts on it. With its low center of gravity, the handling was top-notch and I felt like I could do anything I wanted on that bike.

Wes was adamant about me using the new stuff. The engineers start to take things personal if you don't use it. But he came in from another division and wasn't in a position to start throwing shit out of the window. There was a lot of pressure on me to use the current bike, but I wanted to stick with what worked. For the first three races of the '95 Supercross season I used the '95 bike. Yeah, I won those races but I

Jeremy McGrath

wasn't grabbing holeshots like I could with the '93 chassis. I felt like I had to fight the bike to get it to do what I wanted. After I complained enough about it I was allowed to go back to the '93.

Party Central

My new house in Canyon Lake was fast becoming known as the place to go if you wanted to party. It was the perfect bachelor paradise. Lew and I were both single and were rarely without the company of women. I'm the kind of person who doesn't want to spend an afternoon alone. I want my friends around me having a good time. To me, my success was nothing if I couldn't share it with my friends. After a while it just became a blur. There would be hot chicks at my house who I didn't even know, but it was all good because they wanted to party. I'd invite a handful of friends over and it would balloon to fifty. Music would blast and the beer would flow.

Girls were never shy about their intentions either. We'd find panties in the mailbox with phone numbers attached. Sometimes they would even come in the mail. It was so easy because nine times out of ten they were the aggressors.

One time Lew answered a knock at the door at three in the morning. Two girls showed up at the house saying they had just driven up from San Diego State where they were students and wanted to meet me to get an autograph. If I know one thing, girls don't come to your house at three in the morning looking for autographs.

But chances are they probably wanted to spend some quality time in the Dungeon. I had a 15'-x-20' room in my basement that I totally pimped out with black carpeting, stereo, leather couch, and a full bar. It was where you went if you wanted to be, uh, alone with a friend.

I dated several girls while I lived in Canyon Lake and had a lot of fun with all of them, but because of the atmosphere I didn't want to get serious about any of those girls. Another reason was because to me they were playing the field just as much as I was. They were into me because of who I was, so I never really felt a love connection.

Jeff Talks the Talk

After Mike LaRocco ended my win streak at five races with a win in Atlanta, I won my sixth race of the season the following week in Indianapolis. By the time the series rolled through Houston for round eight, most of the field believed they had no chance to win.

Except Jeff Emig.

He was confidently telling anyone in the pits who would listen that he was going to win the main. That was a bold statement for someone who had never won a 250 Supercross. Early on it looked like he was going to make good on his word. He started second behind Kyle Lewis and was in the lead by the end of the first lap. Just after Jeff took the lead, I passed Lewis myself for second. For two laps Jeff was blazing and sliced up the Astrodome track like salami. I'll give it to him, he was fast when he wanted to be. Houston was one of the most technical tracks of

the year. It was packed with a ton of jumps, turns, and lines. In an effort to level the playing field, the track builders gradually started making the tracks more and more difficult. The idea was that it would slow me down and prevent me from running away from the field. This was akin to lengthening the fairways because of Tiger Woods' power or widening the lane because of Wilt Chamberlain's dominance under the basket. But no matter how technical the track, it didn't take me long to get it wired. What the builders didn't count on was the diminshing numbers of local pros who showed up for qualifying. (After the factory riders and privateers, local pros round out the field.) The tracks were too difficult for them, especially since most local pros only ride one Supercross track a year.

I caught up to Jeff by the third lap. I could tell my footsteps made him nervous. He reverted to blocking all the fast lines instead of making forward progress and turning low lap times. He tried everything to hold me off, including numerous brake checks, in which the lead rider slams on his brakes to throw close following riders to the ground.

By the fifth lap he was desperate. When I passed the mechanics area, Skip held out his pit board, which read "Get Him!" Two corners later, I leaped over him when he failed to clear the triple.

And that was the the end of that.

History . . . Check

With a win in Charlotte, I tied the legend Bob Hannah for second on the all-time Supercross wins list with twenty-seven. On the back of my pants I had the word "Hannah" with a check mark next to it. It took Hannah nine seasons to amass twenty-seven wins. I did it in two and a half.

History . . . Check, Again

In Cleveland, two rounds later, I tied my boyhood idol, Rick Johnson, atop the all-time Supercross wins list with twenty-eight victories. Just like I had checked off Hannah, I did the same thing to RJ. It would have probably taken me a bit longer to catch him if it weren't for an injury that prematurely ended his career. In 1989, privateer Danny Storbeck landed on top of RJ after a jump in practice during the Gainesville National in Florida. RJ's wrist was shattered. He had won the first five Supercrosses that year and most likely would have won his third title. RJ never won another Supercross and retired two years later. He needed six seasons to get his twenty-eight wins while I was able to do it in half the time.

I was only twenty-three and I had a long way to go.

CHAPTER TWELVE

Everyone was pointing the finger at me and I had nothing to do with it. Well, not everyone. Just the very people who run our sport. At the 1995 Supercross season finale in Las Vegas, the AMA officials on hand had steam coming out of their ears. And they wanted my head on a platter. Forget that I already wrapped up my third straight 250 Supercross title and people were referring to me as the Michael Jordan of motocross. And forget that I was responsible for putting 50,000 people in the stands week after week.

The AMA thought that I had committed the greatest sin in their eyes. They thought I stood up to them.

At a time when my career began to take off from an operational standpoint, the sport was in a downward spiral. Riders, promoters, and the AMA were at each other's throats preventing the sport from running as smoothly as it should have. The riders were treated like crap because the promoters knew they would never take a stand. Both riders and mechanics had issues with money, the travel schedule, and a laundry list of other complaints. No one would listen to anyone, let alone cooperate, and as a result very little could be accomplished by way of negotiation. Communication between these parties had never been completely clear, but it had been going downhill for several years.

Many insiders knew exactly how it started: Murder.

In the sixties and early seventies, off-road motorcycling was strictly an outdoor activity. The sport was born in Europe and migrated to America in the form of cross-country races called scrambles. In 1972, Mike Goodwin, who was a flamboyant concert promoter, figured out a way to build a track inside the L.A. Coliseum. As the legend goes, he diagrammed the first track on a napkin in a bar. He brought in tons of dirt and a half dozen bulldozers and fashioned huge jumps and hairpin turns. At the time it was a dramatic idea, somewhat of a gimmick, but it was a hit right off the bat. It was dubbed the Superbowl of Motocross. And it made Goodwin a lot of money.

He sold loads of tickets and generated tons of interest in the sport of motorcycle racing. The success in L.A. led to other races in domes and stadiums around the country. A few years later, the series had blossomed to ten races and was selling out gigantic football domes all over the country.

But Goodwin had a little competition in event promoter Mickey Thompson, who was considered by many the godfather of American motorsports. He'd pretty much done it all. Good and bad.

In 1953, during a cross-country road race in Mexico, the car Thompson was driving skidded off the road and killed six spectators. Seven years later he was labeled "the fastest man on earth" after taking his hot rod up to 406.6 MPH on the Bonneville Salt Flats. He set almost 500 records of speed and endurance. Thompson helped design some of the early Indy cars and even invented the modern racing slick.

By the early eighties, Thompson and Goodwin were two of the biggest motorsports event promoters in the country. They formed a partnership to promote Supercross and other stadium events that wouldn't even last a year. In 1985, Thompson sued Goodwin for

$514,000 and the exclusive right to promote events at Anaheim Stadium, which is located right in the heart of motocross country. When a judge ruled in Mickey's favor, Mike had to file for bankruptcy. He was ruined and his lavish lifestyle quickly dried up. Goodwin was basically tossed out of the sport he helped create.

After he won the lawsuit, Thompson often claimed that he received death threats from Goodwin stemming from their legal troubles.

Three years later in 1988, when Mickey and his wife Trudy were leaving for work from their palatial estate in San Gabriel Valley north of Los Angeles just before six in the morning, they were ambushed by two gunmen and shot to death. There was no shortage of motorsports insiders who thought the hit was Goodwin's payback for muscling him out. (While the Los Angeles District Attorney never brought charges against Goodwin, the Orange County District Attorney had Goodwin arrested in 2001 for planning the murders in Orange County. Goodwin has pled innocent to the charges and moved to dismiss the complaint against him on the ground that Orange County lacks jurisdiction over the alleged crime. The dismissal motion is on appeal, and no trial date has been set.)

The murders sent the state of Supercross promoting into complete disarray. But that was only the beginning, because riders were already fed up with the bureaucratic leadership that was taking the sport down the toilet. If murder wasn't enough, the greed that followed would be.

Over the course of the year, the riders' concerns that we weren't getting a fair shake reached a fevered pitch. A lot of guys felt that purses were way too low. Actually, every rider felt that way. You got just $5,000 for winning a main. But only one rider can win. For the guy who finished tenth, things were quite different. If you were a privateer and you drove from Dallas to finish eighth, you would barely be able to pay for the gas your round trip cost. If a privateer makes the main every week and finishes out of the top ten (which is where privateers usually finish), he'll earn $15,000 for the season. The clerk at 7-Eleven makes more than that.

The total purse for an event was about $30,000. For every rider on the gate. That's forty-two 125 and 250 riders. Considering the risk involved—paralysis or even death—that amount of money is a joke.

Motocross racers do not have a union and there is little rider comraderie when it comes to dealing with major issues that affect us. They think once you've got a factory ride your problems are solved. That's in part because a lot of guys don't even know what the issues are. For example, Pace, which promoted Supercross at the time, and the AMA, the sport's sanctioning body, were always at odds over how to divide up gate receipts and other profits. The AMA wanted to take 100 percent of the back gate money. That is the money that riders, mechanics, team managers, sponsors, and industry execs shell out for pit passes and race entry fees. Why are we paying to be the show? We're talking upwards of $250,000 per season. The money is normally divided by the promoters and the AMA. In '95, most of the money went to the AMA. In '96, the AMA wanted to pocket it all. Why not turn that money into purses and let the riders race for it?

Pro motocrossers have to pay an entry fee of $55 to compete, which is ridiculous. Imagine Kobe Bryant or Randy Moss paying to play.

But money was just the tip of the iceberg. There were complaints about the quality of tracks as well as the quality of rider/promoter relations. Many of the riders felt the tracks were too technical. Even though I thrive on courses with a lot of jumps, it was hurting rider participation. In 1995, rider turnout was at an all-time low because no local pros wanted to come out for qualifying for fear they would embarrass themselves on tracks that were way to difficult for them. Many factory riders complained the less experienced riders just got in the way. Earlier in the year at San Jose, promoters asked the riders if they knew any local pros who wanted to race, because only thirty-six 250 riders turned out.

One of the most pressing concerns was the absurdity of the race schedule that saw the Supercross series start in Orlando then go from Minneapolis to Anaheim to Seattle, back down to San Diego, then back across the country to Atlanta. That is completely ridiculous. How could anyone put out a schedule like that and not think it wasn't going to greatly affect every single person who works in the sport?

"The schedule couldn't be worse if an orangutan drew it on a map with a crayon," Pro Circuit's Mitch Payton once told *Motocross Action* magazine. And he was right. To get to Orlando, the mechanics had to drive the box vans and semis over 3,000 miles from the factories in California. When the race ends on a Saturday night in San Diego, the mechanics have to tear down the bikes, load everything up, and leave Sunday morning for Atlanta. They are on the road for three and a half days when they arrive in Atlanta. That gives them a day and a half to test and rebuild the bikes, as well as pump their riders up. This has to be done twenty-seven times in thirty-two weeks. It wasn't unusual for them to be in four different time zones in a week. Needless to say many of them operate on very little sleep.

The massive driving schedule was very dangerous for overworked, sleepy mechanics. (And illegal according to many state laws.) It wasn't like today, where all of the teams have big rigs and drivers to go with them. Drivers are paid to drive. Mechanics are paid to work on bikes, not to drive trucks. Nowadays mechanics fly home with the riders during the middle of the week to test at team practice facilities. But back then it was murder on them.

Everyone was just plain fed up. Enough was enough. The sport was a tinderbox on the verge of a catastrophic explosion.

All Las Vegas did was provide the spark.

The Riders Strike Back, or the Night the Lights Went Out in Vegas

There had been talk all day about a rider strike. A letter circulated throughout the day urging riders to unify and form a union. The AMA immediately thought my parents and I were behind it. They couldn't believe the sport's biggest star would try to cause such a disruption. But I had nothing to do with the letter. I never even saw it.

LETTER FROM VEGAS

Here is the letter, verbatim, that caused the controversy at the 1995 Las Vegas Supercross.

To the riders,

If you're a rider, you need to read this. We've been unhappy with the AMA for a long time. We've bitched about it amongst ourselves, but, if we are ever going to change things we are going to have to do it together. Today, we're taking the first step.

The people who run Supercross do it for a profit. If you think they're going to share any of the profits out of the kindness of their hearts, you're wrong! When was the last time they increased the purses? For that matter, when was the last time they ever did anything for you? Do you know what they think about us? They think we're young and dumb. And by the time we realize this, we're already out of the sport! They think we'll never come together, because we're not "joiners." They think we're afraid of the factories, to stand up for ourselves. They think we can easily be replaced. They think they've got us by the short hairs.

What do you think? Do you think they're doing a good job? Do you feel well paid for the risks you're taking? Would you like to see things change?

Today, we're asking them some basic questions. Today, we're asking you: Are you with us?

Jeremy McGrath

We're forming an association—not a union. Its purpose will be to bring riders' issues before the AMA to help promote the growth of our sport. We will also be exploring sponsorship, endorsement, and other income opportunities that we can all share in.

Now, you can be cute and sarcastic and make fun of this, or you can show some real courage and join us! The AMA is counting on you to say no. That's the way it's always been. We're hoping you'll say yes. If your answer is yes, please leave your name, phone number, and address with the person who gave you this. This will be kept confidential and we'll be in touch very soon. Take a chance—stand up and be counted.

Race time came around and, despite all the tension, I raced like it was any other day. I had a great battle in my heat race with Doug Henry, then went back to the trailer to get ready for the main. That's when chaos would rule. Just before the 125 main, the power in and around the stadium went out. Black as night. Remember that scene from *Ocean's Eleven?*

For a two-mile radius there was nothing but blackness. No one knows for sure how, but the generators just blew.

The promoters hastily rigged up lighting all around the track with whatever portable generators and lights they could find. After an hour and a half delay, they were finished setting up their makeshift lights and made the decision to run the race. That was a joke. The lighting was better at your local fairgrounds than it was at Vegas that night. The track was so dark and there were huge shadows everywhere. You couldn't see where you were landing on the triple.

It was time to race the main and the riders were heading for their spots on the gate. I had such an uneasy feeling. These conditions were flat-out unsafe.

That night for the main, I was decked out in eighties retro Fox gear as a tribute to my hero, Rick Johnson. I had special all-white Alpinestars and had my helmet painted just like RJ used to. I was still really looking forward to racing. But it wasn't worth the risk.

I was so nervous because of what I was about to do. My stomach was tied in knots, my mind was conflicted. After a couple minutes of just sitting there, I pulled my bike out of the starting area. I talked it over with Honda team manager Wes McCoy and he totally supported me. I was met by promoters who told me that I should only ride if I felt safe. I didn't, so I said I wouldn't ride. They were not happy. As soon as I announced my night was over, Jeff Emig was one of the first ones to the starting gate. That was a total bitch move. Complete chickenshit. This was a perfect time for the riders to unite and bring about change. Understandably though, most of the guys who decided to race were privateers and not in a financial position to sit out. Privateer Larry Ward had put together a miraculous season and was second in the points going into Vegas. When Jeff, who was third in the points, chose to ride, it left Larry no choice.

I got in my car and left the pits. Some assholes started throwing beer bottles, cans, balled-up pieces of paper, and water at me. Many fans had sat for hours drinking in ninety-degree heat. You get the picture. I was freaking out and seriously worried about my safety. My dad urged me to get in my car and get the hell out of there. It was the first time I didn't have fun driving my NSX, that's for sure. Everyone knew it was me because of my license plates: 93 CHAMP. I pulled out of the pits and ran smack into a traffic jam. Without missing a beat, I pulled around the traffic and took off up the shoulder. When I got back to the hotel I didn't go out that night. I didn't want to take the chance that some kook would start something, so I just laid low.

There were rumors circulating that I left because I had planned a big bash back at the hotel. That was total bullshit. Couldn't have been further from the truth. Why give up the chance to earn $50,000 in bonuses just to get to a party an hour earlier. I don't care if the party was at the Playboy Mansion.

Jeff winning Vegas when the lights went out.

Back at the stadium, Jeff ended up winning his first ever 250 Supercross. "I rode motos all week so I wasn't going to sit out," said Jeff afterward. "Plus I earned $50,000 for that win."

But that win didn't count. Everybody in the world knows it. He tries to justify it by telling himself that the bank doesn't care who was on the starting line that night. He's only trying to convince himself because he knows the truth.

The AMA felt now more than ever that my parents and I were the ones who sent the letter around. They were so pissed that someone would challenge them that they went crazy trying to figure out ways to ban, punish, or fine me. They actually had it in for me, thinking that I was planning some big conspiracy. It was totally ridiculous. To this day I have no idea where that letter came from.

The promoters are very scared of the riders forming a union, because it would disrupt their total control over the sport. They don't want their power tampered with in any way. But I wasn't worried about anything because there was nothing they could do to me. Even if I had circulated the letter, I hadn't done anything illegal.

The decision to race should have never been left up to the riders. The promoters weren't looking out for our best interest. I think their main concern was that the crowd would go mental if there wasn't going to be a race. Not to mention refunding everyone's money.

I'm not saying I have the answer for what happened that night, but you would never see that in any other sport, where the sanctioning body treats the safety of its athletes with such disregard. We were like cattle being led around.

The next day I felt the heat from the still smoldering tempers of the race promoters. Honda scheduled a commercial shoot at the stadium that I couldn't get out of. For whatever reason, several of the promoters were on hand. When I walked by them, they wouldn't even speak to me. They truly believed that the previous night's fiasco was my doing.

At the same time, many industry insiders were starting to bat around the idea that I should be considered the greatest Supercross rider ever. I didn't care about any of that. I just wanted to get out of

Vegas and put the whole thing behind me. All I could think about was getting back on the track.

Little did I know that Emig's next Supercross win would be the biggest loss of my career. But first, the outdoor national title was up for grabs.

This time I would definitely show up.

CHAPTER THIRTEEN

I was a conflicted man. Something inside was bothering me, but there was no one to tell. Girls continued to flow in and out of my Canyon Lake crib as if I had installed a revolving door. I loved playing girls, but deep inside I knew this wasn't really who I was. I had lots of relations but I hadn't loved a girl since my high school sweetheart Jennifer Thomas back in 1990. Part of that was because in the back of my mind I knew that most of these girls were trying to play me, too. I'd dump somebody and next week they would be dating one of my boys. Most of them were hypnotized by fame and money. That was more important to them than who I was. I got what I wanted, but I couldn't deny that I was having some moral issues.

Despite my conflicted personal life, I had the '95 250 nationals to worry about. My personal trainer of four years, Gary Semics, always tried to push me extra hard when it came to preparing for the outdoors. He felt like I was a bit of a slacker as far as nationals were concerned, and it didn't sit too well with him. I knew he was right. I was also getting tired of hearing people say I couldn't race outdoors. After I finished third in the 250 nationals in 1994, I decided that I was finally going to get serious about the series, so I had Gary come out and train with me in the off-season with the express purpose of winning the 1995 250 nationals. It was time to prove to myself and the sport that I could be the best outdoors if I wanted.

By 1995, I had won five straight SX titles, including my two 125 championships, and no outdoor titles. The fact is, I never really gave motocross a chance until '95. I just wasn't that into it. Up until '95, I had only won two outdoor races ever. Both of those were on a 125.

I worked with Gary harder then I ever had before. Any chance I got, I practiced in the rain, because I knew that if I was going to win the outdoor championship, sooner or later I would have to perform well in the mud.

Honda stepped up their efforts, too. They hired a separate mechanic for Steve Lamson and I while we were practicing during the week. Hondaland was shut down by now, but there were plenty of out-

Jeremy McGrath

door motocross tracks to practice at in Temecula and San Bernardino. Steve and I went two times a week, Tuesday and Thursday mornings, and rode two forty-minute motos in the blazing heat. Much of Southern California is desert, which gets up near triple-digit heat in the summer. On Wednesday, the Honda mechanic took our bikes and prepped them for the next day with new tires, chains, and sprockets.

In my quest to win the 250 national championship—and get the monkey the hell off my back—there was a huge obstacle in my path: Jeff Emig.

In 1995, Jeff moved up to 250s for the outdoor nationals and was approaching the series with a renewed vigor. Jeff was a lot more competitive outdoors and thrived on tracks that were fast and rough. Just as I had, he stepped up his workout regime in the off-season and was in the best shape of his career.

On March 5, I won the season opener at Gainesville. The site of my first 125 national win was now home to my first 250 win. It was exactly how I wanted to start the season, and I could feel my training sessions with Gary totally paying off.

Henry Crashes at Budds Creek

June 18, 1995, started out as a beautiful sunny day ripe for motocross at round seven in Budds Creek, Maryland. But it would end up being host to one of the most terrifying moments in AMA history.

The Budds Creek track is carved out of a picturesque hillside that offers great sightlines and is dotted with huge oak trees that provide shade to those unwilling to watch the action from the trackside fences. The course is complete with uphill doubles and super fast, sweeping downhills.

In the first moto, I was battling Yamaha's Doug Henry for first place as we rode into a small dip that was followed by a jump that led to a monster downhill. Going into the dip, there were some breaking bumps that I used to slow down. I rolled off the jump and got about ten feet of air before I glided down the hill.

Doug planned to do the same but something bad happened. His throttle stuck wide open. All I saw was Doug sail straight up in the air like a rocket. It wouldn't have been so bad if he was over flat land, but he was over the downhill, which went almost eighty feet straight down.

It seemed like he was a mile above my head. I didn't know what he was thinking. It had to be that he was going to die. In the air he moved in slow motion. My eyes followed him the whole way down. When he hit the ground he just exploded. The sound of the impact was unearthly. He didn't have a chance. Seeing him smash down like that scared the shit out of me. It was just . . . the scariest thing I've ever seen.

I rode by him, lifeless and sprawled out on the side of the course, and I started to freak out. I'm in the lead but my mind was not on something as trivial as the points chase. I was wondering if Doug was still alive. On the next lap, the yellow flag was out and I looked over at the dozen paramedics and team people who surrounded Doug. I couldn't even see him, so I had no idea of his condition. If he were up walking around I would have felt relieved.

But who was I kidding? There was no way he was walking away from that. Doug was Medivaced to a nearby hospital and after the race we learned he had broken his back. He was incredibly lucky to escape paralysis. The damaged verteabrae were in his lower back. The higher the damage on the spine, the more likely paralysis is to occur. His season was done and doctors told him he would never race again. From that day on that downhill was dubbed Henry Hill.

Seeing a friend go through that really scared me. It made me think that my own career could be over with one mistake.

Where Are Your Manners?

It's not easy being in a points battle with Jeff Emig. It seemed like he was always trying to take people out. He'd cut you off at the last second and ram you when he tried to pass. On the start, he would cut over in front of you and do whatever else he could get away with. "That's just racing," was the way Jeff defended his tactics. To me it was dirty riding. Even in the darkest moments of the '97 Supercross series, I didn't resort to stuff like that.

Aside from all that, battling with him outdoors was fun. The thing was, Jeff didn't need to resort to all those dirty tricks to win because he was one of the most talented outdoor guys around. His ability to get holeshots was legendary. He thrived on rough courses and was one of the most difficult riders ever to pass. Like I said before, Jeff used the whole track, so you had to expend a ton of energy to get by him. Especially in Supercross. But at the nationals he had so much confidence and could ride any track fast instead of worrying about blocking you.

There was no doubt he was one of the best. If he just concentrated on riding hard we would've had fewer problems. Each time I beat him it felt like a championship in itself. I had a real sense of accomplishment when I would cross the finish line ahead of him.

Despite all of that, I won the last three nationals of the year—Washougal, Binghamton, and Steel City—to win my first 250 national championship.

After what happened in Vegas, it felt great to be able to run with him and beat him consistently. Winning the '95 Outdoor national championship was one of my biggest accomplishments ever. No one thought I could do it. In the beginning, I wasn't even exactly sure I could. But the outdoor monkey was finally off my back.

WHERE THE TRACKS ARE

Supercross gives the sport its glitz and glamour. Nighttime races make way for mega-watt stadium lights to sparkle off of highly polished front fenders and Troy Lee–painted helmets. But the grit and grime of outdoor motocross is the lifeblood of the sport. That's because outdoor nationals are held at racetracks that are home to the everyday Joe. One magical Sunday a year the course is manicured and prepped for the big boys. Weekend warriors will never set foot on the whoops of Anaheim or the sand of Daytona, for the locals who live within distance of one of the national tracks, they've got plenty of stories about the ruts of Southwick and the clay of Red Bud. Here's a list of the twelve tracks that both AMA championships and local glory are won and lost.

Glen Helen
SAN BERNARDINO, CALIFORNIA
The Dirt: Decomposed granite with sand mixed in.
MC's Best Finish: First place

Hangtown
SACRAMENTO, CALIFORNIA
The Dirt: Clay, ranging from very slick to super rutted.
MC's Best Finish: First place

High Point
MT. MORRIS, PENNSYLVANIA
The Dirt: Thick and clumpy with grassy sections and the occasional baseball-sized boulder.
MC's Best Finish: First place

Budds Creek
BUDDS CREEK, MARYLAND
The Dirt: Loose and dusty
MC's Best Finish: First place

Southwick
SOUTHWICK, MASSACHUSETTS
The Dirt: Deep sand
MC's Best Finish: First place

Jeremy McGrath

Red Bud

BUCHANNON, MICHIGAN

The Dirt: Tacky, midwestern clay

MC's Best Finish: First place

Unadilla

NEW BERLIN, NEW YORK

The Dirt: Grass; thick, dark brown loam

MC's Best Finish: First place

Troy

TROY, OHIO

The Dirt: Fine and moist

MC's Best Finish: First place

Washougal

WASHOUGAL, WASHINGTON

The Dirt: Soft, moist soil

MC's Best Finish: First place

Spring Creek

MILLVILLE, MINNESOTA

The Dirt: Hard-packed clay to sand to loose dirt

MC's Best Finish: Second place

Broome-Tioga

BINGHAMTON, NEW YORK

The Dirt: Rich and sticky with plenty of grab;
tons of rocks

MC's Best Finish: First place

Steel City

DELMONT, PENNSYLVANIA

The Dirt: Rough and hard-packed

MC's Best Finish: First place

What's French for Stop Sign?

For the second year in a row I attended the Bercy SX in Paris. As usual, people were more interested in the party scene than the race. Bercy is really fun because the riders are so well taken care of. This year there was a post-race banquet at the Hard Rock Cafe then partying at an exclusive club called the Locomotive.

To get the riders to the various events, the promoters hired vans to shuttle them and their mechanics all over the city for the week. The guys who drove the vans were pretty cool. They were just like us, looking to have a good time. Wherever we went, we'd race the vans all over the city on roads that were small and tight and had no lane markings. Driving on the "wrong side" of the road was a trip to us even though the drivers were used to it.

Fans at the Paris Bercy SX.

Occasionally, we would try to gain advantage over another van by tossing out whatever we could get our hands on. There were always plenty of parts left over that were perfect for chucking. If a van followed too closely I would toss out a perfectly good pair of Renthal bars or a Pro Circuit silencer. When the parts ammo dried up we would pull off the headrests and toss them out. The guys in the vans behind us would be dying laughing while trying to swerve a hailstorm of aftermarket products.

On our way back from the Hard Rock Cafe, we had two vans driving side by side down a small street. We were about to make a right-hand turn when a guy and a girl on a motorcycle going about thirty MPH drilled the side of our van. The motorcycle smashed right where I was sitting. Both the guy and the girl were ejected and landed in the middle of the intersection. They both had on helmets, so luckily no one was hurt . . . which is more than I can say about the side of the van.

Starring Davey Coombs as the Cookie Monster

When you travel to foreign countries for weeks at a time you learn a few survival rules to get by. I think I speak for most riders when I say getting edible food is the biggest problem when traveling abroad. Our American taste buds are so out of tune with other cultures that the first thing you do when you get off the plane is look for a Wendy's.

It's no worse than in Japan. If you're not into sushi or noodles then you're in trouble. Being the experienced traveler, I started to pack a duffel bag full of snacks that I would ration over the course of the trip. I brought cookies, Pop-Tarts, candy, potato chips, everything. In Italy and France it wasn't so bad, so I didn't resort to my bag of snacks much. But when we landed in Japan I tore in.

After the Bercy race, I returned to my room to find my bag of snacks completely empty. Wrappers were thrown all over the floor and there were crumbs everywhere. Someone totally macked my food, and I was getting more and more pissed off by the second. I immediately began to search the hotel for whoever poached my snacks. Everyone knew

I had brought the bag with me. On a trip like this, snacks were a luxury item. This was *Motocross Survivor*.

I was furious as I went from floor to floor looking for the culprit. In the lobby, one of the guys who drove the vans told me that Davey Coombs was the guy I was looking for. Davey was one of the most respected motocross journalists around and the son of race promoter Dave Coombs, Sr.

I had told Davey about the food in my room if he wanted to grab something to eat, so he went to the front desk and got a key. But word had gotten around the hotel lobby that I had a bunch of snacks in my room. Since there aren't a lot of fast food restaurants open in Paris in the wee hours of the morning, my room turned into a drive-thru!

By the time I got back and found all my food missing, I went straight to Davey's room to find out what happened. I was raging mad and called him out, but he apparently didn't realize that I had two more weeks left away from home and needed that food. He apologized, but the whole ordeal upset Davey's girlfriend, Shannon. She was the one who invited some of the other girlfriends there to have some of my food, and we got into a pretty good shouting match over it. Looking back, it was actually pretty funny, and Davey even tried to smooth things over by sending a box of groceries to Japan for me.

Despite Davey's chip-munching shenanigans, the post-race festivities were the highlight of the weekend, and I partied hard with Skip, Button, and Mitch Payton. For the record, I was no longer afraid of Mitch. He's one of the coolest guys in the business when the racing is done. Even though he was bound to a wheelchair, his reputation for partying was legendary. Everybody's got a favorite Mitch Payton story, and there are few that can match his pace.

About six in the morning we all fell out of a cab onto the steps of the hotel where the riders stayed. There were about a dozen Americans packed and ready to leave for the airport. They were stunned to find out that we were just arriving back from the night before.

What's Left?

Without a doubt, 1995 had been my best year. I won a personal best seventeen out of twenty-eight AMA races, both the 250 Supercross and 250 Outdoor National championships. Financially, I was also at the top of the sport. Along with my $450,000 Honda salary, I earned another $400,000 in bonuses and $70,000 in purses. Throw in another $500,000 from endorsing clothes, helmets, gear, and accessories, plus European start money, and I was beginning to make a serious living riding motorcycles. But as always, I never raced solely for money. I took advantage of all the trappings that came with success, but it was always about winning races. Bottom line. With all the winning and glory, something happened that I didn't even really understand or appreciate at the time.

I had become the best rider in the world.

CHAPTER FOURTEEN

The 1995 motocross season disappeared into the record books and took with it another motocross career. Mike Kiedrowski retired from racing at age twenty-seven. The MX Kied got along with pretty much everybody (except Mike LaRocco and maybe Kawi team manager Roy Turner) and was well respected by his competitors. But despite winning four national championships, Kiedrowski was one of the least heralded champions of our sport. Maybe it was because he never won a Supercross title. Whatever the reason, there was one less competitor nipping at my heels. Still, there were plenty of guys willing to take his place.

As was the case with my previous championship defenses, 1996 was supposed to be the year someone was going to knock me off. But that wasn't going to happen. The Supercross season started out great. I won the first couple races and my confidence was skyhigh. Skip had my bike working great and it felt like

I could do no wrong. Even if I didn't pull the holeshot, it only took a couple laps to take the lead.

When I passed people, I did it with ease. I almost never got tired, as if my body was on a permanent adrenaline rush. I couldn't make something go wrong if I tried. I think I was still on a high after winning the outdoor title the season before.

Race after race after race I continued to smoke everybody. Sometimes it felt like my wheels never even touched the ground. Everyone else was racing for second and they knew it. My fastest competitors labeled me "unbeatable."

I won six straight races to open the season, but it didn't stop there. Atlanta, Houston, Dallas, Indianapolis. The more I won, the more non-motocross mainstream media began to show up every week. The Supercross ratings on ESPN were higher than they'd ever been. The crowd of cameras and made-up morning show reporters who didn't know the difference between a silencer and a swingarm multiplied weekly.

Many people credit this season as the one that put Supercross on the map. To elevate a sport, there has to be an athlete that is able to tran-

Anaheim, 1996.

Jeremy McGrath

scend and bring in outside interests. I guess people felt that guy was me. When I notched my sixth win at Daytona, my 1996 campaign officially became known as the streak. Everyone had one question. Could I win them all?

It was a feat that had never been done. With each passing week, each win, the pressure mounted. If it were up to me, I wouldn't even think about it. But that was impossible when no one would let me forget it. Highlights started popping up on ESPN's Sportcenter. Supercross coverage went from a blurb buried in the *L.A. Times* sports section to front-page news. *Hard Copy* even did a feature on me.

After the races, Skip would get me a lawn chair, a few hundred posters, and a box of Sharpies to meet the astronomical autograph requests.

Things were starting to get to me, but I did the only thing that would shield me from the distractions. I put my head down and raced.

Pro vs. History

Going into round thirteen at St. Louis, the pressure to win every race was almost unbearable. I had already won a record twelve straight races, but that wasn't enough. People wanted me to win them all. Everywhere I went people would ask me about the streak. Before and after every race. The media hype surrounding that season definitely added to the pressure. Instead of just concentrating on one race at a time, I found myself thinking about the streak instead. It was really becoming a burden.

I remember April thirteen as clear as day. The promoters in St. Louis were trying to tie up some outside sponsors for next year's series and they had me running all over the stadium that night meeting people and giving potential sponsors some face time. After I won my heat race, I was ushered clear across the stadium to a suite to meet with Coca-Cola or some other big company. I wish I could redo that night because I would have met the sponsors after the race. By the time I got back to the pits, I was drained from walking and being on my feet. I made the walk in full gear, boots and everything, which, as any racer knows, is not made for walking any kind of distance. I barely had time to get changed for the main. I didn't even look at the tape of my heat race to find better lines to use for the main.

Despite the distractions, the race was an incredible battle. On the starting gate, I was able to regain my focus. Skip was in my ear pumping me up as usual. "Forget about the heat race. Just get a great start, ride like yourself for four laps, then do what you want," were Skip's last-minute instructions. But it was to no avail. After rocketing off the line all year, I got a lousy, mid-pack start. Emig holeshot with Mike LaRocco in tow. I didn't panic, though. I quickly settled into a zone and started picking off riders one by one. After a few laps, I was in third. A lap later, I gained control of second place.

The track had very soft dirt and the jumps were rutted after the first heat race. Jeff was great whenever track conditions were less than optimal, and true to his rep, he was at the front of the pack. Barring a fall, the only thing that stood between me and perfection was Cam Jeffrey Emig. Talent and ability aside, Jeff had one thing on me that night—St. Louis was his hometown track. There is an unexplainable aura that goes along with racing in front of your hometown fans. It can carry you to victory. It's no coincidence that Larry Ward got his first SX win in his hometown of Seattle in 1990. Ezra Lusk, Kevin Windham, Doug Henry, and Brian Swink have all won races in their hometowns. I experienced the same thing at Anaheim.

Emig ordered dozens of tickets for family and friends. And they were all at their highest noise decibels that night.

Jeff was hitting every groove just right. He darted in and out of corners, it seemed, without even touching his breaks. Still, I was able to close the gap between us by lap fifteen. I looked for a line to make a move, but one never opened up. I waited for him to make a mistake, but it never came. Jeff was blocking me and taking all the fast lines. It's tough to get by someone when they use the whole track the way Jeff did.

One thing Jeff and I have in common is that we never rode over our heads. St. Louis was a perfect example. He was composed and rode a

Jeremy McGrath

safe race. I, on the other hand, was doing everything I could to catch him. I did not want *him* to beat me. At one point, I went off the track and dropped back down to third. I had to ride even more aggressively to regain second.

Going into the last corner, a 180 right-hand turn, I grabbed a handful of throttle and lunged forward with everything I had. The finish line was just two jumps away.

Jeff crossed the finish line about a wheel ahead of me. You couldn't read this sentence in between the time Jeff's back wheel and my front wheel crossed the finish line. Jeff jumped off his bike and began to celebrate with his mechanic and old Reche Canyon pal, Jeremy "J-Bone" Albrecht. I was disgusted with myself. I wanted perfection and it wasn't going to happen. "The moon, stars, and planets were all lined up perfectly for me," said Emig about his win.

I hated that Jeff won. It really irked me. If it had been anybody else it wouldn't have been so bad. But I was pissed that it was him.

Jeff will forever be remembered as the guy who broke the Streak. I'm not one to make excuses, but if I had done things a little bit differently I probably would have won the race. I should have never been made to entertain potential sponsors during a race. As far as Jeff goes, he won the race fair and square. This wasn't Las Vegas. He rode hard, so he deserves the credit he got.

Immediatley after St. Louis, the pressure was gone. It felt like a tremendous burden had been lifted off of my shoulders. At the season finale the following week in Denver, I won by a mile. I won the title over Jeff by a record 132 points and became the first rider ever to win four consecutive Supercross championships.

Retire? Who Me?

Strangely enough, during the first half of '96, rumors had begun to circulate that I was nearing retirement. Jimmy Button came up to me after one race and said he heard a bunch of guys talking about it. Most racers are no longer physically able to compete at such a high level when they reach their mid-twenties. Even if they can, burnout will usually get them. Most top guys have been racing since they were five years old. The travel, pressure, and injuries get old. At twenty-five, when you're in the prime of your life, a motocrosser can feel like an old man. Not me. I felt great mentally and physically. At that point in time, I planned to race at least two more years, when I'd be twenty-seven.

When Foxes Fly

In the spring of 1996, the freestyle video craze was beginning to take off. Most of the riders in the videos were top-flight racers spending the day play-riding at exotic locations. One of the hottest videos was *Fly*, which was put out by Fox. It featured Damon Bradshaw, John Dowd, Steve Lamson, Doug Henry, Kevin Windham, Mike Metzger, and myself.

Fly had some of the biggest air anyone was getting at the time thanks to riding areas like Glammis and Dumont Dunes in Southern California.

These days, with the exception of Mike Metzger, you would never see guys like that in a FMX video.

Jeremy McGrath

Starting line at Day in the Dirt.

Wakeboarding and going for a railgrab.

Right: Heading to another podium.

Opposite: Stadium shots just before opening ceremonies.

McGrath superfan.

Me, Mouse McCoy, and Jeff Emig battling it out at Day in the Dirt, 2001.

Me at my first-ever supermoto race at California Speedway, Spring 2003.

Me, Mouse McCoy, Jeff Emig, and Eric Kehoe after the Stunt Celebrity GP race at Day in the Dirt, 2001.

More nac-nac action.

Ryan Hughes, me, and Lew on Lake Havasu.

Dad wearing the lucky crown.

Victor Sheldon, Piper Lindgren, Kim, and me.

Above: Filming the documentary A Day in the Dirt, 2001.

Truck racing, 1999.

Just a few of my race helmets—all created by Troy Lee Designs.

Toyota Pro Celebrity Grand Prix, 2003.

Carmichael and me, 2003.

Me, after just moving into the new house in Encinitas.

First pitch at the 2002 season opener for the Cardinals at Busch Stadium in St. Louis, Missouri.

Some of the history of the McGrath butt patches.

The McGrath mascot.

Me and Jimmy Button.

My last SX win, Anaheim #2, 2001.

Hanging out with my fans at Day in the Dirt.

Me and Kim: our engagement photo, shot on Laguna Beach.

After racers dominated most of the footage in early freestyle videos, the late nineties saw a subculture of former racers, mostly failed privateers, turn freestyle into a profitable career and a national phenomenon. Nowadays a whole new generation of kids, who have never raced and were raised on FMX videos and the X Games, populate the subculture.

Motocross is a very conservative sport. There are rules and regulations and always corporate types of promoters forever regulating our sport. Part of the lure of freestyle motocross is that there are few rules or boundaries. The FMX environment totally encourages the free spirit and individual expression.

Also, freestyle motocross riders don't have to train outside of practicing their tricks. Their bikes don't have to be perfectly dialed, so there is no need for exhaustive and expensive testing. The sport gives young kids an opportunity to have fun earning a living on motorcycles without dealing with the high-pressure world of racing. Those kinds of things must really appeal to the Y Generation, as freestyle motocross is the fastest growing action sport today.

And in This Corner . . .

It wasn't hard to shift my focus back to the nationals. I was entering the series for the first time as defending champion, so my confidence was still sky-high. I had won back in Gainesville on March 2 (don't forget, they used to start the nationals in the middle of the SX series) and the week before that at Hangtown, so I already had an early points lead. If I could hold off Jeff two straight seasons outdoors, I would be carving out my place in MX history. Plus, I'd continue to destroy everyone's low expectations for me on the national circuit.

After the Hangtown race, Lew and I took my boat out on Canyon Lake for a little wakeboarding. I wadded myself bad on a pretty gnarly wave and hurt my knee. I got scared because it was to the point that I could barely walk. At Glen Helen the following week, I was still walking with a severe limp. To make matters worse, it was about 110 degrees and super smoggy. If you look at any picture of me at the nationals in '96, you'll notice that my jersey is shredded up. It was so hot that I cut holes all over it for better ventilation.

Luckily, my knee didn't affect my riding, just as long as it didn't get caught in a rut. I won both motos for my third consecutive national win. (Six in a row if you count back to last year. At that time you could count on two fingers the number of people who'd won six in a row—Bob Hannah is the other—but still, I always got flak for my production outdoors.)

Jeff won the next round at Mt. Morris and I responded with two wins of my own at Budds Creek and Southwick. Fro countered with a W at the Red Bud track in Michigan in round seven of thirteen.

Going into round ten at Millville, Jeff and I had won all but one of the first nine races. In practice on Friday, two days before the race, I was feeling invincible. There was this uphill double that even to this day wouldn't be considered jumpable. Actually, it wasn't even a double, but a single followed by a tabletop. But that's how good I was feeling. You were supposed to single the first jump, then jump the table. I launched off the single straight into the air with the intent of landing on the tabletop. Not smart. Right away I knew I wasn't going to make it. When I returned to earth, I smashed down so hard that my neck slammed into my handlebars. There's a pad on the crossbar, but it did nothing to cushion the blow. Feel your Adam's apple, then imagine it slamming on steel with ridiculous force. Now you've got it. My throat was swollen to the point that I had difficulty talking.

I landed on the face of the jump and my left foot got folded underneath the footpeg. It was a miracle no bones were broken, but it wouldn't have made a difference. My foot was swollen so bad that I had no use of it the rest of the weekend.

I was rushed to the hospital and treated for both my injuries. I had no business racing on Sunday, but I was in the middle of the closest title chase in AMA history. And there was no way I was going to let Jeff win the championship because of an injury. I wrapped my foot in tape as a makeshift cast before I put my boot on. I had to shift with my heel because I couldn't bend my ankle. I would take my foot off

the peg and place it in front of
the shifter. On outdoor tracks
you have to shift gears
about twenty times a lap.
We're talking almost thirty
laps here. Do the math.
Riding in intense pain, I
finished ninth overall. With
no one to challenge Jeff, he
won both motos for his third
win of the series.

That was completely
my fault. There was no
reason I should have
tried to make that
jump. Up to that point
everything was going
so well for me. The
bike was unbelievable.
I had never been more
confident. I thought
I could do anything.

"He had the
most confidence any
motocrosser has ever
had at any time," Jeff
said about me that
season.

But one careless
moment can change
everything. Jeff gained
a bunch of points on me and with only three rounds remaining, I had
to finish the season with a bum foot.

The next week at Washougal, my foot had barely improved. I

couldn't put any pressure on it whatsoever. I would just fall over if I tried to put weight on it. In the first moto, I got off to a mid-pack start and crashed a couple of times because I was favoring my foot. I got so frustrated I pulled off the track and left the race. I didn't even race the second moto. It bothered me so bad that I couldn't ride like I knew how to.

I just gave up. It would prove to be a huge mistake.

I should have just dealt with the frustration and gotten another ninth- or tenth-place finish. Instead, I earned zero points while Jeff rode to a solid podium finish.

Seven days later in Binghamton, New York, I witnessed nothing short of a minor miracle. With lingering soreness in my foot, I rode one of my best races of the season, capturing both motos for a runaway win. To this day I can't explain how it happened. I smoked everybody. There was no time to bask in the glory of that win because I was now leading Jeff by a single point. There was one race left. Steel City in Delmont, Pennsylvania, is where Jeff and I would decide the championship.

This would be motocross history. Because this *never* happens.

Steel City is a really high-speed track with a lot of fast jumps. I was still afraid to put weight on my foot, so my confidence wasn't where it needed to be. Going into a situation like this, you know ahead of time that you have to be perfect to win. If you crash back a few places in either moto, the championship is gone. But at the same time you can't be conservative. You've got to put everything on the line.

When you're in the pits or sitting on the gate before a race like this, so much is going through your mind. You've got to concentrate on what you have to do and not the things that could possibly go wrong. I always operate best when I don't think about things. Jeff's always been good at handling pressure when it comes down to a single race. When he has to get it done in a day, he has a history of coming through in the clutch.

There was nothing else Skip could do to my bike. I couldn't sneak in any extra training. I had to use what I had.

Jeremy McGrath

When the gate dropped, I rose to the occasion. I ripped off the line like John Force and got the holeshot in the first moto, and despite my nagging foot, I rode nearly flawless for three-quarters of the race. Jeff was in second and pushing hard. It was almost like I could feel him breathing on the back of my neck.

I had to put my foot down several times and bobbled in a corner when Jeff raced by me. I gave chase but couldn't catch him. He took the checkers and I got second. At the end of moto one, we were tied in the points. Whoever finished higher in the second moto would take the championship.

When the gate dropped for the second moto, Jeff cut over on me (typical Jeff) and got the holeshot. I followed him closely for half the moto. I was a bit more tired and had to set my foot down a few times. Each time a burst of pain shot up my leg. Jeff was riding great and started to pull out a bit of a lead. He was wheeling out of corners and whipping the bike with confidence. Just as I was about to make a charge, Greg Albertyn passed me, knocking me back to third and giving Jeff a much needed cushion.

After a few more laps, Jeff's lead was too much to overcome. He took the checkered flag and with it the 1996 Outdoor Motocross National championship. He won the title by just ten points. It was a huge letdown for me. After the race, I congratulated him. He rode a smart series and showed he was the better man.

I couldn't help but think back to Washougal when I left the race. Even though I still had the points lead, I lost the championship right there that day. Not only did it cost me the title, but also hundreds of thousands of dollars in bonuses and incentives. If I had finished tenth, I would have earned about twenty-two points instead of zero. Since I lost the title by ten points, well, it doesn't take a genius to figure it out. I reminded myself of Damon Bradshaw when he lost the Supercross title to Stanton back in '92.

It made me realize that every single point counts. Every lap, every moto, every turn, every start. The difference between winning and losing in this sport is so small it's easy to take it for granted.

They say that no one remembers second place, but that's not true. For decades motocross fans will talk about the day Jeff Emig beat Jeremy McGrath in the last moto of the last race for the 1996 Outdoor National championship.

HOW TO RIDE RUTS

Ever find yourself in a rut? If you race Supercross you do. Track builders spend lots of time designing triples, step-ups, and whoops. But the riders themselves create the obstacles that can be the most menacing. Ruts are formed in corners and the faces of jumps when riders take the same line over and over again. The deeper the rut, the more tricky it can be to negotiate. Here are a few tips to help you get by unscathed.

Step 1

This first thing to focus on is getting your wheels squarely in the rut. You'll want to lean slightly into the turn and extend your inside leg in front of you. If you start to lose your balance you can use that foot to dab the ground to keep momentum.

Step 2

Keep your eyes forward. You never know what will be in the rut. There might be a huge rock or a crashed rider could have torn up the groove. Look into the rut or just inside it. Just like you wouldn't look at the headlights of oncoming traffic—don't look outside the rut. You go where you look!

Step 3

Stay loose and neutral over the bike. Too far forward and the back wheel could bounce out of the rut. Too far

Jeremy McGrath

backward and you'll wheelie due to too much traction. Don't brake in the rut—the bike will stand upright and slow your forward progress. Get that out of the way before you dive into the rut. On your way out of the rut get on the gas hard.

Step 4

Above all, pay attention! You could be the fastest rider on the track, but if you're not concentrating it won't mean a thing. Track conditions change. A rut that was there in the main might not have existed in the first heat. Late in the race, conditions may deteriorate by the lap. Keeping your focus will keep you on the bike and off your butt.

Things to Keep in Mind

All of this is happening at race speed. Oftentimes you'll have someone right on your tail. Or maybe you're trying to make up extra time. Perhaps you've got serious arm pump. Either way, the more practice you get, the more these steps will become second nature. Learn to ride ruts like you're on a rail and they'll be an advantage, not an obstacle.

The Reign in Spain

Two weeks later, I was off to Jerez, Spain, for the 1996 Motocross des Nations. The United States had won the des Nations a record three times from 1981 to 1993. But we faltered with second place finishes in '94 and '95. I was our 250 representative, Jeff rode the 500 class, and my Honda teammate, Steve Lamson, handled the 125 duties. The U.S. team dominated the international competition by winning every moto of every class. This was one of the greatest moments of my career. Partly because it made up for my poor showing at the '93 des Nations. Winning the way we did also helped erase some of the negative feeling I had about losing the outdoor nationals two weeks earlier.

Skip Retires

Skip decided that he wanted to spend time with his wife, Kristi, and their newborn son. He was pretty drained after spending nearly forty weeks of the year on the road. He took a job at No Fear that rarely required him to travel. Man, I hated to see him go. Skip is more than just my mechanic, he's one of my best friends. He cared about my success. About our freindship. People like that are hard to find. Now he was leaving. Getting through a year of racing motorcycles can be extremely grueling. I needed someone like Skip to carry me through. There is a special bond that a rider and his mechanic share, and I was heartbroken to have it end. But I knew that he had to do what was best for his family and that we would remain the best of freinds.

Three, Two, One . . . Contract

My contract was up at the end of the '96 season. I had been in rather informal negotiations with Honda since about June and didn't forsee any difficulty in getting the deal done quickly. I had planned to sign my usual two-year deal that would take me through 1998. We agreed in principle to about $1 million a year. All we really had to do was change the dollar amounts from the previous contract and we would be good to go.

When October rolled around and the deal still wasn't complete, I didn't think anything of it. Negotiations had gone well, so I just waited for them to send me a contract to sign. Nothing about the delay felt unusual.

That month we were about to begin testing the all-new '97 CR. This was the first year Honda went with the all-aluminum perimeter frame.

I knew the bike was going to be a big change from what I was used to, so I was eager to get started to work out any kinks before January.

A week before testing, Honda sends me the contract. I was more than a little surprised when there was an extra twelve-page section with restrictions on what I could do off the track. On top of that, it was written in some sort of legalese that no one in my family could decipher. We spent about $8,000 on a lawyer just to put it in language we could understand. When I read the interpretation I couldn't believe it. The more I read, the more pissed off I got. In plain English, the contract stipulated that I couldn't ride Jet Skis, snowboard, BMX, or anything of that nature. These are things I've done my whole life. These are my hobbies. They were asking me not to be me. They were trying to tell me how to live my life away from the track.

They had fines written in for everything. It was possible that I could win the title and end up owing them money. They must have thought I was just some stupid racer.

This was a total shock to me. Something way out of the blue. I've always done everything I had to as far as honoring every contract I've ever signed. I've never caused my employers any grief whatsoever. Once they were annoyed that I appeared in a Jet-Ski magazine on a Kawasaki

My last race ever aboard the Honda.

watercraft. It wasn't a big thing because Honda didn't even make a watercraft. Another time Honda sent me a letter chastising me for not wearing a helmet in an ad for Spy glasses. That was about it. And that ad was computer-generated. Maybe they were paranoid because of my wakeboarding crash before the Glen Helen National.

If they were, they never said anything.

I'd never done anything to warrant discipline with regard to conduct. These restrictions were slapped on me for no reason. My parents and I were totally confused. But mostly I was really mad.

They were dragging their feet on the contract, but we had no idea this was brewing. I felt like they were taking my life away from me and I wasn't having it. As long as I did my job they had no right to tell me how to live. The culprit behind those twelve pages was a Honda suit named Ray Blank. He was the VP of Honda's Motorcycle Division, but he wasn't involved with the team. He never even went to the races. They thought they were going to sit back and tell me what I was gonna do. No way. I don't play that game.

As things dragged out, October turned into November and the contract matter was still unresolved. Every factory rider was signed to a contract for '97 except me. Regardless, I went ahead with testing the new bike because I just figured things would get worked out. It was a good thing I did. I quickly discovered that I hated the new bike. I remember the day we took it up to Glen Helen, just outside San Bernardino. I almost literally couldn't ride it. The new frame design was so rigid and stiff I was afraid to ride it at speed because it handled so poorly. It was just terrible. It vibrated tremendously and was unruly in the corners, unlike my point-and-shoot '93 chassis.

It rutted corners with a lot of choppy holes, it would shake right out of my hands. It also had a very low footpeg design that made my riding postion feel awkward. That same month at the Tokyo Supercross on really soft dirt, I was crashing all over the place. One thing I'm known for is my ability to stay on the bike. I rarely crash, but I couldn't stay upright on that thing. I came up short on a double and my chin hit the crossbar, knocking me unconscious. I was bleeding all over the place

Jeremy McGrath

and it was just a mess. To this day, I still have a half-inch scar under my chin from that crash.

That day at Glen Helen is when I decided that I wasn't going work it out with Honda. It was a very somber realization. I was simply afraid to ride the bike. Around that time, Honda launched a huge ad campaign for the '97 CR 250. In one four-page print ad, Honda boasted that "The future of motocross has just been recast." They weren't kidding.

My time with Honda was at an end. Honda made it clear that they weren't going to budge as far as their new restrictions were concerned. That killed all possibility of working out a deal. I felt like they sold me out.

All my life, all I ever wanted to do was ride for Factory Honda. Not only did I live my dream, but I was their all-time winningest rider. I loved racing for Honda, and to have everything come crashing down so unexpectedly was such a sad way for me to end it. It ate me up inside. I used to pretend to be Rick Johnson. Now I was leaving Honda on bad terms. I had a sick feeling eating away at me for months after everything ended.

Hello, Roger, My Old Friend

With about a month to go before the start of the 1997 Supercross season, I still didn't have a ride. My parents decided to call Roger DeCoster, the elegant motocross legend. Roger, a former Honda consultant and current team manager at Suzuki, was more than happy we contacted him. After about two or three long days at Suzuki headquarters in Brea, California, we ironed out a one-year contract with Roger and his boss Mel Harris. At one point my parents sat for twenty-seven straight hours to hammer out a deal.

Both my mom and dad really went to bat for me in this situation. No one else wanted to battle Honda when things got tough. The Honda execs in Japan bullied Suzuki and tried to intimidate them into not signing me, but my parents wouldn't budge because no one was gonna screw over their son.

With the deal we had, I wouldn't exactly be riding for the factory team, which already had Greg Albertyn, Mike LaRocco, and Frenchman Michael Pichon. Instead we arranged a deal where I would be a team unto myself with the same support from Suzuki the factory guys got.

Motocross was in an age where fledgling support teams were popping up in the form of hybrid privateer/factory-supported efforts. I just took it a step further when a "team" was created solely for me. Phil Alderton, who at the time owned a dealership called Suzuki of Troy (he also owned Honda of Troy), chipped in another $200,000 to beef up my

ULTIMATE AEROBATICS: One of the most stylish riders ever, Suzuki rider Jeremy McGrath does his famous "nac-nac" maneuver on his RM250 while high up over a triple jump.

New team, new Suzuki.

salary. The official team name was 1-800-COLLECT/Suzuki of Troy/No Fear. On race days I was to operate out of the factory Suzuki semi.

I really have a lot of respect for Roger and Suzuki for taking me on with such short notice. It was huge for my dad, too. When he was coming up he read every magazine with DeCoster on the cover. When he first met him in the early nineties all he could do was stare at him. Now Roger was helping get his son a ride.

They brought a bike over to my parents' house, which I tested on the Supercross track I had built a few years ago in their backyard. The bike didn't blow me away, but it was the only option I had. We had very little time to test and set it up for the season opener on January 11. It normally takes about three months of rigorous trial-and-error testing to properly dial in the suspension and tune the motor to race standards. We had less than two weeks. That was not good considering that I had some serious issues with the power of the new Suzuki. Simply put, it was sorely lacking. For the last four years, I felt my Honda was the fastest thing on the track. Now I was at a disadvantage.

It seemed after so many years on top that everything in my life had been turned upside-down. I had a brand-new team and mechanic, my relationship with Honda was in shambles, and the bike I was riding just wasn't working for me.

It felt so strange riding a yellow bike. Each time I looked down I expected it to be red and it wasn't. But what was done was done. I made a promise to always be true to myself. Honda tried to take that away but it's something that was too important to me.

Slammed in L.A.

Blow the doors off the competition. That's what I needed to do at the first Supercross of the year at the L.A. Coliseum. There was no other way. Whenever you switch teams there is a ton of pressure to perform. (As if there isn't enough pressure on factory guys already.) You want to keep your numerous sponsors happy, justify the team signing you to a megabucks contract, and most important, beat everybody on your old team.

There was a ton of media, motocross luminaries, and all forms of industry observers who came out to see whether or not I could deliver. Honda was definitely on my mind all week. I wanted to show them they fucked up big by letting me go. But things went bad from the get-go.

I got the holeshot, but before I could make it out of the first turn, Steve Lamson, who still rode for Honda, smashed into me from behind, knocking me off the back of my bike and onto the ground. When I picked myself up off the Coliseum floor, I was in second to last place. Lamson was in last. I was still trying to collect my marbles and went down again two corners later. About five turns later, Lamson slams me to the ground again by completely stuffing me in a ninety-degree turn! I never had any problem with Steve in the past, so I couldn't figure out why he was doing these things. Could Honda have sent him on a kamikaze mission to take me out because of the way our relationship had ended? That was all I could think of. I ended up getting fifteenth, the worst finish of my career. So much for blowing the doors off the comp. That night was absolutely miserable. Whether or not Honda sent Lamson to get me, Honda took other measures that suggested it was trying to get back at me.

Honda Pulls Support from Troy

In their effort to get back at me, Honda was willing to wipe out the less fortunate. Honda pulled Honda of Troy's bonus program, $80,000 in parts and factory recognition, in retaliation for Phil Alderton helping me out with Suzuki of Troy. This unprecedented takeback would mean Phil had to cover the HoT costs out of his pocket. The funny thing is, HoT team rider Larry Ward took third at L.A. Then they pull the plug!

It was going to be a long year for Team Honda. For the oft-considered "greatest team of all-time," their race effort was maybe its weakest ever. It consisted of Steve Lamson, who had never won a 250 race (and never would), and the unproven Scott Sheak in the 125 class. Honda's brand-new $400,000 semi was a lonely place to be in '97.

A year later Phil would cut his ties with Honda completely. He now runs the Yamaha of Troy racing team.

Bike Troubles and More Bike Troubles

A good craftsman never blames his tools. This is true. But in Supercross, if your tools aren't perfectly (and I mean perfectly) tuned, you are starting the race at a severe disadvantage. The Suzuki was giving me problems I wasn't sure I could overcome. It handled poorly and was really slow. How's that? Compared to my CRs, the RM was a turtle. Handled like one, too.

Mitch Payton and Roger DeCoster spent long hours in the dyno room at Pro Circuit testing horsepower, but Mitch will tell you that usable power on the track is a lot more important than wicked dyno curves.

The bike didn't hit hard enough anywhere in the powerband. It was sluggish coming out of the corners and just didn't have the mid-range to run with other bikes on the straightaways.

Frustrating doesn't begin to describe it. But one of the things that bothered me even more was the front fork. For '97, Suzuki still ran conventional Showa forks. (In the mid-nineties most factory and production bikes were equipped with upside-down forks, which offer better

handling and a more stable, all-around feel.) My fork had a lot of flex in it that robbed me of confidence to go fast on technical tracks. Suzuki installed some sort of fork brace to lessen flex, but it was no substitute for a better fork.

I pleaded my case to Roger DeCoster that I needed something better, but he was slow to make a change.

The clutch was no good either. In Phoenix it went out and I had to roll everything and ride around stuck in second gear. We brought in Ron Hinson, who builds aftermarket clutches, to work on the bike, and it was a big help. But there was still a shitload of work to do. These are the kinds of things that are normally taken care of in October, so I was still feeling the fallout from the Honda implosion. Basically, we were testing at the races while everyone else was totally dialed. The bike was never the same twice. I couldn't get used to anything whether it worked or not. Surprisingly, the one thing the bike did well was get decent starts. But that's only because the damn thing was so slow there was almost no wheel spin.

That the bike didn't live up to my standards was not a reflection of the people who were working like hell to get it right. Roger DeCoster, Mitch Payton, and my mechanic, Wyatt Seals, did their part in getting me the best possible machine when I pulled up to the line. But they were fighting an uphill battle.

Wyatt Seals, Hired Wrench

One of the biggest adjustments going from Honda to Suzuki was working with a new mechanic. Particularly someone I didn't know that well. Had I stayed with Honda, I would have been assigned a mechanic from within, since Skip retired. Someone I already knew. Wyatt Seals had been Ryno's mechanic for a year. They had a good working relationship but both were looking for a change. Wyatt parted ways with Kawasaki, so I hired him to wrench for me while I rode for Suzuki. Contrary to popular belief, Wyatt left Kawasaki, not Ryno.

Wyatt told Ryno that wrenching for me would allow him to be

closer to his sick mother. Ryno was sympathetic to Wyatt because his dad died from cancer in 1994. As tough as Ryno is, he was devastated by the loss of his father. When Wyatt started wrenching for me it still may have bothered Ryan a little. "If Wyatt decided to work for Jeremy because he could better take care of his mother, then fine," says Ryno, "but if he was doing it just for the number-one plate, then fuck him."

Jimmy Moves In

One of the best friends I've ever made in motocross is Jimmy Button. In '97, he rode for Team Chaparral Yamaha and was one of the up-and-coming riders on the 250 circuit. Most people around the industry know the tall and lanky Button for his inquisitive personality and easygoing demeanor. There are a lot of people crawling around the pits with smiling faces and ulterior motives, but Jimmy was someone I could count on to be real.

Jimmy and I first met in 1987 at the amateur nationals in Ponca City. He was this super-fast mini rider from Phoenix who was supported by Factory Honda. His CR 80 was tricked out with aluminum triple clamps and sub-frame and other prototype parts. Mitch Payton's Pro Circuit race shop tuned his motor and suspension. In other words, he was getting full support. Not bad for a thirteen-year-old.

Back then he was faster than I was even though he was two years younger. In fact, he was one of the few kids who could beat Damon Bradshaw.

Up to this point, Button's career has been almost the exact opposite of mine. While I struggled to get both support and attention as a mini pilot, Button was the toast of the amateur world. Now that we were pros, I'd won sixty races and four championships, while Button had yet to earn his first win. Since turning pro, Jimmy played the role of the scrapper, constantly fighting to get and keep a factory ride. In 1995, there were no takers and he was forced to race in Europe to make a living.

In an industry of overblown egos, Jimmy's mellow temperament and like-minded warped sense of humor made him easy to hang out with. In the early nineties, when I raced 125 West Supercrosses, Jimmy used his aunt's address in New York to race the East SX series, so I didn't see him as much. But we'd hang out at the East/West shootouts and in the summers on the 125 national scene. His strength was a fluid riding style and he wasn't afraid to hang it over the edge. After he finished a promising second to Ezra Lusk in the '94 East SX series, Suzuki canned Button for no apparent reason. Unless you count Suzuki team manager Roger DeCoster bringing in three-time world champion Greg Albertyn from South Africa. In the following weeks, Button called Honda, Yamaha, and Kawasaki inquiring about a factory ride. But every roster was booked. Jimmy would have ridden for free if all they gave him was a bike.

In March of 1997 at the Gainesville national, I approached Jimmy about coming to live with me at my new place in Canyon Lake. He was still living in Phoenix at the time and had just gotten married, but his relationship with his first wife was deteriorating to the point that it was affecting his riding. After a year of marriage, he went through an ugly divorce and his mind was fried. "I was just wandering through life aimlessly at that point," Button told me. I could tell Jimmy was emotionally drained. Button is one of the most upbeat and friendly people in the industry, but he just hadn't been himself with everything going on at home. At the end of the month he packed his bags, got rid of his excess baggage, and headed for California. I told him he could stay as long as it took—a week, a month, a year, whatever. It didn't matter. He needed someone there for him and I was just doing what any friend would do.

Having him around did both of us plenty good. We trained, ate, rode, partied, and scammed on girls together. After about ten months at my house in Canyon Lake, Jimmy moved out and bought his first house in Tuscany Hills, where he still lives today.

Getting It Right in Minneapolis

We were still having major horsepower issues. Every other bike was just plain faster than mine. To alleviate the problems with the forks, we

took the upside-
downs off of a
practice Honda
I had in my
garage. While
we were at it,
I snagged the
front brake
off that bike
because the
Suzuki binder
didn't grab hard
enough and
faded when it
got hot. As soon
as we made
those changes,

I won round eight at Minneapolis for my first win of the season. This was the deepest I've gone in a season before getting a win.

When I crossed the finish line it felt like I had just won my first race ever. I was so incredibly relieved to get a win on the Suzuki that I felt like a little kid in a candy store. It's a feeling I can't even explain. I'm actually surprised I didn't cry tears of joy. The year before I won fourteen out of fifteen Supercrosses, but none of them compared to this. People considered this season the beginning of the end of the Mc-Grath Era. Everyone was gunning for me. They treated me like a bloody piece of meat in a tank full of starving piranhas. My back was against the wall. And Minnesota was where I came out swinging. Minnesota was also Jimmy's first race after moving in with me. He rode without the weight of the world on his shoulders and finished on the podium for the first time in his career.

After nine rounds, I was second in the points behind Emig and hoped to use the next round in Minneapolis as a springboard to get back on track. But that proved to be wishful thinking.

WIDE OPEN

They're At It Again

On the Thursday before the Pontiac SX, Team Suzuki rider Mike LaRocco called Roger DeCoster and asked to be let out of his $350,000-a-year contract. The next day, Jeff Stanton, my former teammate and current Honda consultant, sent LaRocco a brand-new CR 250 to try out. LaRocco thought he would get out of his Suzuki contract mid-season and sign with Honda. Team Red was desperate for someone when Steve Lamson went down with a broken thumb by mid-season. They were without a single 250 rider.

But LaRocco did the unthinkable and failed to show up for the race on Saturday. DeCoster told him the only bike he was going to race that season was a Suzuki.

Honda had bigger problems. Rumors began to circulate that they were going to pull the plug on their race program if things didn't turn around.

If It Weren't for Bad Luck . . .

My woes continued at round twelve at the Pontiac SX. I grabbed the holeshot and led the race for eighteen laps when I pushed too hard into a corner and flew over the bars. It was the kind of mistake that loses championships. Emig finished a lackluster seventh. Had I won, I would have taken an eleven-point lead in the standings. Instead, I headed for the next round in Charlotte trailing 234–232.

I was leading the pack again in Charlotte and riding in a really comfortable groove. Finally, I was starting to feel at ease on the bike. Just as I'm thinking this, my rear tire blows out. You have got to be kidding me. I don't even know how the tire went flat. I couldn't believe this because flats during Supercross races are extremely rare. I felt my frustration level rising, but I wouldn't make the same mistake I did at Washougal last summer when I pulled off the track. I kept riding hard, even jumping the triples with a flat, to finish seventh. Emig got fourth so I lost even more points.

It was just one more heartbreaking race in an already trying season.

As a side note, Yamaha West 125 SX rider Kevin Windham won the race, marking the first time in AMA history an active 125 rider won a 250 event.

. . . I'd Have No Luck At All

Jeff won the following week in Dallas for his career-best fourth win of the season. His formula was similar to mine in '93—get the holeshot and win wire to wire. He was always known for his starts and, true to his rep, had the quickest trigger off the gate all season. After Dallas there was a rare three-week break in the schedule before the season finale in Las Vegas. As poorly as things had gone all season, I still had an outside chance at the title. It was a long shot but I was still alive. I had to finish six spots ahead of Jeff to earn my fifth straight championship.

During the break, Button, Lew, and a few other friends of mine had

a big day out on the lake then headed for a restaurant near my house. We had a few beers and kept things chill, but a couple of guys started horsing around and a table got knocked over. Broken beer bottles ended up all over the floor. I was wearing thongs, so I stepped back to get out of the way of the ruckus.

I stepped on a broken bottle half with my heel and it rotated up and gashed my Achilles tendon. This was all I needed. I went to the doctor and had eight stitches put in and had to keep it elevated for the rest of the week. I sat at home with my foot wrapped in ice wondering how low things were going to get.

Losing Las Vegas

I couldn't bend my foot. That should give you an indication of my confidence going into the season finale in Vegas. Since I couldn't flex my foot, I had to stand on the footpegs on my heels instead of the balls of my feet. I needed to finish ahead of Jeff by six places to win the title, but he was in front of me the whole race. My longshot airballed. I finished seventh and Jeff rode to a conservative fourth. It was all he needed to win the 1997 Supercross championship, ending my four-year run of titles. At twenty-six, Jeff became the oldest rider ever to win his first championship.

When he rode past the mechanic's area on the last lap, his mechanic Jeremy "J-Bone" Albrecht's pit board read PAY DAY CHAMP. I crossed the finish line in pain and totally disgusted with myself. Thankfully this season was now the past, but I had no idea what the future would bring.

Brother, Can You Spare a Win?

I wasn't the only one on hard times in '97. After winning the 250 Supercross title an astonishing nine years in a row, Honda failed to win a single 250 race in 1997. But that didn't really help ease my pain, because that season had been a miserable experience from the start. I had to play catch-up all year and suffered one demoralizing blow after another.

Jeremy McGrath

I had never been lower in my life. Even to this day, thinking back to '97 can still conjure up negative feelings.

Secret Ops On the Strip

Over the course of my six years at Team Honda, I had developed a very trusting relationship with Cliff White, Honda's chief engineer. At first he was really quiet, tough to get to know. He did not let people in easily. But after spending so much time together racing, we eventually became close. Skip also had a tremendous respect for Cliff and saw him as a mentor. When it came to working on motorcycles, Cliff's knowledge and ability was unparalleled in the business. Whether it was porting a cylinder or setting suspension, he operated with a flawless precision. He was well regarded for his cerebral approach to tuning a motorcycle. He'd worked for Honda over twenty years and was one of the main reasons they reigned for so long.

About a month prior to Vegas, Cliff and I began talking to each other about life in general. I'd call him at home or he'd call me. After a while the subject of me returning to Honda came up. The wounds inflicted last winter were still fresh, but I knew I had to go in a different direction than the one I was headed in.

Cliff knew I wasn't happy and really wanted to see me back in red. I did, too. So I called Honda in Japan to arrange for a top-secret meeting between myself and a high-powered executive from the factory about a possible return to Honda. But I needed someone I trusted to help me. Since Cliff wanted to see Honda back on the top of the podium, I asked for his help.

During the failed talks last fall, the Japanese execs had no idea of the sorry state of negotiations between myself and the American execs. They saw me on their bike at the Tokyo Supercross, and even though I wadded myself up, they figured things were fine.

When they found out I had signed with Suzuki, they were pissed. Like I said earlier, a factory motocross team is nothing more that a marketing tool. The bikes that win get the most exposure and publicity. The bikes on the podium are the ones that the public buys. Honda knew their championship streak was going to end, which would have a negative affect on sales.

There is a Japanese custom understood by the riders that says once you leave a manufacturer, you aren't going back. It happens, but it's rare.

Cliff was scared when I told him about the meeting, but I needed him. In the weeks leading up to Vegas, I was walking on eggshells but arranged it nevertheless.

After the race, Button drove me back to the hotel, the MGM Grand on the Strip. When I got out of the car, I told him to wait for me, but to stay out of sight. I went to my room and called the front desk and asked for Mr. Honda. With the room number of his suite in hand, I cautiously made my way there.

Walking through the halls toward the elevator bay, I was so freaked out. I was nervous as hell and my palms were sweating because I didn't want anyone to see me. What was I doing? This kind of thing was highly unusual.

I was so afraid someone was going to spot me and ask where I was going. On a Saturday night at the MGM Grand, there are thousands of people gambling, milling about, and just living it up. A ton of motocross folks were also staying there. But when you're the most recognizable person in the sport, you need a little luck to go unseen at the Grand. I jetted to a little-used elevator in the back of the hotel and prayed no one I knew would get on. The ride up to the top-floor suite took forever.

When I got to the suite, I was greeted by the Japanese exec. He was casually dressed and puffing on a thin cigarette. I walked in and Mr. Honda extended his hand gently and said, "Ah, Jeremy-san, how are you?" When I saw how laid back he was, all of my fears instantly went away. Despite the unwritten rule of never returning to a former team, he welcomed me back with open arms.

I explained to him that I never wanted to leave in the first place, that the unnecessary restrictions forced my hand. He wasn't worried about that in the least and assured me steps would be taken to get me back on a Honda for '98. The meeting lasted about forty-five minutes and ended with a handshake and the promise that we'd get back in touch at the end of the season in September.

On my way back to the lobby, I tried to remain as inconspicuous as possible. Outside, Button was waiting where I had left him. I got in the rental car and we drove off into the sea of neon lights. As Jimmy quizzed me, I stared out the window thinking to myself, "This meeting never happened."

Keepin' It Clutch

Ever since Lawrence Lewis and I have hung out together, we've gone riding together. Sometime in the early nineties Lew started bringing a video camera to our riding sessions. He would film us doing some pretty crazy things like hill climbs, jumping huge gaps, and just horsing around. After a while we had all this footage we didn't know what to do with. So we started Clutch Films, a small production company, to produce videos of our riding sessions.

We hired some other riders and put together a collection of highlights and called it *Steel Roots*. But we needed some help polishing the finished product and learning the ropes of the MX video craze. So we called on Dana Nicholson and Jon Freeman of Fleshwound Films to help us produce it. A year or so earlier they released the *Crusty Demons of Dirt* series, which featured myself, Ryno, Factory Phil, Joel Albrecht, Buddy Antunez, Seth Enslow, Mike Metzger, and Tommy Clowers.

Steel Roots did well, selling about 60,000 copies. But it also meant that me and Lew's relationship took on another dimension—business partners. It would prove to make things a bit more complicated than I hoped. My dad was already weary of the fact that Lew was living with me. Now that we were in business together, Big Jack had even less love for Lew. He still felt Lew was leeching off of me because "he ain't bringin' anything to the table but he's still collecting money."

My dad never stopped resenting the fact that I gave Lew a stipend when he hung out with me. Looking back on it, he was as hurt by it as he was pissed. "I've never had two or three hundred bucks just to throw

away like that," he once said. "To me a twenty-dollar bill is a big deal. I was a poor bastard growing up. And I was still poor when Jeremy started racing. I struggled to buy eighties for Jer to race and he never gave me three hundred bucks a week. Hell, I was only making three hundred bucks a week as it was."

FIVE RACERS TURNED FREESTYLERS

Bet you didn't know at one time or another your favorite freestyle motocross riders tried their hand at racing. Here are five guys who traded in holeshots for heel clickers.

Mike Metzger

2002 X GAMES GOLD MEDALIST

Best SX Finish: 1997 Dallas 125 WSX, sixth

Best MX Finish: 1993 Glen Helen 125 MX, fourteenth

Claim to Fame: Nicknamed the Godfather of freestyle

motocross; threw down huge back-to-back

backflips at the 2002 Summer X Games for the first successful backflip in competition aired on national television, self-proclaimed "King of the Two-Wheeled Deal."

Mike Jones

2001 WINTER X GOLD MEDALIST

Best SX Finish: 1991 Foxboro 250 SX, second
Best MX Finish: 1992 Budds Creek 500 MX, fifth
Claim to Fame: Has invented many of the tricks that are staples of the FMX world.

Carey Hart

2002 X GAMES SILVER MEDALIST

Best SX Finish: 1998 Minneapolis 250 SX, twentieth
Best MX Finish: 1998 Glen Helen 250 MX, fourteenth
Claim to Fame: First rider to pull a backflip in competition (2000 Gravity Games).

Tommy Clowers

2002 X GAMES STEP-UP GOLD MEDALIST

Best SX Finish: 1993 Anaheim 125 WSX, fourth
Best MX Finish: 1993 Hangtown 125 MX, twelfth
Claim to Fame: At the end of 2002 Tomcat was 21–2 all-time in the step-up competition.

Brian Deegan

WINTER X GOLD MEDALIST

Best SX Finish: 1997 L.A. 125 WSX, first
Best MX Finish: 1997 Troy 125 MX, fifth
Claim to Infamy: Upon crossing the finish line at the L.A. Supercross, Deegan ghost-rode his bike; founder of Metal Mulisha freestyle crew.

Lew Too Many

Lew and I were still hanging out and training nearly everyday. When we weren't throwing parties at the house we were wakeboarding or taking a spin in my new powerboat. We were pretty inseparable. My parents had hoped by now that I would have outgrown wanting Lew around all the time.

They were skeptical when I tried to explain the situation—that it was hard for someone in my position to find another person who I could hang out with me because of my schedule. And Lew and I got along great, so it worked. But they were hard on him nonetheless. After a while I found myself constantly being a mediator between Lew and my parents. They saw him as a moocher while I saw him as my best friend. It pissed my dad off when Lew would take out my boats or drive my cars when I wasn't there. "You got to take care of that problem before something happens," my dad would warn. My response was to tell him I'll just get more insurance. This infuriated him to no end.

To make matters worse, whenever I was away at the races, Lew would throw wild parties at my house and I would always get an earful from my parents. The cops would call them and say there was a raucous party at my place and my dad would lose it. I talked to Lew about the parties and pretty much let it slide, but as stuff like that continued I started to get a little frustrated.

We were beginning to head in different directions. I was becoming less and less interested in nonstop partying and emotionless relationships with girls who were more interested in my money than me as a person. I wanted to grow up but Lew couldn't let go. To him, life was a constant party. I didn't look at it like that anymore.

It didn't help that I was going through the most emotionally draining year of my career. I lost the Supercross title to Emig and was not mentally prepared for the nationals, which started the following week.

My parents continued to tell me that it was time for Lew to start living his own life. "Let him cast his own shadow," my dad would say. He often referred to Lew as Kato Kaelin. My dad didn't want Lew at the races or anywhere around me when they were present. But I didn't want to sell out my best friend. Sooner or later something was going to give.

In a big way.

Cruel Summer

Despite my miserable year, Button and I managed to have a ton of fun in the summer of '97. He was one of the main reasons I was able to keep my sanity that season. Just to give you an idea of where my mind was that summer, take the race at Mt. Morris. The rain was coming down in sheets, making conditions nothing short of a mud bath. Button and I are a lap down, running fourth and fifth, respectively, when we both go down in a sloppy, rutted-out corner. It's taking us forever to get our bikes up and riders are flying by us, roosting mud all over the place. Larry Ward and Damon Bradshaw passed us like they were riding on the pavement of Daytona. Our jerseys and pants were thoroughly waterlogged and clinging to us like baggy wetsuits.

Our bikes were overheating and barely running properly. Button yells to me, "I can't wait till we get to Havasu tomorrow!" I was thinking the same thing. I had no idea what I finished. I didn't care.

My attitude had a lot to do with how much the people around me were putting into their jobs. I don't want to put the blame on anyone else for my results, but I was dealing with a level of frustration I wasn't used to. My mechanic, Wyatt Seals, was a cool guy, but his focus wasn't always there. And sometimes *he* wasn't even there. He met this girl Holly, who worked at the AMA, and got whipped real quick. He started spending all of his free time (and some of his work time) with her. He'd be in the Bahamas or the Keys with Holly when he was supposed to be at the Suzuki test track with me.

I can't remember how many times I got to the Suzuki test track only to find out I was the only one there. I had to call the suspension guys at Showa myself and tell them to meet me there.

It was times like that I really missed Skip. He would always have everything ready when I got to the track. All I had to do was ride. A lot of the time with Suzuki, I ended up bringing my own tools and working on my bike at the track. I'd set up my own tent and everything. I just stopped caring, because you can't properly test a bike by yourself. At the factory level, that's just plain ridiculous. It's a collaborative effort, and one person is not a collaboration.

At Honda, when you needed a part it was there the next day. If you thought you had the best bike ever, they would make it even better. It's an experience that I'll never forget. With Suzuki, I learned not to hold my breath. Whether it was lack of technology or factory support, something was missing.

Daytona Bike Week, 1997.

When the Suzuki execs from Japan visited their factory in California, orders went out to hide the race team's eighteen-wheelers and just about anything that showed that Suzuki was fielding a team. The trucks weren't allowed within 100 miles of the factory in Brea, California, when the head honchos were in town. It was the most bizarre thing I've ever seen. Almost as if they were running a program behind Japan's back.

Jeremy McGrath

By mid-summer there was still a lot of work to be done to the bike. By then I knew that it wasn't going to get done. I was just fed up. I stopped practicing altogether. Instead, I would take the boat out or go wakeboarding. During the middle of the season all I did was show up at the races. I got third at Washougal and didn't even pick up my trophy. I had lost all enthusiasm for what I was doing.

Even though Button was riding for Chapparal Yamaha at the time, he would ride at the Suzuki practice track with me whenever I decided to practice. Even when the Japanese engineers were visiting. All of the tracks are located within a square mile of each other in Corona, California. Usually riders stick to their own team's track, but '97 was such a bizarre year that all protocol went out the window.

On a Roll

Since I lived in Canyon Lake, I spent most of my golf outings at the Canyon Lake Golf Course. Lew and I were still into racing golf carts because that was half the fun of playing. But by '97 most of the golf courses had converted from gas-powered to electric golf carts. There was no longer any way to rig them to go faster. But that didn't stop us. At Canyon Lake, there was a huge downhill in the middle of the golf course with a bridge at the bottom. I learned that if you turned the cart off you could get it to coast up to about thirty miles per hour down this particular hill. One day that's exactly what Lew and I did.

We were flying down the hill, cracking up all the way, when I jammed on the brakes at the bridge at the bottom. Immediately the cart fishtailed and started to slide sideways to my left. I thought we were going to get out of this one until the wheels on the right started to lift off the ground. They rose higher and higher until I realized that this baby was going to roll. The cart started to flip and ejected me out of the front while Lew went sailing out the passenger side. The cart went tumbling across the bridge but stayed in one piece. Luckily, we did too.

The Return of Skip

With Wyatt not taking his job as seriously as he should have, I started laying down on the job, too. This was totally not what I was about, so we had to make a mid-season change. Halfway through the summer, Roger DeCoster called Skip and asked him if he would wrench for me for the rest of the season. Skip agreed to come back for the six or seven remaining nationals. Wyatt was demoted to pretty much changing tires for the Suzuki team for the rest of the nationals. He took it really hard, but it was a change that needed to be made.

There's no way Skip would let me get away with not practicing. All the nonsense ended as soon as Skip came back. His return pumped fresh air back into my lungs, but I knew it was only temporary.

Goodbye, Cliff White, My Old Friend

Nothing ever came of my secret meeting with the Honda bigwig. There were some communication problems between Cliff and I over the summer and we never quite connected. If I went back to Honda for '98, my situation would be similar to what I had at Suzuki. I wouldn't have been on the factory team but I would have gotten my own deal plus bikes from the factory. That sort of setup wasn't the norm like it is today, so there were a lot of risks involved.

After the meeting yielded nothing, Cliff and I didn't speak for almost six years. And as a result, our friendship had become severely fractured. The relationship that was built on mutual respect and admiration disintegrated to nothing. During that time, when I saw him, he would just look away or walk by without speaking. It's not like I didn't ever see him either. He was at all the races. It was like I didn't exist to him. Cliff has a very corporate mentality and is a Honda lifer, fiercely loyal to his employer. It's not far-fetched to say he was probably instructed not to talk to me after things went sour.

Once after a bad race with Suzuki, Cliff told a friend he felt good when I lost. A statement like that is so out of character for him it just shows how cold things got between us. I think he felt like he put his ass on the line for me and I left him hanging. I thought about that every time I saw him.

For a while it was really hard to take. He made a lot of things possible for me. He believed in me so much that he was willing to risk a lot to get me back on a Honda. It just killed me when we stopped speaking. It went on for so long because it was hard for either one of us to break the silence. After so much time passes, it's not an easy thing for grown men to do. I knew deep inside that I was going to have to make the first move.

In April of 2003, that's what I did. Team Honda was testing at my new track, McGrath Proving Grounds, when I dropped by and was startled to see Cliff. It was incredibly awkward, but after six years I walked up to him and said hello. We spoke breifly, mostly just small talk, but the ice had finally been broken. I'm still planning on having a real sit-

down with him so we can really find out what went wrong and hopefully repair our friendship. (In June of 2003, Honda sponsored me to race Pro Vet and Supermoto. In a strange twist of fate, I'm back with Cliff and Honda after all these years. It's been way too long.)

In a sport where so much is at stake, so much is on the line, it is not unusual for relationships between people who genuinely like each other to wilt and die. The strongest friendships can hold up to anything, but other times, close bonds suffer seemingly irreparable damage.

Losing Cliff White as a friend for good would have definitely been one of the biggest regrets of my career. Thankfully, I have the chance to make sure that doesn't happen.

End of an Error

When I crossed the finish line in the last moto at the '97 season finale in Steel City, I was so relieved. Not because I had won (I finished fifth; third in the final points standings) but because the season was finally over. Jeff Emig won the title, becoming the seventh rider to win both the 250 Supercross and outdoor national championships in the same year.

I knew that things were going to change, but I wasn't exactly sure what direction they were going. Since I had signed a one-year deal with Suzuki last December, they had already put another offer on the table. That season they had just paid me a record $800,000 base salary to ride for them. They were willing to pay me even more to stay on for '98. I would get less if I signed with anyone else. But I knew I was gone. I didn't want to sacrifice my results for money. Suzuki and I were a match that just wasn't right. After being with a program like Honda for six years, riding for Suzuki was a step backward.

The funny thing is, had I won the Supercross title on my RM, I think I would have stayed with Suzuki. I would have felt like I owed it to them. But that was a moot point now. I wanted out. Jimmy and I had always talked about how cool it would be to be teammates. We imagined finishing the Supercross series 1-2 and all the other stuff that kids dream about. But this business is so unstable for a rider that things like that rarely ever come together. Even so, during the course of the season I had been ever so slightly entertaining the idea of riding for Team Chaparral Yamaha in '98 if things fell into place. Button casually tossed the idea out to Chaparral's team manager, Larry Brooks, who had retired from racing a year earlier. As the season wore on, I started to think of it as a realistic option.

Dave Damron, the owner of Chaparral Motorsports, which is one of the biggest accessories companies in motocross, had been talking with Yamaha team manager, Keith McCarty, about whether or not I could get bikes and support directly from the factory if I signed with Chaparral.

Randy Lawrence, Larry Brooks, and me with Team Chaparral.

After Steel City, Brooks, Button, and I talked things out in the rental car on the way back to the hotel. The more we talked, the more I liked the potential scenario. But this was back when satellite teams weren't really much of a factor in the 250 ranks. They were around but were usually small, underfunded efforts that yielded few podium finishes, fewer wins, and no Supercross championships.

That was exactly what Chaparral Yamaha was at the time. So I was still feeling a little bit nervous about the whole thing. Dave Damron had a nice race shop and a great business, but his team wasn't exactly Factory Honda. But it seemed like my best option at the time. So right there in that Ford Taurus, I decided that I would get my Supercross title back on a midnight-blue Yamaha YZ 250.

Dave agreed to pay me $500,000 and Yamaha came through with the factory bikes, so it was on. When I got back to California, I tested the YZ just to be sure. I loved the bike and the deal was sealed.

The official team name was Chaparral/1-800-COLLECT/Yamaha. If you're wondering about how long the team names are getting these days in Supercross, just know that it's the way things are heading. As the sport grows in popularity, more outside (read, mainstream) sponsors are getting involved. In exchange for some pretty big checks, the sponsor's logos find new homes on radiator shrouds and become prefixes to team names. Going into the '98 season, we were lucky enough to have some great support from them.

Even though I rode for Chaparral, part of my deal was that I would get parts directly through the factory by way of Keith McCarty. That was to ensure I wasn't at a disadvantage. I got everything Factory Yamaha riders Kevin Windham, John Dowd, and Doug Henry did. (Although I decided to go with the '94 cylinder as opposed to the '98.) My new mechanic, Randy Lawrence, and I tested at the Yamaha test track, as well.

Upper Management

When Team Chaparral was created two years prior, Dave Damron needed a team manager able to deal with the ups and downs that would accompany any fledgling race effort. About that time, Larry Brooks was looking for a ride for his twelfth and final season as a professional motocrosser. When Larry inquired at Chaparral for a job, Damron said sure, but I need a manager, too. So at the age of twenty-six, Larry became the first ever rider/manager in U.S. motocross history. LB is a no-nonsense pro who has earned the respect of many in the industry since he began his career back in 1984. In his dual role, Larry would not only have to race but put together press packages, handle sponsors, order parts, troubleshoot on race day, and motivate his riders.

Damron felt he was the perfect personality to deal with Chaparral's young and reckless 125 rider Brian Deegan. FMX fans know him as the controversial leader of the anti-establishment Metal Mulisha freestyle crew. But Deegan began honing his outlaw ways even under Brooks' tutelage. Originally from Nebraska, Deegan is responsible for one of the most notorious moments in AMA history. After winning his first and only 125 SX in Anaheim, Deegan ghost-rode his bike off the finish-line jump in celebration and was fined $1,000 by the AMA.

Later that year, Deegan was also accused of twice cutting the course at the Budds Creek National on a section of the track out of race officials' view. Larry's mild-mannered persona helps him deal with athletes like Deegan, but Brooks' own once-rowdy past allows him to relate even better.

Button Flies, Parties in Geneva

Now that Button and I were both on Chapparal Yamaha, we were hanging out more than ever. If you saw one of us, the other wasn't usually

Jimmy Button and me.

far behind. In October we went to Geneva, Switzerland, for an exhibition race. It was a one-night deal where we flew in Friday night, raced Saturday, and flew out Sunday morning. Button was on fire and won both motos for his first ever 250 win. It won't go down in the AMA record books, but it was still a win. I rode like a dork and crashed out. I think I ended up fourth, but it was cool to see Jimmy ride the way he did. After the race we were ready for the usual European post-race hijinks.

The promoters arranged a dinner at a banquet hall that Button and I gladly attended. The tables were like fifty feet long and had elaborate place settings. When we got there, much to our surprise, they didn't serve beer. Only wine and champagne. Not long after our entrance, Button and I make quick work of a huge bottle of red wine. Then another and another. An hour in, we were pretty liquored up. We scarfed down mountains of pasta to chase the wine, and by the time our mechanics got back from tearing our bikes down and boxing everything up, we were completely annihilated.

My new mechanic, Randy, Factory Phil's brother, dared Jimmy to take a bottle of champagne and wet down the whole place. On command, Jimmy shook up the champagne and let everybody have it like he was still on the podium. After that, he chugged what was left of the bubbly like water and told everybody he owned the place. Randy had a bit of a history as a prankster, so I guess he felt it was time to pass the torch. He didn't drink but he was the biggest instigator. "I bet you won't run and clear the table," Randy prodded Jimmy. Too late. Before Randy even got the words out of his mouth, Button dove on the table and started pulling himself along, knocking everything to the floor.

There were tons of people eating at the tables who all of a sudden ended up with meals in their laps. His initial dive only took him about ten feet, so he started to pull himself along by the edges of the table. When he got to the end there was nothing left. But instead of getting all pissed off, everyone loved it. The next thing you know we had started a massive food fight.

Jeremy McGrath

Champagne was sprayed everywhere and salad bowls sailed through the air like Frisbees. We were taking pots of spaghetti and dumping them on our heads and chucking biscuits as far as we could. It was the most insane thing we had ever seen.

Somehow, Jimmy lost his shirt, shoes, and socks in the process and had to walk back to the hotel half naked in the snow. I was so red-wined out, Randy had to guide me, step for step, back to my room. Luckily, the hotel was only about a hundred yards away.

We got back to the hotel but couldn't find the key to our room. So naturally, we tried to bust the door down instead of going to the lobby for an extra key. We had planned to hang out with the trophy girls, so we had to get changed and sober up quickly. I decide to kick in the door, which was a stupid thing to do. One well-placed kick and the door just exploded. My plan was to change, but minutes later I found myself passed out on my bed naked. Randy had the girls meet us at the hotel. He invited them all up to my room and they found me naked on my bed. Luckily, I was too out of it to care.

The next morning I had the worst hangover I've ever had in my life. While everyone was checking out I was laying in the middle of the lobby floor on this beautiful, white Persian rug feeling like I was about to die. I started heaving my guts out all over the place. The concierge was yelling at me in French, but I didn't care. (It was all for Button's first win!) I did learn my lesson, though. To this day, I haven't touched a drop of wine. Neither has Button.

CHAPTER SIXTEEN

There was something that occurred to me that I couldn't bring myself to admit for a long time. I was a lonely man. Even with a seemingly endless flow of chicks, the phone ringing off the hook, and the Dungeon a high traffic area, I couldn't lie to myself. I was very alone.

I hated that, too. I was tired of living that life. I wasn't a player. That's just not how I was raised. Ever since I can remember I was always taught family values, but when a certain lifestyle is available to you it's easy to get pulled in. I always knew inside that I wanted to be like my parents, totally in love and married to one person for the rest of my life. Besides, it was too much work to constantly juggle so many women. Having one girl on hold while you click call waiting to lie to another was becoming old. I always hated lying, too. The more girls there were, the more tangled the web would become. I started to feel really bad about it.

With Button gone and the Chaparral Yamaha

deal completed, my life was going through a serious transitional period. I was twenty-six years old and I had played my share of the field. My dad was always amazed at my ability to have no emotional attachment when it came to female conquests. He was also weary of it. But it was kind of getting time for me to look for someone to settle down with. I mean, I wasn't actively looking for Mrs. Jeremy McGrath. I just thought if it was meant to happen it would. So I went about life as usual, which meant one thing—Lake Havasu.

After the European exhibitions, Button and I headed for the lake. There were tons of MXers there as always, including Buddy Antunez and his wife, Shelly. They were staying in this little resort that had a bunch of really cool condos where a lot of us often stayed. Shelly's friend Kim Maddox was with them that particular weekend, but it wasn't like I knew who that was. I just liked what I saw. She had long blond hair and a great smile. It just so happened that we had a chance meeting outside my condo that night.

Their crew had just gotten back from a local bar called Kokomos, lit out of their minds, when they started horsing around. Someone ended up breaking Buddy's kitchen table. Everybody felt sorry for Buddy and decided to embark on a mission to find him another table so he wouldn't have to pay for the busted one when he checked out.

So they walked across the courtyard to the room of Ricky Carmichael's mechanic, Chad Watts, who happened to have the same exact table. Guys were passed out all over the place, so Kim and her cohorts helped themselves to Chad's table. Fifteen minutes later they returned with the busted table, set it up, and snuck back out undetected. On their way out, Button, Lew, and I were just getting back from a night of partying ourselves.

My condo was next to Chad's, so they passed us in the hallway. Kim was wearing these orange wide-legged pajama bottoms that I thought looked pretty funny. "Nice curtains," I called out, mocking her pants. She thought I was pretty much a jerk.

About six months later, by a strange twist if fate, my friend Victor Sheldon, a pro jet-ski racer, set us up on a date. I definitely remembered her from the hallway and hoped she didn't remember the curtain pants remark. She did. Kim was a bit wary of me because she thought I was a player. She had heard about my legacy. Even my dad thought I was a super pimp, so I can understand Kim's reservation. But it took her not having anyone on Valentine's Day to get her to agree to go out with me. On February 17, 1998, Kim and I went out for the first time. It was one of those things where there really wasn't any pressure on anyone to entertain, so we could just relax, have fun, and get to know each other. Victor and his girlfriend, Piper, double-dated to make things more comfortable. At dinner, Kim and I ordered the same thing and kept each other laughing. Afterward we headed over to a billiards hall, got a drink, and talked to the wee hours of the morning. She was quick-witted, smart, funny, and just finishing up her public administration degree at San Diego State. I guess I must have done something right, because at the end of the night we both decided that there would be a second date.

Yogi, Kristi, and Getting My Speed Back

I started the 1998 season with the same agenda as last year's ill-fated Suzuki voyage. My goal was to win early on the new Yamaha. Although, I had no intention of showing up Suzuki or Roger DeCoster. I was racing to get back the championship. I didn't care what color the bikes behind me were. Before the first race, Pace, who produced the series back then, gave Jeff Emig a T-shirt with him whipping his bike out and flashing the No. 1 plate. "We'll see how heavy that plate is," my dad said to himself at the time.

After riding to a lackluster third in the opening-round mud of the L.A. Coliseum, I finished second at Houston and Phoenix to twenty-two-year-old Georgia native Ezra Lusk.

A new challenge to the throne had begun to emerge. In the off-season, Team Honda signed Lusk as their No. 1 rider. When the likelihood of my returning to Honda began to fade, they went full-throttle

after Ezra. In just his third season on 250s, Ezra, along with the talented but inexperienced Kevin Windham, was supposed to have the best shot at keeping me from regaining my title.

Ezra was one of the more aggressive riders on the circuit and wouldn't hesitate to swap paint with whoever happened to be in any given corner with him. And unlike most, he didn't fade late in the race. He was just as fast on lap twenty as he was on the first lap.

He's been factory-supported rider since he was a six-year-old member of Team Green. His 1986 works KX 60 cost about as much as two 1998 KX 125s and was almost as fast. Lusk was groomed to be a Supercross champion. In 1998, he was out to make it a reality.

Ezra is a soft-spoken introvert. Friends nicknamed him Yogi because of his hairy arms as a child. I never had any problem with Yogi in the past, but that was soon to change.

Despite Ezra's budding confidence, I put together a four-race win streak, the longest since the tail end of 1996, my last season with Honda. My Yamaha got great holeshots and had tons of power. The suspension and chassis provided handling reminiscent of my old CRs. My confidence was rapidly beginning to climb to pre-Suzuki levels. Wins at Seattle, San Diego, Indianapolis, and Atlanta put me at the front of the points race for the first time in two years.

Meanwhile, things were looking up for Button, as well. He was riding much better and he was beginning to establish himself as a guy factories often inquired about. His second in San Diego was his best 250 Supercross finish ever. With my win, Chaparral Yamaha team manager Larry Brooks called it the best night of his life.

In Indianapolis, there was the usual logjam going into the first turn. The result? I got a second-place start and Ezra got knocked to the ground and suffered a broken left hand. "Basically, what happened was that a Chaparral Yamaha knocked me down from behind," said Ezra in disgust. He tried to point the finger at Button when in reality it was Honda of Troy's Michael Craig that sent him to the dirt.

I went on for the win, my sixty-fourth career victory, to set the all-time mark for combined Supercross and motocross wins. When I pulled off the track my mom, dad, and sister Tracy were waiting for me with tears in their eyes. It was one of the most emotional moments of my life.

Button's personal life was also getting back on track. A week before my first date with Kim, he started seeing Kristi Sampson, who was Brooks' sister-in-law. Jimmy was riding so well he decided to invite Kristi to the Atlanta SX. There's always a natural tendency to show off when you ride, but for some reason when there's a girl at the races that you want to impress, you always manage to fall on your ass. Kristi came to practice the day of the race and Jimmy crashed no less than five times. Larry was pretty pissed because he knew Jimmy's focus wasn't on the race.

When Kristi showed up at the race with her sister, Terri, Larry was reluctant to let them in. Since Larry was married to Terri, he didn't have much choice. In the first heat race, Button crashed in the first corner and had to go to the semi to qualify. In the main, I got the holeshot with Button starting about fourth.

On lap ten, Button snapped by me in a right-hand hairpin turn to take the lead. He was really feeling it and built up what had to be a ten-second lead—that's a lifetime in Supercross. But it wouldn't hold up. His mechanic, Brian Kinney, held up his pit board with the message: MC IN SECOND AND COMING.

As soon as Jimmy saw that, rather than riding to win, he rode not to lose. That rarely works. He made several mistakes and I caught him in the rhythm section. He passed me back in the following turn, but I recaptured the lead for good three corners later. I got the win and JB managed to hold on for second, proving that San Diego was no fluke.

I didn't rag on Button too hard for losing it in front of Kristi, because I knew sooner or later that Kim would be coming to the races, too.

Kim's Birthday

I scored some early points with Kim by remembering her birthday. It was only a week after we first went out, but at least I remembered. I made Kim cover her eyes and guided her into my bedroom. On the bed was a powder blue and white Shift jacket I had gotten for free. (Shift is a motocross apparel company owned by FOX.) The way I laid out the jacket made it look like I had intentionally posed it even though I didn't. I put a card with no envelope on top of it. When Kim uncovered her eyes, she thought it was so cute that I made the effort. Giving her a free, unwrapped gift was such a bachelor thing to do, but she loved it anyway.

I would come to find that Kim takes anniversaries, holidays, and birthdays very seriously, which is the exact opposite approach I take. Kim remembers important dates of all her friends (mine too) and basically everybody else she comes into contact with. She operates with the thought that no one should be forgotten on his or her birthday. Just the thought alone is enough for her not to want anyone she knows to go empty-handed. Even if it's just a card, Kim will put something in the mail for everybody. But not me. For starters, I'm terrible at remembering important dates. I just don't get that excited about holidays or exchanging gifts. Besides, I'm just not that good at gift giving. I never have been. It seems whatever I give is always the wrong thing. I've tried to get better but I always seem to fall short. I'm the kind of person who would just as soon rather not get anything. It wouldn't bother me at all.

But this stuff was important to Kim, so I knew I had to concentrate on it in the future. Unfortunately, it would get a lot worse before it got better.

Jeremy McGrath

The First Six Months

You know how when you first meet a girl you really like, you'll go out of your way to do anything to impress her? That's how the first six months with Kim were. I was head over heels in love with her and did whatever I could to make her happy. No dinner was too expensive. Nowhere was too far to drive. No wait was too long while she tried on clothes when we went shopping.

Instead of putting in extra practice time at the track, I regularly made plans to hang out with Kim. Concerts, movies, and dinner came nonstop. We went out five times a week and I thought about her almost every second we spent apart.

Even though I wasn't good with birthdays and gift giving, I got the little stuff right. I regularly surprised Kim with flowers and candy for no reason. I left notes on her car and phone messages telling her how much I loved her. She would write me inspirational notes before every race that I would tape up in the dressing room in my semi.

Kim and me.

Because I was spending so much time with Kim, my mom got a little worried. She was looking at it from a mother's perspective and knew that my life was undergoing a big change. Sometimes it's hard for a mother to let her only son grow up. At the same time both my parents were happy because they thought Kim had replaced Lew.

Things were going so well between Kim and I that there was nowhere to go but down.

St. Louis Smackdown

Ezra hadn't won since round three and came to St. Louis looking to turn the momentum in his favor. On lap nine, Ezra T-boned Suzuki's Mickael Pichon, sending him flying ten feet through the air. For the next ten laps, Lusk and I engaged in a heated battle for second that climaxed in the last turn of the race. In a left-hand hairpin turn, I went high and wide while Ezra took the inside line. But instead of holding the tight line, he went wide in front of me as I was diving out of the berm, causing us to collide. Yeah, I left the door open, but he almost went backward on the track just to slam me. We both crashed, but my bike went flying five feet in the air. Mike LaRocco passed us both and Ezra got up and finished third. I got a lousy fourth. It was a total cheap move and I was fucking pissed after the race.

The crowd pounded him with boos afterward. Back in the pits, I waited for him to come through the stadium tunnel. When he emerged, I rushed him and asked him what the hell his problem was. About ten Honda guys formed a human shield around Ezra so I couldn't get to him.

"That's racing, man," he said. But he sounded like a chicken with no conviction.

Pontiac Excitement

The next week in Pontiac, everyone was expecting another altercation between me and Ezra. But I just put it out of my mind and thought about the race. On the starting line for the main, Ezra and I were side by side. We didn't speak a word or even glance at one another. I was intent on making a statement by winning. But instead, disaster struck. Landing off a jump, the triple clamp that held my bars in place snapped like plastic, body-slamming me to the ground.

It's a miracle I wasn't badly injured, but I was dazed and out of the race. As I was struggling to get to my feet, Larry Ward tried to squeak by on the outside and accidentally decked me with his elbow. I went down again and got the message: Tonight was not my night.

It was the only time in my career I failed to finish a 250 race.

My wrist was killing me after the crash, but I didn't realize for another couple of weeks that I had broken a bone.

When Ezra won the race he also won a bet with his mechanic that had prevented the normally clean-shaven Lusk from shaving his mustache until he won. Ezra got to shave and

Ezra Lusk.

Gossealar had to lose his trademark cookie duster, too. If it were up to me, I'd have had them both looking like ZZ Top by Las Vegas.

After my body slam at Pontiac, we had a week off before the round at Charlotte. Button and I decided to take Kim and Kristi to Hawaii. I hoped a trip to the Pacific would silence the school bell ringing in my head. We stayed at the Hyatt Regency Kauai in Po'ipu and just tried to forget about Ezra, the points race, and pretty much everything related to motocross. Some surfing and a little tennis took care of that, but it was impossible for me to stay away from motocross. We ended up at the Wailua motocross track and signed autographs for a couple of hours. I didn't mind. It was just cool to see how stoked the fans in Hawaii were about our sport.

When the series picked back up in Charlotte, my bad luck continued. I crashed in the mud and ended up in last place by the fifth lap. I rode to a wet, cold, and lonely fourteenth place.

Better Than Ezra

Even with those two bad races, all I had to do was finish in second place at the Dallas Supercross to win my fifth 250 SX championship. The fans in Texas Stadium were rabid that day. This was a big day for Supercross because we were being broadcast live on ABC. A few minutes prior to the start, Art Eckman asked me a couple questions for a live interview, but there were so many knots in my stomach I didn't have anything to say. I just wanted this thing to start.

Once again Ezra picked the gate right next to me. Down the start straight we tore off. We were neck and neck going into the first turn. Our bars banged so hard we nearly took each other out. There was no way I was going to budge, and we made it out of the first corner alive. I snagged the holeshot, but barely. Ezra made it clear that he wanted the lead by smashing plastic with me in the corners. And after St. Louis, I just didn't trust him. After showing me his wheel a few times, he made a mistake in the longest whoop section of the year and dropped to third. Doug Henry and I traded leads (he had the whoops wired that day) for the better part of four laps before Ezra came from nowhere to reclaim second. I had to give Ezra a lot of credit for his gutsy effort. He was riding with a separated shoulder and wasn't able to practice all week. Yet he was still turning fifty-eight-second laps, the fastest of the

'93 win.

Jeremy McGrath

night. He used a clever inside line to snake past me on a ninety-degree left-hand turn on lap twelve, and I fought feverishly to regain the lead.

I decided rather than risk crashing by trying to win the race, I would hold second and seal the championship. Ezra won the race but that didn't matter to me. As I crossed the finish line to capture the 1998 SX title, I felt like crying tears of joy. It was a tremendous load off my shoulders. I thought about how things went sour at Honda and the terrible season I had the prior year with Suzuki.

My mechanic, Randy Lawrence, used a Sharpie to draw a line canceling the No. 2 on my YZ's number plate. On the podium after the race, Fox gave me a T-shirt that had a No. 1 plate and the words I BELIEVE THIS IS MINE. Damn right it was.

Paging Jeff Emig . . . Are You Out There? . . . Anywhere?

Jeff Emig and I were heading in two directions. No former champion had fallen off the podium as fast as Jeff had. He went through a myriad of problems during the '98 season that included bad starts, injuries, and an overall lack of confidence. After a second at the first round in L.A. his results took a nosedive: fourteenth in Seattle, thirteenth in Atlanta, and assorted DNFs. In the semifinal at New Orleans, he slammed hard in the whoops, a microcosm of his lack of concentration. He injured his back and was officially out for the season.

Jeff would never win another AMA Supercross and was in danger of losing his factory ride. And that was the good news.

Good-bye to Lew

Back at home things between Lew and I were not going well. His constant partying had gotten completely old. It got to the point where my mom and Lew had gotten into it several times. I had mentioned it to him before but didn't really express how I felt. But that's how I am. I'll let things build up until everything comes bursting out. And

Lew and me.

that's exactly what happened with Lew. We had a huge blowup. Worse than we had ever argued about anything before. That's when I decided I couldn't deal with it and kicked him out. I gave him time to find a place, but we were through.

It was really emotional for me because, outside of Skip, Lew was my best friend. Before he left we had one of those talks that is so deep you realize what your friends mean to you. But we had to go our separate ways for now.

That wouldn't have been so bad for him, but I told him Clutch Films was done, as well. That got him. Up to that point, we split the money we made from Clutch. Shutting down the company wasn't a big deal to me at all because it was a side project. I wasn't going to miss the few hundred thousand we had made up to that point. But Lew helped to create Clutch and it was all he had, so he was pissed.

Things Go Sour at Fox

I had originally signed a two-year deal with Fox to wear their race gear. They were contracted to pay me $320,000 in '98 and no less then $175,000 for '99. I had it written into my deal with them that my contract would become void if my race schedule was significantly altered. Basically what that meant was if I was healthy and didn't ride both Supercross and the nationals, my contract would be no good. There were rumors for years that I secretly harbored the desire to race Supercross only. It's no secret that I wasn't crazy about riding nationals, but I did it anyway and felt I was the best when I fully concentrated. Anyway, at this stage in my career I felt the best thing for me to do was ride a Supercross-only schedule. I would, however, race selected nationals. And now that I had a Supercross-only contract, Fox claimed that my deal was void.

They were right. But here's the thing. We had agreed that they pay me my '98 wages on a quarterly basis. When they got word of my '99 SX-only deal, they stopped paying me for '98. They made their last payment on July 15, 1998. They still owed me $220,000.

With my new race schedule voiding my '99 Fox agreement, I was free to sign with another gear company. I chose the No Fear brand, which had just thrown its hat into the MX clothing wars.

When the No Fear contract was being put together it wasn't exactly a big secret. This industry is an extremely close-knit collection of people. If one person knows something, it won't be long before the rest of the MX community does. Since they knew I was leaving, Pete Fox really wouldn't communicate with me when called.

When I did sign with No Fear for '99, it was perfectly legal. But there was a hitch. Under the rules of my '98 agreement I obviously couldn't be photographed wearing anything but Fox. Enter Donn Maeda. The editor of *MXracer* magazine wanted to do an interview and photo shoot for an upcoming issue. I agreed, since I was friends with Donn at the time, but I told him that the only way I would do it is if he promised not to run the photos before January '99. My Fox contract was ended on December 31, 1998. He

Me in Fox gear.

agreed, so I headed to Barona Oaks and *MXracer* shot me wearing my brand-new No Fear gear. So what happened next? The issue of *MXracer* came out in the first week of December and Fox sued me for breach of contract. Maeda disrespected me big-time and caused me a lot of trouble. He basically cost me a shitload of money.

When I look back on it now, I probably should have done things differently. The biggest thing I would have done was never leave Fox. I could have made the most money with them. I just should have renegotiated a deal to ride Supercross only. If I had done that it's quite possible I would have finished out my career with them. I guess you live and learn.

Steel Roots

To produce *Steel Roots*, the first video from Clutch Films, it really only cost about $70,000. You're looking at costs for travel, film, and editing. Riders get about $1,000 for a day of riding, which is about the going rate in the FMX video world. But sometimes there are expenses you don't count on. We rented a chopper for some aerial shots and headed for Beaumont, California, where a series of massive doubles were built with the specific purpose of spending some quality time in the lower atmosphere.

When I saw the jumps I got a little chill. And I wasn't cold. I was scared to jump those things before I even got out of the car. There was a 110-foot double that required an entire afternoon just to work up the confidence. So you can imagine how I felt about the 120-foot double right next to it. To make matters worse, there was nothing around to warm up on. No 50- or 60-foot gaps, rhythm sections, or anything.

I was nervous about the whole thing, but with an entire crew I felt a ton of pressure to go through with it. I headed for the 110-footer in about fourth gear and lofted into the sky. Right away I knew I wasn't going to make it. When you don't have the distance on a huge jump like this all you can do is hang on. There's not even time to pray. Coming up short on big jumps is one of the leading causes of injuries. On an 80-foot double, freestyle ingenue Travis

Pastrana once landed short and separated his spine from his pelvis. On the videotape of the crash you can hear his mother scream, "Oh my God, I know he's dead this time!"

As I hit the crest of the second double (the object is to land smoothly down the backside), I slammed with a wicked force but managed to stay on the bike. The fork, however, was bent to hell. It cost Yamaha about $40,000 to replace it. I didn't even attempt the 120-foot one. I came back about a week later and made the first double, but not without going through another fork. Needless to say, Yamaha was pretty pissed.

The action jump that inspired Mattel's Tyco RC McGrath.

The most important skill a Supercross racer can possess is the ability to jump with technical precision. The more jumps there are on a track, the more time riders will spend in the air. And you want your wheels on the ground. There are two basic methods of jumping that you may want to choose from on any given lap. One will keep you as low as possible, the other will send you sailing.

Body Language Method

It's in your best interest to stay as low as possible over a jump. As you approach the face of the jump, lay off the throttle just before you take off.

You want to be in a squatting position with your weight forward. Lean the bike over slightly as you sail off the lip. The more you lean into the jump, the more it will go sideways. Use your right arm and leg to determine the amount of whip you'll need. This will keep you from sailing straight into the sky. With the throttle off, the rear wheel will instantly begin to slow down. It will also cause the rear end to rise. This will set you up to land on your front wheel with the gas on without losing forward momentum.

Rear Brake Method

This technique is one you will use less often. Its main purpose is getting you as much airtime as possible to clear a mammoth jump. It comes in quite handy when there is a big jump with very little runway. In this situation, you'll be on the throttle all the way to the face of the jump. When you take off, your bike will be at approximately the same angle as it was on the takeoff: The front wheel will be much higher than the rear. At the peak of the jump, tap the rear brake. This will stop the rear wheel causing the back end to rise giving you a floating sensation. You are now ready to land on your front wheel. Keep your head up to prepare for the next obstacle. Keep in mind: If you start to endo, crack the throttle to even the bike out.

Things Get Rocky with Kim

After the first six months, I kind of throttled back on my devotion to Kim. I was so crazy about her that I was running myself ragged trying to impress her. Things were moving a 100 miles an hour all the time, and I knew I couldn't keep up that pace. I was taking time away from my job to be with her and I decided that's something I could no longer do. I felt I needed to make some more time for myself, as well. Racing, sponsors, media, and friends were already putting tremendous demands on my time. Now Kim was in the mix. There was no time left for me. I thought toning things down would just be a natural progression of our relationship. But just as quickly as our love had sparked, hard feelings and resentment began to creep up.

I realized that I needed to look in the mirror and ask myself if this is what I really wanted. Yes, I was crazy about her, but I still needed to make sure that I was willing to go into this with a real sense of commitment. I felt like I had an angel on one shoulder and a devil on the other. The angel was telling me to start a life with Kim while the devil wanted me to party with naked chicks on the lake.

It didn't make things easier that my old girlfriends were so jealous. They would call my house and leave obscene messages. Sometimes when Kim would answer they would ask if they could come over and pick up their toothbrushes and panties. Once a couple of girls came over when Kim was home and made a scene out in front of my house. They peed in the bushes, rolled around in the lawn, and flashed themselves.

Just a bunch of really immature stuff. It was easy to see that I had made the right decision when I chose Kim over them.

Stuff like that just brought out worries Kim had about whether or not I would be completely faithful to her. My Canyon Lake lifestyle was no secret. She knew my friends and saw their party agenda. And because of that she hated that place. She just wanted both of us to get away from that environment.

She wanted this. I wanted that. We both were just really confused. Everything came to a head. We had a huge argument and emotions just poured out everywhere. The argument was really painful because it was the first time we had ever raised our voices at each other. Even so, I took care not to say anything that I would regret. I don't believe in cursing at someone you love even when things are not going well. In the past I would have thrown a girl out on the spot, but not with Kim.

The argument ended with us breaking up. Kim told me she was moving back to Colorado to start over. That really caught me off-guard, but I felt we just couldn't see each other's side.

Was that the end of us already? The next day Kim started to pack for Colorado and I left for Ryno's wedding in Las Vegas. Two days later, I called her to see if she had packed her things and made travel arrangements back to Colorado. Before I could even ask we both just poured out our emotions. Neither of us wanted this to end, but we needed to make compromises and get everything out in the open. I flew her to Vegas and from there we drove to the lake in Parker, Arizona, to spend the weekend ironing out our differences.

Kim had to understand that I was taking too much time away from racing to be with her and that would have to change. She also had to understand that it was impossible to keep up the pace of our first six months together. And I had to make it clear to her that I was in this for the long haul.

I knew that this was the girl I was going to marry. She was the one who was going to have my kids. At the same time, I knew I wanted to put my player past behind me, but I still felt the same temptations. I never cheated on Kim, even in the early stages of our relationship, but

I had to fight some of my old ways. I could have easily caved in but I was crazy about her and I didn't want to blow it. After all, it took me twenty-seven years to find her.

I realized I just had to concede and throw away my black book and all the numbers I accumulated over the years. I was scared to do that because it represented such a drastic change in my life, but it had to be done. When I did that our relationship blossomed. I thought focusing on one girl was going to be a difficult task, but it got easier every time

My 29th birthday.

Kim and I hung out. The more time I spent with her the more I loved her. I could be myself around Kim. I had a newfound security that didn't leave me wondering whether she really wanted me or my fame. She was real. For the first time in my life, the love was reciprocal.

But I still had to do more. I had to remove all doubt in Kim's mind (and mine) about me straying off the path. I decided to move out of Canyon Lake. Living there was too hard on our relationship. Too many distractions. I didn't need *Girls Gone Wild* in my backyard, so I put the house on the market.

The Dungeon was closed for business.

By 1999 there was almost nothing left to accomplish in my career. I knew where my bread was buttered, so I negotiated a Supercross-only contract with Yamaha. I would race a few select nationals, but I was all about the stadiums from here on out. Winning the title back in '98 proved to me that I was still the fastest, smartest, and most consistent rider on the track. I had won more races than all other riders combined and 55 percent of all the races I'd entered. That's twice the percentage of Jeff Gordon, who has owned NASCAR for the last five years. And with the exception of Mike LaRocco, no one has more second-place finishes than me either.

Motocross was the fastest growing sport in America. Bike sales had risen steadily since the late eighties and rare was the Supercross that didn't sell out. The sixteen-round series averaged over 50,000 fans per race. The television package with ESPN was the richest ever and the ratings were the highest since ABC used to air the USGPs at Carlsbad back in the eighties.

As a result of the higher visibility, I was able to bring more mainstream sponsors to the sport. Sponsors with deep pockets meant commercials that were seen by many. In 2000, I shot a 1-800-COLLECT spot with Alyssa Milano.

The expanded exposure was cool, but the shoot wasn't exactly the most memorable experience. It was out at Glen Helen on a really cold and miserable day. It was raining on and off and the crew had set up a bunch of heaters to keep everybody warm. I grew up watching *Who's the Boss?*, and to me Alyssa was always this hot little chick I was totally into. But when I met her on the set she wasn't nearly as cute as I remembered. I actually thought she was a little bit out of shape and her butt was kind of big. She was chain-smoking like crazy, so I wasn't impressed by that either.

When she came out of her trailer for our scene she promptly told the director that no one was taking a break until her scene was done.

Jeremy McGrath

She copped a total spoiled diva attitude. Her only goal was to get out of there as soon as possible. She pretty much regulated everybody and got the total princess treatment. We made small talk between takes, but I could tell she thought she was on higher ground and really only talked to a bunch of her friends that were on the set that day.

The cool thing about it was that my friend Andy Harrington was the stunt double for Alyssa when her character pulled the wheelie at the end of the commercial.

Even though the experience was a disappointment, I was pretty stoked to see the ad air during Wimbledon, Sportscenter, and a bunch of other shows I watched regularly.

With added exposure, I had to continue to deliver on the track. I won eight races in '99, which translated into a sixth Supercross championship. My eighty-three-point margin of victory over Ezra Lusk was the second largest of my career. Despite being twenty-nine years old, ancient by Supercross standards, I felt like I was at the top of my game.

On the podium with 1st place wins in Phoenix, Michigan, and Vegas, 1999.

Remember Me?

Do you ever wonder what happened to all your friends from high school? Well, that's what high school reunions are for. Actually, I really didn't want to see what the Perris High Class of '89 was up to, but Kim thought it would be a great idea so I let her talk me in to it. The reunion was held at the Embassy Suites in Temecula, not far from school. When I got there I was still pretty apprehensive about the whole thing. Whether you're into it or not, you still want to look your best and put your best face forward. That year I was in my best physical condition ever. Kim looked hot that night, so at least we had that covered. We drove my Acura NSX to the reunion and people started staring at us as soon as we pulled in the parking lot. When we got inside, the first thing that struck me was how different so many of my former classmates looked. More than a few hairlines and waistlines had changed. Most of them had stories about how they hated their 9–5 lifestyles or that they got dead-end jobs right out of high school, but some people were super cool.

So many people came up to me and congratulated me on my success and said they followed my career. Everyone was like, "I tell all my friends that I went to school with you." It made me feel good to see that everyone was so positive about my success.

One guy with a huge Afro I vaguely remembered was pretty pumped that I came. "When you won the Supercross title in '93," he said, "I was like 'damn!' In '94, I said, 'Damn, damn!' In '95, I was like, 'Daaaaamn!' In '96, I was like, 'You the man!'"

I was really curious to find out what had become of a girl named Kim Harris. I had big crush on her my senior year, but she wouldn't give me the time of day. She was so hot back then and to her I was just some weird motorcycle guy who was nowhere near her league. When she saw Kim and I, she came up to us, congratulated me, and asked for a picture.

I looked at her with a blank stare and said, "Too late, you had your chance." She stopped in her tracks and looked as if someone had just broken her heart. Even Kim was caught off-guard, but I was only kidding around. She snapped a picture and we quickly caught up on old times.

Jeremy McGrath

After the reunion was over, Kim and I talked all the way home about everything that happened. Kim was so excited about it and it wasn't even her high school. Driving home I thought I had made some pretty good decisions since I graduated high school.

And I was really glad Kim Harris never gave me the time of day.

Jenny from the Past

Over the next few days following my high school reunion, I started to wonder what became of other people from my past, particularly my first real girlfriend, Jennifer Thomas. She was the first girl I ever loved. It's hard to forget someone you experience so many powerful emotions with for the first time. I ran into her about six or seven years before and she had fallen on some tough times. Even though we had long since broken up, I didn't want to see her struggle, so I lent her about five or six hundred dollars.

I couldn't help to wonder what she was up to now. Her number was still in my Rolodex, and I gave her a call just as a friend. The vibe was really good, and we made plans to meet for lunch one afternoon. Even though I had good intentions, I still felt a little uneasy about trying to reunite with Jennifer. The couple times I talked to her I had to make sure Kim wasn't home. I wasn't cheating, but I felt bad because I was hiding something from her.

We both made a promise never to hide anything from each other, so I decided not to go through with the lunch. Even though I was curious about how Jennifer's life was, Kim's peace of mind was more important to me.

Next Stop, Encinitas

After I sold the Canyon Lake house, Kim and I moved back into my first home in Murrieta. The renters moved out and we stayed there while we hunted for a new house. I was all prepared for a long, drawn-out search when we began by checking out properties in a brand-new development in Encinitas, thirty miles north of San Diego.

A two-acre lot on the highest hill in the neighborhood just felt like the right spot, so I decided that was where we'd build our new house. With the help of an architect, I designed a gated 6,000-square-foot house with a pool, Jacuzzi, tennis court, and a separate garage that would house a weight room and more living space.

In the fall of '99, Kim and I moved out of the 1,400-square-foot Murrieta place and into our new home. Getting the house completed was an unbelievable undertaking. Kim was fully responsible for the house and decorating and I was responsible for the garage and the yard.

We spent so many hours picking out cabinets, paint, tile, furniture, and carpet that I felt like an expert. We went to this interior decorator place to pick out some carpet and the people were basically just a bunch of snobs who cater to even snobbier people. They looked at us like, "Who the hell do these young punks think they are?"

Picking out the carpet was an important step, because the carpet I had in Canyon Lake was not soft. When I watch TV I don't always want to sit on the couch. Sometimes I want to lie on the floor, so I had to make sure we got really soft carpet. They had all of these sample but they were packed in this huge book of samples. I took the book, set it on the floor, and rubbed my knees on each individual carpet sample page to simulate lying on the floor watching TV. The people there thought I was crazy, but at least I got the softest carpet.

Baggin' It

On one of her forays to the mall, Kim came across a Louis Vuitton bag that she couldn't be without. The bag had a pretty hefty price tag, so she thought that she would shop around to try to get it cheaper. With Christmas two months away, I looked at this as the perfect opportunity to improve in the gift-giving department.

After she first saw the bag, she looked everywhere but just couldn't find it. Even the first place she saw it had sold out. She was pretty bummed out but thought she'd have a good chance to find the bag in Europe while we were at one of the off-season exhibition Supercrosses.

On an off day at the Bercy SX in France, Kim and I walked all over Paris looking for the elusive bag. We covered over 100 blocks, going in every boutique and major department store, but our searched turned up nothing. We did everything but put out an all-points bulletin. Kim had pretty much given up on it.

Back in the States a couple of weeks later, we were at a local mall in Santa Ana when, much to our surprise, we found the bag in a women's clothing store. Kim was pretty shocked. I thought it would make a great Christmas present.

"I don't want you to get me something just because I want it," she said. "I want you to get me a Christmas present because it's something you want to get me."

I was a little confused but I took that to mean that she wanted the bag for Christmas. (That was my first mistake.) I got the bag for her that day and she was so happy to finally have it.

A month later we made plans to celebrate Christmas at my parents' house in Menifee, a forty-five-minute drive from Encinitas. A few days before Christmas, Kim had flown home to Colorado to spend time with her family. On Christmas Day she flew back to Southern California and drove to my parents' house. She arrived with a huge bag of gifts for everyone, including my sister Tracy, that looked like they had been professionally wrapped with heartfelt handwritten cards. There were unmarked packages and cards just so no one would be left out. But someone was left out: Kim.

I didn't get her anything because I thought the bag was her present. Kim was hurt because she thought that I forgot her. Almost instantly she looked as if she was about to cry. She was pretty pissed like any woman would be. The only thing that saved me was that she didn't want to make a scene in front of everyone. I was in deep shit. On the ride home she didn't say a single word. I thought she was going to rip into me when we got home, but she was too upset. I could tell that she was simmering for days.

A couple days after Christmas, I asked Kim why she wasn't carrying her bag around with her.

"I took it back," she replied. Every time she looked at the bag it reminded her of "The Night I Forgot Christmas." When she told me that, I did the smart thing. I kept my mouth shut.

Jimmy Is Paralyzed at San Diego

There have been many memorable dates in my career, but January 22, 2000, is one I'll always remember. Even though I wish I could forget it. The Supercross series was a good one for me so far after winning the first two events of the season in Anaheim. It was a typical Saturday afternoon practice session. Larry, Randy, and I were going over some adjustments from the first practice. They were trying to work out the

Jimmy Button and me.

kinks in the rear suspension while I tried to clear my mind of everything but the track. I still needed to figure out what was the fastest line through a couple of back-to-back hairpins because my corner speed wasn't where I wanted it to be.

The afternoon practice session was just getting underway when my teammate Jimmy Button headed out for the second session. He rolled onto the track in second gear and was kind of putting around looking for any changes in the track. Just looking for new lines, checking the condition of ruts that could cause a problem later that night.

He was riding about five MPH down the left side of the whoops on the first straight when his front tire got lodged in a hole and tossed him over the bars onto the ground. At 6'4", he was one of the tallest racers ever. Now he lay crumpled on the track. It was a total freak accident. I mean, he was going about as slow as you can go on a Supercross track. He barely even got dirty. But when he hit the ground he knew it wasn't good. His body went cold. Nothing worked. He couldn't move. He was paralyzed from the neck down. He had bruised the C-2, C-3, and C-4 vertebrae and torn the interior and posterior ligament in his neck. He was going five MPH!

When Brooks saw his body go limp, he also knew right away what had happened. But he didn't want to believe it.

"Get up, Jimmy! Get up!" Brooks screamed. He had hoped by some act of God that Jimmy would stand up and brush himself off. But Brooks knew that wasn't going to happen. Normally, when Button goes down he takes the moment to maybe wallow in the bit of attention a downed rider gets from anyone who's trackside. There had been plenty of times in the past when he washed out and his mom, Anita, went running over and he popped right up. But this was serious. In seconds, paramedics immobilized his body. At motocross events there's an ambulance on site at all times. He was rushed to nearby Sharps Medical Hospital in fifteen minutes. They put him in an MRI and gave him steroids to reduce the swelling. He stayed in intensive care for about two weeks.

After the ambulance took Jimmy away, a dark cloud fell over the afternoon. Everybody was just numb. Jimmy is always so full of life and always keeps the mood in the pits light. Now he was unconscious in a hospital bed instead of blasting the track on his thumper. The fact that his life changed in less than a second was sobering. All I could think about was Jimmy. My concentration was shot. Did they expect us to race that night? I finished fourth, but it meant nothing. Jimmy's accident was a grim reminder of the reality of motocross. Every time you throw a leg over a bike could be your last. That is scary.

He ended up staying at that hospital for sixteen days before being transferred to Barrow's Neurological Center in Phoenix to be close to his parents. The doctors listed him as an incomplete quadriplegic and fitted him with a halo to stabilize his neck. He spent the next five months with other spinal cord and stroke patients learning how to do simple things like tie his shoes and dial a phone. His early rehab was nothing more than opening and closing his fist. He'd do that all day long. Jimmy lost about 65 pounds of muscle and got down to 115 pounds. Remember that Jimmy is 6'4". His original prognosis was that he would be able to walk again, but not for two years at the earliest.

Jimmy shocked everyone when he began to take baby steps after a few weeks. One day, about two months after the crash, he took about five unassisted steps. The next day it was ten. Then fifty yards. Then a hundred. Around that time, Kim and I went to Arizona to spend a few

days with him during his rehab. His spirits were pretty high. We didn't even talk about the accident. He was just glad to see someone other than his doctors and therapist. Jimmy and I talked nearly every day when he was in Phoenix. To keep him motivated to come all the way back,

Jeremy McGrath

we decided that if I won the Supercross title he would have to present me with the supercross championship trophy at the season-ending AMA banquet in Las Vegas in May. Going down the stretch run in April, I had a pretty big point lead and sealed the deal with a win in Joliet, Illinois, at the second to last round. The 2000 Supercross title was my seventh.

My last championship celebration.

To hold up his end of the bargain, Jimmy was in therapy ten hours a day, seven days a week. "Just to get up four stairs and onto the stage," he told me. Even though he had a miraculous recovery, he was still very weak and frail. At the banquet, Jimmy struggled to climb the stairs with the help of his trainer, Cory Worf. As Jimmy painstakingly took his wobbly steps, Cory kept him steady by gently pulling him forward by his belt loops. When Jimmy made it to the top, the crowd erupted with a standing ovation. There wasn't a dry eye in the place. It was heart-wrenching to see how someone who was once so free was now so dependent on others to do simple things like walk and tie his own shoes. Many riders saw their own mortality in Jimmy. At the same time it was uplifting to see what kind of fighter Jimmy had become and that his spirit and willpower were very much alive. I'll remember that day as one of the special moments of my career.

Getting back on his feet financially was almost as difficult as his rehab. His bills soared to $14,000 a week and he wasn't working. He had

Jimmy Button and me (front row) at the 2000 awards banquet In Las Vegas. This was Jimmy's first appearance since the accident.

a brand-new house to worry about, so I paid his mortgage until he got back on his feet. When he went looking for a job in the motorcycle industry, a lot of people turned him away because they were afraid that his body was still too frail. He went from being given everything to people refusing to even take a chance on him. The job prospects were slim until Bell Helmets signed him as a rep to make sure its riders were taken care of on race day. That was cool for me, because Bell was one of my main sponsors, so Jimmy and I got to hang out at the races.

About a year and a half ago, Jimmy got back on a motorcycle for the first time since the accident. He just putted around a parking lot in first gear, but it was a huge milestone. He'll probably never be able to throw on a helmet and go play-riding on a Sunday afternoon, but he's come to terms with that.

Today Jimmy runs one of the largest action sports management firms, named, appropriately, Action Sports Management. His talent roster includes almost thirty of today's rising MXers, skateboarders, BMXers, and snowboarders.

Jeremy McGrath

Emig Breaks His Back

Unfortunately, Jimmy wasn't the only rider to suffer a career-ending injury in 2000. On May 4, while practicing at Stephane Roncada's practice track, Jeff Emig broke his back when his throttle got stuck and sent him sailing thirty feet into the air. When he crashed to the ground he thought he was going to die.

In the fall of that year, DC Shoes ran a two-page ad in *Racer X Illustrated* that had Jeff and Jimmy sitting side by side displaying the halo and back braces they had to wear during their arduous rehabilitations. The copy had a cryptic reality and read in part as follows. "Greatness has a price. More so than any other sport, motocross is the ultimate combination of man and machine. Dangerous and brutal in nature, when juxtaposed against the teeth-chattering racing background, it can be poetry in motion. DC recognizes the beauty and reality and understands the sacrifices some of the best have made to elevate motocross to a new level."

"Nobody rides for free," Emig was quoted as saying in the ad. It's a simple truth.

Jeff decided that after twelve years of professional motocross it was time to throw in the towel. His career went through a series of unexpected ups and down in his later years. In the summer of '99, he was arrested for marijuana possession in Lake Havasu and was fired by Kawasaki. For the first time in ten years he was without a factory ride. He bounced back with a surprise win a month later at the '99 U.S. Open of Supercross. He had won four championships (125 MX, 250 MX twice, 250 SX) and amassed thirty-seven Supercross and national wins, which was good for eighth on the all-time wins list.

Despite our differences and our sometimes rocky relationship, Jeff was one of the toughest guys I've ever faced. When we weren't feuding, we were putting in some of the best battles in motocross history.

Jeff's official farewell party was thrown in typical Jeff style—glitz, glam, and Armani suits—at the MGM Grand in Las Vegas at the U.S. Open the following October.

MC'S FIVE WORST CRASHES

If there is one thing I'm known for other than winning, it's not crashing. I rarely crashed because I was always in control. I was always in control because I never rode above my head. But here's what happened when I did:

1992 Mt. Morris MX
MASSIVE ENDO

Injuries: Separated left shoulder, broken right leg, concussion, blurred vision.

Foggy Memories: It was real muddy that day and my ignition kept cutting in and out. Over a huge sixty-foot downhill double it cut out for good, sending me over the bars. My bike landed on top of me and packed me into the ground.

1997 Steel Roots I
MISSING THE LEDGE

Injuries: Total body soreness.

Foggy Memories: We were shooting some jumping scenes for *SRI* at Ocatillo Wells when I flew over this huge jump onto a small landing area. I came up short and my front wheel went over a little ledge, causing me to endo off of it. It didn't look that bad but it knocked the crap out of me.

1998 Pontiac SX
CASING THE TRIPLE

Injury: Broken right wrist, concussion.

Foggy Memories: While leading the race, I came up short on a triple, cased the landing, and got slammed into the berm. I was completely dazed and struggling to my feet when Larry Ward, going

Jeremy McGrath

high in the berm, accidentally knocked me down again.

1998 Steel Roots II
COMING UP SHORT

Injuries: Torn chest muscles, bruised shoulders.

Foggy Memories: I cased a huge uphill step-up. I didn't
actually crash, but it hurt so bad I wanted to cry. I
was holding on to the bars so hard my pectoral
muscles tore away from the bone. My bike was toast.
I ended up bending my frame, handlebars, and forks.
The forks bent so bad they stuck in permanently.
I still can't believe I saved it.

2002 KTM Practice Crash
OVER THE BARS EJECTION

Injury: Dislocated hip.

Foggy Memories: Much like Mt. Morris in '92, my bike
sputtered but I kept going. I landed on my feet but
folded over so far that my hip popped out. Definitely
the worst pain I've felt in my life.

Motocrossed

Another cool experience I had that year was shooting some riding scenes for the Disney movie *Motocrossed* starring Alana Austin. *Motocrossed* has kind of an odd cult following in the industry. Even though the movie is geared toward kids, most moto people dig it because it's another step into the mainstream. The movie is about a girl named Andrea Carson who takes her injured brother's spot on their family's motocross team and is able to hang with the big boys. At the

same time she has to hide the fact that she's a girl despite falling in love with her main competition. The shoot was at Barona Oaks, where I won those scooters back in '88. Steve Lamson was the other stunt rider that day. Travis Pastrana also rode for the shoot. It was pretty easy. They put me on a YZ 426 and we just did a few jumps and rode the whoops. In the movie, a French rider is hired to take Andrea's spot on the team and portrayed as a stereotypical rude Frenchman. It would have been much easier if they had just gotten David Vuillemin to play the part.

Teen Choice Awards

Later that year I was asked to be a presenter at the Teen Choice Awards in L.A. I thought that would be a pretty cool thing to do, so Kim and I got all decked out and headed up the 5. The ceremony was held at this huge hangar at the Santa Monica Airport. When I got there I saw nothing but kids everywhere. I've never felt so old. I didn't realize until I got there that I was way overdressed. I was rockin' my Rolex with a nice shirt and some dress shoes. Talk about really feeling strange and old.

All the kids there were all decked out in skater gear. I would have felt better in a T-shirt, baggy jeans, and some DC Shoes.

When we got to the airport, we had to go to a designated parking lot about a mile away. Then we got in a limo and they drove us to the red carpet. They had about a dozen limos all on a continuous loop that all the celebrities had to use. It seemed like everyone was big pimpin' in a limo, but they were only going a block.

On the red carpet, I bumped into Stone Cold Steve Austin, who knew who I was right away. He was such a cool guy and super excited to meet me and vice versa. In turned out that he has a house about fifteen minutes from Kim and me. He actually lives about ten minutes from Skip.

Inside it was funny to see how they have people fill in empty seats between takes. I presented an award, which was a hollowed-out surfboard, to Blink 182 with Rachel Leigh Cooke, who starred in *She's All That*. She was super nice and a cutie, but I was really surprised at how tiny she was.

An Evening with Jay

Shortly after the Teen Choice Awards, I headed to Burbank for a guest spot on the *Tonight Show* with Jay Leno. The producers wanted me on but decided to spice up the show beyond the everyday sit and chat. They brought in Travis Pastrana, a dozen tons of dirt, and the Dirt Wurx track builders. We had an old-fashioned race on the back lot. Travis had shot to dizzying heights in the freestyle motocross world in '99 thanks to

the X Games when he launched his RM into San Francisco Bay the previous summer.

The stage and back lot of the *Tonight Show* were turned into a mini Supercross course. We each ran one timed lap around the track that

started on the stage, went out of the studio doors to the mini track on the lot, then back inside. Travis, a natural-born showoff much like myself, nearly lost it several times around the track, drawing huge oohs from the studio audience. After Travis' run, I negotiated the makeshift track a good five seconds quicker than he did for the crown of Late Night Supercross champ. Riding through the tight studio hallways was a little sketchy, but I haven't worked on my throttle control the last fifteen years for nothing. Jay presented me with a trophy and promised to invite us back next year.

The Rodman Experience

One time I was in Las Vegas with my close friend Grayson Goodman, who I've been racing with since the eighties, and another buddy of mine, Pepe. Both of those guys are good friends with Dennis Rodman and introduced me to him that weekend. I was totally shocked at how normal he was. People have this idea that Dennis is this out-of-control partier who is constantly living over the edge, but in reality he's super relaxed. Everyone always put a ton of pressure on him to "act like Dennis Rodman," but he just likes to have fun like anyone else. We all ended up going out and drinking Kamikazes that night. Dennis easily pounded about eight without flinching.

After that night, we became pretty good friends and Lew and I occasionally go up to his bar, Slocum's, in Newport and down a few with him. I'm a huge fan of the NBA and try to go to as many games as possible. Button and I usually hit a few Lakers playoff games after the Supercross season is over.

Lakers trainer Dan Garcia introduced Button and I to Shaquille O'Neal, who has been known to throw his leg over a bike every now and then. When Shaq and I were introduced he couldn't get over the fact that I was *only* 5' 10". "Let's go riding, man!" he said. Most people usually say that, but could you imagine all 7' 2" of Shaq trying to make it through the whoops?

The Return of Skip

All that stuff is fun and I'm glad I've been in a position to experience it. But I'm a motorcycle racer. And even though the 2000 Supercross season was one of my best ever, I needed something to raise my game and get my focus back to where it was in the mid-nineties.

Actually, I needed someone.

Skip doing his thing.

For the 2000 season, I left Chaparral Yamaha to become the first rider ever to field his own team, Team McGrath Racing/Mazda/Yamaha. Becoming a team owner was a thrill, but the list of things you have to do to get a project like that off the ground is a mile long. You have to learn the intricacies of running a business on the fly, which includes payroll, insurance, and hiring employees.

Just getting your semi up and running can be overwhelming. There is a mountain of paperwork for that, as well. Proper registration, getting a driver, parking permits, canopies, paint jobs, and periodic maintenance must be kept in check. At about three miles to the gallon at $1.65 a gallon, it cost $20,000 just to drive the rig to all sixteen events. And we didn't even do nationals.

One of the most important steps in running a successful team is securing top-flight sponsors to help fund the venture. We were really lucky to have

Mazda on board. We followed that up with Bud Light. They stepped up the Team McGrath effort with television commercials and an in-store ad campaign that featured life-size cutouts of me. Having high-profile sponsors is one thing that I'm proud to say I've brought to the sport with the help of my former business partner, Jeff Surwall.

After hiring the rest of the staff you can't just leave it up to someone to run your team for you. It's a seven-day-a-week job. I hired Larry Brooks to manage for me, so I felt the team was in good hands. We hadn't yet stepped into the realm of hiring another rider. That was a bit down the road, not to mention a whole new ball game.

Oh yeah, and I had to race, too.

A Kid Named Ricky

In my career I have stiff-armed all comers, roosted in the face masks of nineteen other riders on a weekly basis, and pretty much handed out royal ass whooping to my challengers. Damon Bradshaw, Mike Kiedrowski, Jeff Emig, Ezra Lusk, and Kevin Windham can all speak to that. But going into the 2001 Supercross season, I would face the toughest challenge of my career in a 5'5" redheaded, twenty-year-old Floridian named Ricky Carmichael. As a member of Team Green, RC had racked up more amateur national championships than any rider in history. At twenty, his resume made him a lock for the MX Hall of Fame. He won a 250 national championship ('00), three 125 outdoor titles ('97, '98, '99), and a 125 East SX crown ('98). Since his first full season as a pro in 1997 he has won an outdoor title every year. But he was still working out the kinks indoors. In 2000, he finished fifth overall in the 250 Supercross points standings. He won his first ever 250 SX race at Daytona, which closely mimics an outdoor course.

When Ricky was ten years old, he came out to stay with me for a weekend at my house in Murrieta. He was just happy to be hanging out with the guy whose poster he had on his wall back in Florida. There was something about the way he rode his KX 80 even back then. You could tell he was destined for greatness.

Carmichael reminds a lot of people of Bob Hannah. Sometimes it seems he has no idea when to let off the throttle. Or maybe he simply refuses to. Even with his accomplishments, he was still a super squirrel. In his first 250 Supercross season in '99, Carmichael was a human

Left and page 262: Winning the last race, 2001.

crash-test dummy. He managed to slam himself out of no less than five races. His reckless speed sometimes made him the fastest rider on the track, but he wasn't much of a threat because he couldn't finish a race.

And when he crashed, he bit it hard.

Jeremy McGrath

With the big boys, he found he couldn't get away with the same out of control riding that saw him become the winningest 125 rider in history. But by 2001, he had learned enough self-control to make him a serious contender for the crown. Even though I was ten months shy of thirty, I still felt I was the favorite to win my eighth title in nine years.

In the first race of the season, I took the win at Anaheim, making me seven for of nine all-time at Anaheim. The next round in San Diego saw Ricky win his second career race. I countered with another win at Anaheim, then a second at Phoenix. It seemed like things were about to get real interesting, but Ricky just kept winning. After round five at Anaheim he didn't lose another race. His thirteen-race win streak tied the record I set back in '96. I finished second to RC in the final points standings by sixty-four points. People looked at it as a down year, but I actually had just one fewer podium finishes than when I won the title in '98. And after all, second place is nothing to scoff at, but people look at it as a bad year when you've won as much as I have.

Will You Marry Me?

Kim and I had been dating for about four and a half years, and I knew she was the girl I wanted to spend the rest of my life with. I've never loved or cared about any woman the way I did about Kim. When we first started dating I knew she was the one, even back then. Now it was time to pop the question. We had talked about it but not seriously. We both knew it was eventually going to happen but we had no idea when.

After the '01 Vegas Supercross in May we had planned our annual trip to Lake Mead, where we would spend a week on a houseboat. All of our friends went, including Jimmy and Kristi, Lew and his girl, Lori, and bunch of other people up from Dallas. The actor Jeremy London, who is a good friend of mine, and his wife, Astrid, came too. Jeremy brought his remote control planes and we took turns flying them.

It was a pretty relaxed weekend without a whole lot to do. It was all about being with friends. We'd take the boat out, play horseshoes, barbecue, fish, get some sun, and just try to relax. So I decided that I was going to propose to Kim on our trip. I would take her out on the water, just us two, and ask her to be my wife.

Kim and me at the World SX, 2002.

So the day I planned to pop the question, things didn't exactly work out the way I'd hoped. We were all playing horseshoes and downing some beers. Then Kim started going for it and got a little tipsy. I decided not to ask her then because I wanted her to be a little more aware of what I was saying. I ended up waiting to ask her until the morning. That meant I had to sweat over it for one more night.

The next day we slept in until noon then took a boat ride by ourselves. It was a beautiful afternoon, and we parked the boat in a cove

Jeremy McGrath

and went swimming. The whole time I was completely distracted with the question I was about to ask. Back in the boat we toweled off and I pulled out the ring and waited for the right moment. Sebastian Tortelli's mother-in-law is a jeweler in France and she'd made a beautiful ring, so I couldn't wait to see Kim's expression.

Ever since I was a kid I've always wondered how it would go when I finally proposed to someone. It always looks so smooth in the movies, so I didn't think it would be that hard.

I was so wrong.

I've never been more nervous than I was in the moments leading up to the question. I was sweating, my hands were shaking, and I couldn't concentrate on anything Kim was saying. I was waiting for the right moment to tell her how much I loved her and that I wanted us to spend the rest of our lives together. I had so much I wanted to tell her. But man, I just couldn't get it out. We were talking and talking and I couldn't find the right time.

She knew I was acting a little weird because I was answering her with yes and no answers. Finally, I found the words. It wasn't smooth at all. She thought I was kidding because of the way I led into it. I was trying the best I could, but it was really hard to get it to flow out right. I asked her to be my wife and she said yes. When I gave her the ring she started to cry right away. We set our wedding date for August 3, 2002.

Another Evening with Jay

Two days after Kim and I got back from Lake Mead, we headed up to Burbank for my second appearance on the *Tonight Show*. Last year's episode with Travis was one of their highest-rated shows of the year, so they welcomed us back with open arms. But it doesn't hurt that Jay is such a gearhead either.

Dirt Wurx brought in the dirt and built the track again on the back parking lot. Jay had to park his Corvette about fifty yards away from his personal space, but he didn't seem to mind. This year the big difference

McGrath vs. Carmichael, 2001.

was my opponent. Travis was injured and RC had just won his first Supercross title, so it made sense to match us up. Travis was there to serve as an announcer. After getting used to the course in an afternoon practice session, I headed to my dressing room to get some rest. Kim and my publicist, Cheryl, entertained visitors and talked about the wedding while I stretched out on the floor. Jay arrived about an hour before showtime and popped his head in. "I can see you're really nervous about tonight," he joked when he saw me sprawled out in my racing gear. Jay asked about our wedding plans and Kim proudly showed off her rock. Travis hung out with us and got embarrassed every time someone recognized him.

After Jay left, the show's other guest, Christopher Titus, popped over and talked motorcycles for a while. *Tonight Show* producer Tracy Anderson came in to brief us on how the show was supposed go. Afterward, I signed Jay's autograph book, which he has all of his guests sign. It's cool to flip through and see all the celebrity signatures. I put my John Hancock right under The Rock and Calista Flockhart, who were on the show the day before.

Once onstage, Jay, RC, and I engaged in some playful banter. RC poked fun at my age with a comment about my facial hair. Real funny, but enough talk. Like last year, the course started on the stage where Jay does his monologue. From there it headed through the studio, out a backstage exit to the track, back in, and across the finish onto the stage.

After a quick coin flip, I elected to go first. You have to turn in a pretty flawless ride on a track as short as this. There were two huge thirty-foot jumps on the track and a handful of berms. The track was really tight, but I could do it in my sleep. I blasted the course pretty easily and felt like I got a time that would be tough to beat. When I crossed the finish line, the clock registered 46.7 seconds. RC was up next. He rode pretty well, what you'd expect from RC. When he popped his KX back onstage, the race clock stopped at 46.6 seconds. RC edged me by a tenth of a second. I didn't sweat it. I was just glad our sport was getting this kind of exposure. I'd see Ricky next January in Anaheim when it really counted.

Bag It

To avoid getting air filter oil all over your hands when applying it to your filter, put the filter in a plastic bag then apply the oil. Massage in gently then install filter. Rubber gloves won't hurt either.

Can You Spare a Nickel?

If you've ever crashed (you have) and had the bars tear out the end of your grips, put a nickel in the bottom of your grips before installing them. You'll save a fortune on grips.

Give Me a Brake

Everyone knows how annoying it is when you take your front wheel off and someone pulls your front brake. You have to take a screwdriver and pry apart your brake pads. Just stick a piece of cardboard between your pads beforehand and problem solved.

Feeling Exhausted?

Need a place to keep your rear axle when working on your bike? Just pop it in your silencer (make sure it fits first). Now you won't lose it. If you do, you'll find it. Eventually.

Chain of Events

Proper chain maintenance is a must. Use a wire brush to scrape away any excess dirt from the chain before applying chain lube. This will prevent the oil from seeping inside the rollers and clogging them with grains of dirt.

Jeremy McGrath

Training Daze

Almost immediately following the 2001 season, I began to train for the next season. My focus was total and my attention undivided. I was destined to be in the best shape of my career. I concentrated on improving

my stamina through extensive cardiovascular workouts. I also wanted to target my upper body and arms. I shed about 10 pounds to get down around 165.

My training had gone well all summer, but this particular off-season seemed especially long. I couldn't wait to get back on the track and deal with Ricky Carmichael.

I thought I was preparing myself by training harder than I ever had, but in reality I was hurting myself. While making me stronger, my training had a negative effect, as well. When I rode, my forearms would tighten up and throb with pain to the point that I could barely grip the handlebars. The dreaded arm pump. Every racer has experienced it at some time in his career. It's a part of racing, but sometimes when you overtrain it can render you almost useless on the course. With arm pump, you can't attack the track. You can't dive in and out of the corners or maintain a blistering pace over the course of twenty motos. During the 2002 Supercross season I was feeling it every time I rode.

It was having a devastating effect on my results. For the first three races of the season, I finished thirteenth, tenth, and ninth. I didn't get on the podium until round eight in Atlanta with a third. I've never entered a season with more hunger and desire than I came into this season. As a result, I felt a tremendous mental letdown when I wasn't getting the results I wanted.

The arm pump was taking everything out of me. Meanwhile, RC got off to a terrible start to the season when he DNF'd at round one in Anaheim. By round five he was back on track and had the points lead at the end of March. But I was still suffering. I had hit my conditioning peak back in December, a month before the season started. I was feeling completely drained by the middle of the season. It was so frustrating that all my hard work in the off-season wasn't paying off in the least.

It got to the point that I wouldn't ride during the week to let my arms rest so they wouldn't bother me on Saturday. Toward the latter half of the season the arm pump began to work itself out and I consistently finished fourth or fifth. My best race came at Dallas where I took another third. I ended the season third in the final points standings while Ricky won his second straight 250 Supercross title.

MC'S FIVE GREATEST HITS

Even though I didn't win a Supercross in 2002, I still finished that year with eight more total wins than the active rider in the No. 2 spot (RC's eighty). A win is a win, but here are my top five greatest races of all time.

1992 San Jose SX

SAN JOSE STADIUM

Win No. 13

Bike: Honda CR 125

I crashed on the start and was dead last. By lap thirteen, I passed a stunned Damon Huffman for the lead.

1993 Anaheim SX

ANAHEIM STADIUM

Win No. 14

Jeremy McGrath

Bike: Honda CR 250

My most memorable win ever. It still feels like yesterday
when I passed my teammate Jeff Stanton for good.
This race announced me to the world.

1993 Gainesville MX

Win No. 24

Bike: Honda CR 125

This was my first 125 outdoor win. The race was
special because I battled tooth and nail with Erik
Kehoe (current Team Honda manager). We passed
each other back and forth for thirty-five straight
minutes.

1996 Daytona SX

DAYTONA INTERNATIONAL SPEEDWAY

Win No. 58

Bike: Honda CR 250

There were so many skeptics that said I couldn't win this
race. I won it three times, but the first was the best
because there's nothing I love more than proving
people wrong.

1996 Motocross des Nations

JEREZ, SPAIN

(Does not count toward AMA win total)

Bike: Honda CR 250

In '93, my first des Nations team, I was clearly the weak
link and was so bummed with myself. But in '96, I
dominated, winning both of my motos. I had this crazy
feeling that there was no way I was getting beat that
day.

I Don't Accept Charity. Period.

Going into the 2002 season finale in Las Vegas, I didn't know it at the time, but the 155th time I lined up for a 250 main event was going to be my last. I just wanted to win this race more than anything. By round sixteen, I was finally starting to get my rhythm back. Arm pump was no longer a factor and my lap times in practice were as fast as Ricky's. I won my heat race and pocketed $4,000 (a little cushion for the night of gambling ahead). Even though I finished fifth in the main, I wasn't too worried. Bummed, but not worried. I was already looking ahead to next year.

Carmichael won and capped his second straight 250 Supercross championship by whipping his bike parallel to the earth over the finish-line jump. I didn't care. The only thing I could think about was next season.

I had finished third in the final points standings, which equaled my lowest ranking ever. It was considered throughout the motocross community as a failure. For me. Not for anyone else. Do you know how many guys would die to finish third? At the time there were only four other active 250 racers who had ever finished third or higher. And I did it as a thirty-year-old when most guys twenty-six are

considered ancient in this sport. I had become a victim of my own success. I was competing against my own legend, and the legend got better holeshots and was a lot faster through the whoops than I was.

The next night after the race was the annual season-ending AMA awards banquet at the Joint at the Hard Rock Hotel. All the riders get all tuxedoed out and the wives and girlfriends spend hours on their hair and getting dresses. After RC, Travis Preston, and Chad Reed were given awards for winning the 250, 125 West, and 125 East classes, respectively, I was given the 100 percent Award. It was designated for the rider who showed the most heart and refusal to quit in the face of huge odds.

I felt like they were doing it as if to say "Don't worry about it Jeremy, here's an award just to let you know we still care about you." But I didn't like that. They gave me that award for nothing. When I heard my name called I was caught completely off-guard. I got to the mike and had nothing to say except maybe about ten words. I was too stunned to speak. I've poured my heart and soul into making this sport what it is today and I don't need a courtesy award as an extra pat on the back. The prize that came with the award was an all-expense paid trip for my family to anywhere in the world. But why were they giving it to me? I felt stupid because I was thinking everyone else in the crowd knows that I didn't have my best year, so why would I accept this. It was a nice gesture, but I earn what I get.

More and more people were asking me when I was going to retire. I knew I wasn't dominating the way I did when I was twenty-four, but do you know any athlete who was better at thirty than twenty-four? It's just reality. Even though I was one of only three thirty-plus riders on the circuit, the retirement questions bothered me. Winning is what matters to me, but I was still racing because I loved the sport. I love how my bike feels when it snaps off the line. I love how the exhaust smells. I love perfectly executing a tricky rhythm section. I love the moments of anticipation when I'm riding from the pits to the starting gate while Skip is on the back of the bike hoping our weeklong preparations pay off.

And I still love the hell out of throwing down nac-nacs.

I didn't fear retirement. I never tried to lose sight of the fact that I was blessed to be doing this as long as I had. I believe that everyone has a fifteen-year maximum window to ride at a high competitive level. If you're lucky, that is. I started racing at sixteen and never really raced minis all that much. So at twenty-six, twenty-seven, or twenty-eight my body wasn't wrecked beyond repair and my mind wasn't burnt to a crisp. I still felt fresh. My desire hadn't waned. If anything, my passion had intensified. That's how much I love this sport.

As far as retirement was concerned, I was never afraid that I wouldn't know when to say when. I've got my pride like everyone else. I will never just cruise around in eighth or tenth place to collect a paycheck. No one would want to see that. I was never going to be Willie Mays floundering in the outfield, and by the end of the 2002 Supercross season, I was nowhere near that.

I was still one of the three best riders in the world.

Charlie's Angels

In the summer of 2002, I filmed a cameo in the sequel to the box office hit *Charlie's Angels*. The shoot was in Long Beach where the filmmakers had Dirt Wurx build a pretty gnarly track in a huge coal pit. I was a big fan of the first movie, so I was pumped to shoot a scene in the sequel. Working with Cameron Diaz was such a cool experience. She was so down to earth and friendly. Drew Barrymore was cool, too. I had met them both before when they came out to a race in Anaheim. I didn't get to meet Lucy Liu because she wasn't on the set that day. I told Cameron that I was really nervous about my scene even though I played myself. In the scene, Cameron rides up next to me and I kind of call her out by raising seven fingers to sort of say "I've got seven titles. What do you got?"

The director McG was super rad and made things fun, but I really didn't know what I was doing because I'm not an actor. "Don't worry about anything," Cameron said. "It's got to be a lot harder to do what you do."

"I don't know about that," I replied, "because I have no idea what I'm supposed to do."

Leaving Yamaha

When I left Yamaha, I was amazed at how history repeated itself. Once again I experienced a disheartening fiasco when it came to signing a contract extension when it should have been cut-and-dry. Yamaha was beginning to settle up their roster for 2003 during the middle of the '02 season. Since I was struggling, they tried to use that against me. I didn't want to go to the bargaining table until my results improved.

My plan was to race for Yamaha/McGrath Racing one last year and retire a Yamaha man for life at the end of the 2003 season. For me, 2003 wasn't going to be some sad farewell tour with middle-of-the-pack results. I would have given Carmichael all he wanted. But they didn't see it that way.

Things got delayed for one reason or another and it wasn't until late spring when Yamaha team manager Keith McCarty put a deal on the table. The deal was for $300,000. Not a bad amount of money, but it was less than half the $750,000 they paid me in 2002. All I wanted was the same amount, no more no less. Considering what I had done for their race program, that wasn't asking much. They had guys signed for way more than that who had never won a 250 race.

I was hurt. That offer was an insult. It caught me completely off-guard. It was hard to remain composed and bite my tongue when I saw the contract. Before any of that even came about I was already thinking about strengthening my team, McGrath Racing. We had worked tremendously hard at developing the team, and I felt like it was time to hire a rider. I had my eye on Chad Reed, the twenty-year-old Australian who rode for Yamaha of Troy. Chad had just won the 2002 125 East Supercross title and looked to be a top 250 rider for years to come.

Throughout his career, Chad looked up to me the way I did to Rick John-son. He's often quoted as saying he modeled his style after mine, which explains his love for stadium tracks.

To sign Chad, I needed the factory support of Yamaha in terms of supplying bikes, parts, and other means of support. But I needed to have my own deal done with Yamaha before I could realistically go af-ter Chad. That would be a moot point. Yamaha had forbidden Chad from talking to McGrath Racing because the factory was interested in sign-ing him. They told him that if he rode for my team he wouldn't be get-ting factory support. That's enough to easily scare a young rider away from a situation like McGrath Racing.

When a factory pulls a power play like that it's almost impossible to compete with. I was out of the loop, which sucked because I lost Chad and trust in Yamaha.

Right then that told me that this wasn't a team situation. Yamaha had no interest in helping me or McGrath Racing. They only allowed me to have a team because I was the rider. They totally tried to crush my effort to stay involved in motocross as a team owner. A couple months

Jeremy McGrath

later, Yamaha signed Chad to their 250 team for the 2003 season. I realized how quickly people can turn their back on you when they "find something better." Yamaha left me out in the cold. Nice way to pay back a guy who got them their first title since 1981.

I had won three championships and twenty-seven races for Yamaha, but still left feeling like their program was a distant second to Honda's. At Honda, each year the engineers would lay out ten cylinders for me to test so I could customize the bike's power delivery to suit my needs. In four years at Yamaha, we must have tested three cylinders total. Honda technicians made the bike conform to the rider. Not the other way around.

Ricky Carmichael had ridden Kawasakis his entire life and thought he had it pretty sweet. When he joined Honda in 2002, he couldn't believe the level of commitment he found. Fortunately for him, he found out by joining Honda. I found out by leaving.

But that's nothing more than the past. Now all I cared about was the future. I decided to look for a new home to finish my career. So that's precisely what Larry Brooks and I did. We talked with Kawasaki, Suzuki, and KTM. Everyone at those teams was cool, but KTM stood out the most.

Mrs. Jeremy McGrath

On August 3, 2002, Kim and I got married at the St. Regis resort in Monarch Beach, California. In front of about 300 of our closest friends and family, we said our vows just as the sun was setting. A cool breeze blew off the ocean, which was no more than a few yards away. It was one of the best days of my life. I knew she was the one but that didn't stop me from being completely nervous. I had the same feeling I had when I proposed.

The ceremony was presided over by Minister Steve Hudson, who is known to the motocross community as the Supercross Chaplain and is a really fun guy. It was so great to see so many people that were important to me at our wedding. My parents, my grandma Jeannne, Kim's parents, David and Linnea Maddox, and her grandmother, Dolly, were all glowing with pride. Kim's best friend Piper Lindgren was the maid of honor and Laurie Porter was the matron of honor. The bridesmaids were my sister, Tracy, Button's fiancée, Kristi, Mande Nantkes, Kila Green, and Katrina Gaede. Lew was my best man and Button, Brooks, Skip, Scott Bell, Victor Sheldon, and Doni Wilson were the groomsmen.

We spent the next two weeks in Hawaii on our honeymoon at the Mauna Lani Bay Hotel. For the first week Kim and I played tennis and just chilled by the poolside. There was still a buzz at the hotel because Nicholas Cage and Lisa Marie Presley got married there the same week we arrived. The following week, Jimmy, Kristi, Brooks, and Terri joined us in Maui.

On the plane ride back to California, I started to think about all of the work I was going to have to put in on the new KTM. It was going to be a long road but I was ready to get started.

Hip Trouble

After racing in Europe for three years on a four-stroke Honda, KTM hired Ryan Hughes to work with 125 rider Billy Laninovich and help with testing and setting up the bikes. In August, Ryno was the first person to ride my KTM 250SX to see what the bike needed done to it.

Shortly after returning from Hawaii with Kim, I began to seriously test the new KTM. Right away I loved the bike. It had tons of power and was really fast. It was fast enough that I felt like I had a good shot at winning back the title. Skip and I tested at the KTM track nearly every day. I was really beginning to get a good feel for the bike after about fifteen hours of seat time. Late in September, Skip and I were wrapping up a pretty good practice session when I decided to put in two more laps for good measure.

Through the rhythm section the bike bogs down and sends me over the bars. When I land on the face of the next jump, my body folds over forward and I dislocate my hip as I slam into the dirt. It was the most pain I had ever felt.

For the next two months I spent every waking hour resting and rehabilitating my hip. I hobbled around on crutches. I couldn't go near a gym, so my training suffered. It hurt to sit for more than a few minutes at a time. When I wanted to watch TV, I had to lie on my stomach or my butt would get sore.

As hard as I had been training before the crash, I needed to step it up even further when my hip got better because I had lost so much time. With a brand-knew bike, shaky confidence, and a hip that wasn't 100 percent, I needed to gauge where I was competitively. In December, I headed to Switzerland to race in a World Supercross GP. In my first heat race on the new KTM, I won the race and started to feel that old confidence. Then disaster struck. In the next race I collided with Kyle Lewis over a triple jump, crashed hard, and knocked myself unconscious.

It was the second serious accident I suffered in three months. For the first time in my career I began to feel like I couldn't give 100 percent on the track because I was thinking about getting hurt. My hip wasn't where it needed to be and it was robbing me of my confidence to go fast.

I started to think about the four-year deal I had signed with KTM. I wasn't sure it was the right thing to do. I was so motivated to beat Yamaha in my mind that I wasn't listening to my heart. And my heart wasn't 100-percent committed.

I was thirty-one years old, and for the first time in my career I was beginning to think that the end might be near. It was a hard pill to swallow. I get emotional just thinking about it. I knew when I left Europe after that race that I had a huge decision to make.

2003 and Beyond

When round one of the 2003 AMA Super-cross series rolled around in January, life in Super-cross went on much as it has these last twelve years. The pits were alive and buzzing with energy. Crews scrambled on race day to make last-minute adjustments. RC's dad and Mitch Payton swapped race stories under the Pro Circuit canopy. Jeff Emig cashed in a food voucher for a plate of lasagna at the Kawasaki trailer. Button strolled around the pits telling anyone who would listen about this, that, or the other.

At the Team McGrath rig, Skip and Larry tried to connect a 38" flat screen TV to play *Steel Roots III* for the fans waiting in line for autographs.

Everything was normal with the exception of one thing: I had no butterflies in my stomach for the race that weekend.

That's because I wasn't racing.

I had decided after thirteen professional seasons to hang up my helmet. I knew I couldn't give it everything I had. The hip injury four months prior had prevented me from riding at the top of my game. The crash in Europe was too strong a sign to ignore. I've always said that if I can't do everything at 100 percent out on the racetrack that I wouldn't do it at all.

Coming to grips with this seemed almost impossible, but it was reality. I wasn't going to lie to myself or anyone else. When you race motocross for a living there is constantly a small universe of people swirling around you who depend and count on your success. You never want to let them down. Being at the track and not racing felt so strange. My parents were almost fidgeting because they didn't know what to do with themselves. As always, my dad, in his own way, found the right words. "If it's OK with you," he said, "it's way OK with me."

Normally on race days my parents are doing a million things related to my racing that they don't have time to breathe. About seven o'clock, my dad's blood is going and he won't settle down until about lap fifteen of the 250 main, when I'm comfortably out ahead of the pack. Racing is all we've ever known, be it BMX, Ponca City, or Anaheim. Racing was our lives. And it always will be.

Telling the people closest to me that I was about to change all of our lives was the hardest thing I've ever done. Especially when they work for you, because retirement is going to affect them in a big way. When I told Skip, I basically said, "Pull up a chair. I think I'm going to retire."

"I know that," replied Skip.

"I mean right now," I said.

Skip knew that day would come, but he was still really caught off-guard. All we had ever done was race. Now life was going to be different. I understand why it was tough for him to take. Still, he was happy for me. As always.

I called Ryno a week before the press conference in Anaheim with the news.

"Have you heard yet?" I asked.

"Heard what?"

"I'm retiring."

I had seen him a month before in Europe and gave him no indication of retirement, so he was caught off-guard. It was crazy telling Ryno that I was through racing. This is the guy who had been there through almost every phase of my career. Ryno supported me in my decision as did Button.

"Another $5 million and an extra championship isn't going to change your life," Jimmy told me. I could have easily pocketed another few million dollars for just riding around the track, but I can't stand not winning. Not being at the top of my game. I didn't get involved in this sport for money. I got in it to win. I would never let myself be one of those guys who just collected a paycheck. I've made fun of those guys my whole career. My dad thought I might retire next year and had hoped to see me show my speed of old. But he perfectly understood.

My sister, Tracy, was glad that she wouldn't have to worry about my safety anymore. She was a nervous wreck every time I lined up on the gate. Same goes for my mom.

On January 2, 2003, I held a press conference in the Diamond Club at Edison International Field. I felt composed about my decision the whole time.

I was never really nervous until the drive from Encinitas to Anaheim on the day of the press conference. Actually, I was nervous as hell. Proposing-to-Kim nervous. The room was packed with many of my

Holding back tears at the press conference to announce my retirement.

former employers, sponsors, racers, and friends. To me, it's not hard to give a speech to strangers, but speaking in front of a room full of people you've admired and respected your whole career is really difficult. When I started talking I was shaking, sweating, crying, and everything. I could barely get through my retirement speech. I tried as hard as I could to hold back my tears but nothing worked. I could see tears in the eyes of some of the toughest motocross racers in the world.

Only the riders could understand my attachment to the sport. It's something I've done almost my whole life, the reason people know me, and now I was closing that chapter. The way it turned out was almost storybook. I used to come to Anaheim as a kid with Ryno and Phil, and we'd cheer for Rick Johnson and Jeff Ward. We were just kids dreaming about being down there racing Supercross. We were light-years away but it didn't matter to us. But you know what? We all made it. My first win was at Anaheim. So was my last win. Now I'm retiring there. It all went so fast it's hard to believe. But I'm not retiring from motor-

Kim and me just before the last race, Holland, December 2002.

Jeremy McGrath

cycles, just racing competitive Supercross. In fact, I went riding the very next day.

The night of the race was extremely emotional for me. After introducing the other 250 riders, they played a four-minute video of my most memorable highlights to the Van Halen song "Dreams." The fans went nuts when they saw a clip of me in the winner's circle sporting a mullet after winning the west Supercross title, my first, back in '91. After the video, the place went dark and a spotlight landed on me as I was being lowered on a platform. The place erupted as if the Angels had won the World Series all over again. I can't explain the feeling that gave me.

I rode off the platform and gave one last, slow parade lap to the strains of Nelly's "No. 1" blasting over the PA system. The AMA presented me with the Mickey Thompson Award of Excellence, and I bade the fans a fond farewell. After that, I got dressed and watched the race from the Knothole Club with my family. As a tribute to the fans who have supported me throughout my career, I rode a parade lap in each city of the 2003 Supercross series. It was just a small way to acknowledge the fans of our sport.

One very important thing happened that night that made me feel safe in my decision. When I walked through the pits and heard the ringring of those 250 motors and smelled the exhaust that I love so much, I didn't get all antsy and want to throw my leg over my bike. I had made the right decision.

I feel confident that I'm leaving motocross in good hands. Ricky Carmichael, Chad Reed, and James Stewart, Jr. are more than willing to carry the torch. Along with being great riders, these guys have tremendous respect for the sport.

Back in 1993, an eight-year-old kid asked me for my autograph and my jersey. "I'll give you mine if you give me yours," I told him. Right away he took off running to the pits to retrieve his jersey. Five minutes later he returned with a blue-and-white Fox jersey and signed the front and back with big, looping letters that kids write with when they first learn cursive. The signature read "James Stewart 259."

WIDE OPEN

Just after my retirement, Kim and I were going through my old gear to have some of it framed when I came across the jersey James gave me that day. I couldn't believe how small it was. Today James is a two-time 125 champion and the future of our sport. He's a guy who isn't afraid to be in the spotlight. I didn't mind the spotlight, either. I never did. But I'm looking forward to life after racing. I'm excited about the break from the schedule and the constant travel. I'm a motorcycle enthusiast and I'll race at local races. Just not at this level. I want to enjoy life. I built a motocross track in Temecula and I spend a lot of time there riding with my friends. I've always wanted to see what was on the other side of the fence. Now I'll find out.

I definitely want to start a family someday and so does Kim. I know my parents are really looking forward to grandkids, as well.

THE LAST GOOD-BYE

My retirement speech at the Diamond Club at Edison International Field in Anaheim was attended by hundreds of media, riders, manufacturer representatives, and industry insiders. Here are excerpts from my farewell:

> First and most importantly—it is crucial for not only my peers and members of the industry to know—but for race fans and enthusiasts of this great sport to know—that although I am announcing my retirement, this 2003 season should be looked at as my farewell tour. . . . Kind of a way for me to say goodbye over a four-month period!!!
>
> It is my sincere hope that these efforts, throughout the 2003 supercross season, will allow me the opportunity to meet and greet as many race fans as possible and be able to thank as many individuals as I can for the many, many years of overwhelming and enthusiastic support I have received. This sport truly has the greatest fans!
>
> . . . It is true that my recent injuries have played a role in my decision to retire, but timing has also played an equally important role. By that I mean, after a great deal of thought and retrospect and looking at this wonderful career I have had— this sport has brought me more than I could have ever imagined or dreamed—it just seemed like the right time. I'm closing this chapter, the racing and competition part, and starting to move towards the next chapter in my life.
>
> I know many of you are probably wondering, "Why now?" and to be honest with all of you I

never knew how this was all going to end—I actually thought I would have been retired by now. But . . . during these past few seasons I continued to be motivated and I wanted to be out there—I wanted to win—I love the competition. However, as all of you may or may not know it kills me to be out there and not winning.

To me, this sport is a *lifestyle, a passion* not just a job. I promised myself early on in my career—if and when I wasn't 100% focused or motivated, it was time to step down—and it is important to me to keep that promise to myself. This sport has given me everything and is something I really love. However, if you get to the point where you have doubts and hesitation—it can become your enemy and I could grow to hate it. I love the sport too much to ever let that happen.

The End . . . Or Just the Beginning . . .

A few days after I made the decision, my family and I sat around looking at old Supercross tapes of my career. There was Anaheim in '96. San Jose in '92. Minneapolis in '97. My hair went through more than a couple phases. The early nac-nacs and Supermans made me laugh. I thought I looked so cool back then.

I never lied to myself or my family about the fact that this was someday going to end. They never lied to me either. Even after my first 250 title way back in 1993 my dad told me to be ready for this day. We just didn't think it would come 16 years, 102 wins, and 12 combined championships after I started. He told me back then that all glory is

fleeting. That nothing lasts forever. But that's not true. The memories, the moments, the snapshots of what motocrossers do will be with me for the rest of my life.

ACKNOWLEDGMENTS

Love, thanks and gratitude to ...

My dad, Jack: From that day you rode under the fence I knew we would be a great team. You will always be my hero. Thank you for believing in me. I love you.

My mom, Ann: For all you have given up for me to make my world go round. I appreciate your love, wisdom, and guidance more than you will ever know. I love you.

My sister, Tracy: My biggest fan. Thank you for always taking a backseat to my racing and for living in my shadow. The sacrifices you have made are immeasurable. I love you.

My wife, Kim: My soul mate and best friend, thank you for the love, laughter, and fun you have brought into my life. I love you.

Lawrence Lewis: Best friend, roommate, business partner, and best man; through good and bad our friendship has stood the test of time.

Cheryl Lynch: For all the countless hours of hard work and for always being there for me.

Skip Norfolk: For your brilliant skills; my career wouldn't have been the same without you. Thanks for helping to make great memories.

Larry Brooks: For your outstanding team leadership, loyalty, hard work, and long hours, and especially your unconditional friendship.

Jimmy Button: For being a great friend, a great teammate, and for showing us what incredible will is all about.

Mitch Payton: For that meeting in your office that changed my life.

Gabriele Mazzarolo: For always being true to me; your friendship has meant a lot to me through the years.

Troy Lee: For helping to shape my image on the track and for all of your cool ideas.

Randy Lawrence: For your hard work and dedication.

Mark Johnson: For that wonderful start with the Team Green Amateur Program.

Rick Johnson "R.J." : For the phone call that I never thought would come. Thanks for being a great hero and friend.

Dave Arnold and Cliff White: For believing in me and for giving me my first chance.

Dave Stephenson: For all your great advice and guidance.

Gary Semics: For teaching me that success doesn't come without hard work and sacrifice.

Jeff Emig: My biggest rival and most respected competitor; thanks for all the great races.

Ryan Hughes and Phil Lawrence: Lifelong friends, childhood buddies, and two people I've shared great race experiences with.

Special thanks also need to go to: Jeff Fox, Jim and Dave Castillo, Mel Harris, Derek Natvig, Brian Lopes, Eric Carter, Malcolm MaCassy, the Hinson family, Gary Becker, Charlie Mancuso, Roy Jansen, Duke and Sonnie Finch, Brian Barnhardt, Rodger DeCoster, Mark Johnson, Victor Sheldon, Scott Bell, Grayson Goodman, Cory Worf, Dr. Toy, Dr. Murphy, Kevin Brown, Tracy Jansen, Dave Damron, Jeremy and Joel Albrecht, KTM, Yamaha, Thor, Parts Unlimited, Bell Helmets, Boost Mobile, Kicker Audio, Tige, Hot Wheels/Mattel, Renthal, Dunlop Tires, One Industries, and SPY Optics.

And finally, heartfelt thanks to those of you who helped make this book a reality . . . Chris Palmer, who put my life into words like no one else could, thank you for your time and patience. Ken Faught, who made sure all my facts were right. Cheryl Lynch, who brought the whole book idea together for me. Marc Gerald, my book agent, who knew there was a publishing house out there interested in supercross. Josh Behar, my editor at HarperCollins, for believing in the whole concept. Dawn Di-Censo, for making sure all the buyers knew about my sport and this book. My mom, Tracy, and Kim for spending hours digging into old photo albums for the pictures that have added so much to this book. And to all the pro photographers who contributed their remarkable images—Davey Coombs, Eric Johnson, Chris Hultner, Fran Kuhn, Simon Cudby, Kirk Bender, Mario Marini, Carolyn Abacherli, and especially Ken Faught and Kinney Jones.